MARK
A Gospel for Today

FOR OUR PARENTS

MARK

A Gospel for Today

Simon and Christopher Danes

LION EDUCATIONAL
Oxford · Batavia · Sydney

Text copyright © 1989 Simon and Christopher Danes
This edition copyright © 1989 Lion Publishing

Published by
Lion Publishing plc
Sandy Lane West, Littlemore, Oxford, England
ISBN 0 7459 1504 3
Albatross Books Pty Ltd
PO Box 320, Sutherland, NSW 2232, Australia
ISBN 0 7324 0060 0

First edition 1989

British Library Cataloguing in Publication Data
Danes, Simon
 Mark: A Gospel for Today
 1. Bible. N.T. Mark – Critical studies
 I. Title   II. Danes, Christopher
 226'.306

 ISBN 0-7459-1504-3

Printed in Yugoslavia

Acknowledgements
The authors would like to express their thanks to
Geoffrey and Stephen Maddock and to Rob and
Linda Bygrave for their generous hospitality while
they were writing, and to Catherine for her help
and encouragement.

Bible quotations are from the *Good News Bible*,
copyright 1966, 1971 and 1976 American Bible
Society, published by Bible Societies/Collins.

The modern (Rite A) version of the Lord's Prayer
quoted in Unit 4 is from *The Alternative Service
Book* 1980.

Photographs
Associated Press, pages 22, 151, 164 (above);
Barnaby's Picture Library, page 41; Trustees of the
British Museum, pages 139, 189; Camera Press,
page 180; Cephas Picture Library/Mick Rock, page 14;
DAS Photography/David Simson, pages 48, 91, 192;
Alistair Duncan/Middle East Archive, pages 16,
146/47, 156; Mary Evans Picture Library, page 59;
Chris Fairclough Colour Library, page 169 (below);
Sonia Halliday and Laura Lushington Photographs,
pages 55, 84, 87, 127, 174, 177, 183 (right) /F.H.C.
Birch, page 17 /Jane Taylor, pages 82, 128, 135; Barry
Searle, page 145; Barry Kirk, page 57; Hulton Picture
Company, page 111; Hutchison Picture Library, page
183 (left); Lion Publishing/David Alexander, pages 75,
76, 112, 152, 155, 171, 178 /David Townsend, pages
38, 45; Phil Manning, pages 164 (below), 165 (above);
Alan Millard, page 65; Network Photographers, page
119; Picturepoint, pages 29, 106; Popperfoto, pages
97, 120, 148; Rex Features, pages 33, 117, 143; Royal
National Lifeboat Institution, page 68; Zefa (UK) Ltd,
pages 47, 181, 187.

Illustrations, maps and graphics
Simon Jenkins, pages 31, 46, 63, 79, 115, 191
Lion Publishing, pages 11, 24, 28, 51, 52, 61, 132–3,
159, 160–61, 184
Lion Publishing/Tony Cantale Graphics, pages 9, 12,
19, 20, 34, 54, 70, 85, 93, 113

Design by Tony Cantale Graphics

Contents

Foreword

A man is wanted by the secret police. He works late into the night, desperate to finish the history – the story of the man who started his movement. The movement believes that what its founder did and said will change the world. But it is vital that his life story is recorded. The writer knows that to be caught means death: already, many of his friends have been executed. And the secret police could arrive at any time . . .

This is the most popular theory about how Mark's Gospel was written, nearly 2,000 years ago.

The writer was Mark. The movement was Christianity. The founder was Jesus. The secret police were the Romans. And the history that was written was Mark's Gospel. Now read on . . .

Life in
the Time of Jesus

Mark tells stories about Jesus, a carpenter and a teacher who lived in Israel. Our calendar is supposed to tell us the number of years that have passed since Jesus' birth. For example, 1989 should be one thousand, nine hundred and eighty-nine years after Jesus was born. In fact, it is slightly wrong. We think Jesus was born in about 4BC and died in AD30 or 33.

What was life like in Jesus' time?

Jesus was born in Israel and brought up as a Jew. God had promised Abraham, the Jews' ancestor, that he would be their God. Around 1350BC, some 400 years later, God rescued the Jews from slavery in Egypt, and gave them Israel as their home. (This journey out of Egypt is called the *Exodus*.) The Jews believed – and still believe – that God was the God of the whole world, but that they were his special people. Everyone else was a Gentile (a non-Jew).

By the time of Jesus, Israel was part of the Roman Empire.

In 37BC, the Romans made a man called Herod the Great king of the Jews. He ran the country for the Empire, and was very cruel. When he died in 4BC the Romans divided up his kingdom among three of his sons. Two of them are important for us:

In the time of Jesus, Palestine was an occupied country. The Roman eagle was a hated symbol of Rome's power.

● Archelaus ruled the southern part of Israel, which was called *Judea*. He was such a bad ruler that, in AD6, the Romans got rid of him and put one of their own men in charge of Judea instead. This was the Roman governor (*procurator*). At the time when Jesus was grown up, the procurator's name was *Pontius Pilate*.

● *Herod Antipas* ruled the northern part of Israel, which was called *Galilee*. He also ruled Perea. Antipas was not allowed to call himself 'king'; he was known as the 'tetrarch'. He was a cruel and selfish man, like his father. We find out more about him in Mark's Gospel.

Despite all this, the Jews did their best to remain true to their faith. There were three important things in their everyday lives:

The Torah

This was (and is) the heart of the Jewish faith. The Jews believed that God had given his laws to Moses, the great Jewish leader during the Exodus. The word 'Torah' means 'law', or 'instruction'. They thought that Moses had written down God's laws in five books. These are the first five books of the Jewish Bible, the Christian Old Testament. The Torah also includes some history, but the laws showed the Jews how God wanted them to live.

Other names for the Torah are:
- the Pentateuch
- the Law
- the Law of Moses.

The synagogue

This was the local place of worship, where the Torah was read and explained. There was a synagogue in every town and in most villages. The synagogue also acted as a community centre and a school. In Britain in the Middle Ages most people could not read or write. This was not so in Israel in Jesus' time. Jesus, like every other male Jew, would certainly have been able to do both.

The Temple

There were many synagogues, but only one Temple. The first Temple had been built by King Solomon (970–910BC) in Jerusalem. It was destroyed in 587BC by the armies from a country called Babylonia, but it was rebuilt. Later, Herod the Great added to the buildings and made them much grander. The Jews believed God had told Solomon to build the Temple, and it was the most holy place in the world. Animal sacrifices to God could only be offered there.

We shall be finding out much more about the Torah, the synagogues, and the Temple later on.

It is a mistake to think that the Jews in Jesus' time all believed exactly the same things. They all had the same basic beliefs, but they understood their faith differently. There were four groups to which many of them belonged. These were:
- the Pharisees
- the Sadducees
- the Zealots
- the Essenes.

We need to look at each of these in turn.

The Pharisees

The Pharisees were the largest group. Their name may mean 'people who are separate from others'. Their main aim was to keep the laws of the Torah. Some of them studied it full time, but others had normal jobs as well. They tried to make sure that the laws of the Torah were always kept by 'making a fence around the Law'. This meant they had extra rules to make sure they did not even break the Law by accident. They learned these rules off by heart.

For example, the Torah said that no one should work on the Sabbath, the Jewish holy day (Exodus 20:8). This law was probably designed to give people a day off from work so that they could rest and worship. But the Pharisees made sure it was kept by saying people could not do anything on the Sabbath that might mean 'work'. They said you could not walk more than two-thirds of a mile, and could not even write on the Sabbath. Rules like this got more and more difficult to keep.

Many Pharisees were genuinely religious people who wanted to try to keep God's laws. Paul, the great early Christian missionary, and Gamaliel, his tutor, were both Pharisees. So was Nicodemus, whom John's Gospel says was friendly towards Jesus. Some Pharisees, however, were in danger of looking down on people who did not keep their own rules. Mark says they argued bitterly with Jesus about this.

The Pharisees accepted some ideas that were not in the Torah, but were in the other books that now make up the Old Testament or Tenakh. They believed in angels and life after death, and in the coming of the Messiah (see Unit 4).

The Sadducees

The Sadducees were a very small group. Most of them were priests in the Temple, and they were often very wealthy. They enjoyed being at the top of the tree in society, and looked down on ordinary people. They did not want trouble with the Romans because this might affect their power.

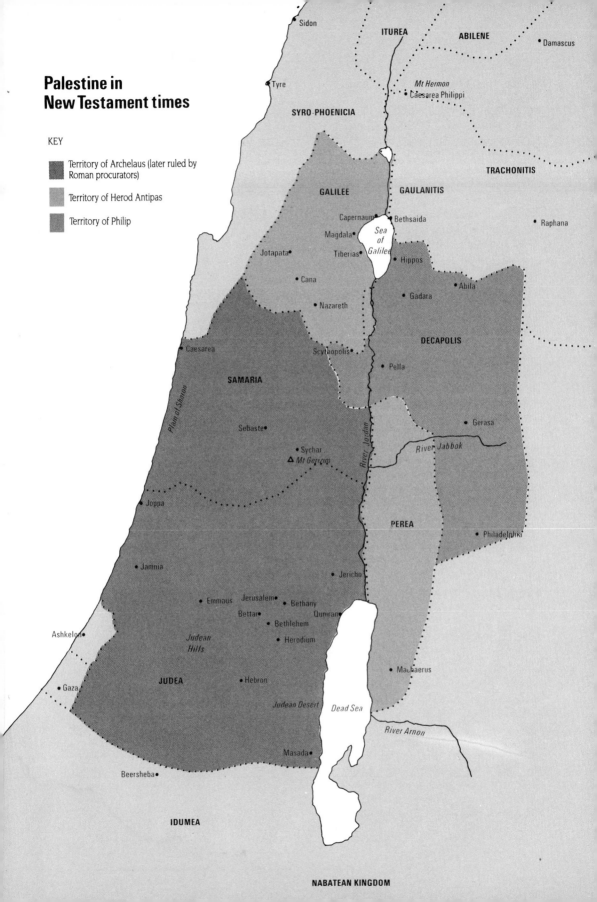

Palestine in
New Testament times

KEY

■ Territory of Archelaus (later ruled by Roman procurators)

■ Territory of Herod Antipas

■ Territory of Philip

Sidon

ITUREA

ABILENE

• Damascus

• Tyre

Mt Hermon
• Caesarea Philippi

SYRO-PHOENICIA

TRACHONITIS

GALILEE

GAULANITIS

Capernaum •
Magdala •

• Bethsaida

• Raphana

*Sea
of
Galilee*

Jotapata •

Tiberias •

• Hippos

• Cana

• Abila

• Nazareth

• Gadara

DECAPOLIS

• Caesarea

Scythopolis •

SAMARIA

• Pella

Plain of Sharon

Sebaste •

• Gerasa

• Sychar
△ Mt Gerizim

River Jabbok

River Jordan

• Joppa

PEREA

• Philadelphia

• Jammia

• Jericho

• Emmaus

Jerusalem •

• Bethany

Bettar •

Qumran •

• Bethlehem

Ashkelon •

• Herodium

*Judean
Hills*

JUDEA

• Hebron

• Macaerus

• Gaza

Judean Desert

Dead Sea

River Arnon

• Masada

Beersheba •

IDUMEA

NABATEAN KINGDOM

Their name seems to mean 'sons of Zadok' or 'members of the priests' party' (Zadok had been a priest under King David, 1,000 years before). They based their thinking entirely on the Torah, and rejected ideas that were not found in it, such as angels, the Messiah, or life after death (Mark says that some Sadducees had an argument with Jesus over the last of these). As a result, they disliked the Pharisees and did not agree with the Pharisees' extra rules. For them, the Torah was enough.

The Zealots

The Zealots (which means 'fanatics') believed in armed resistance against the Romans. The Romans thought they were terrorists, but many Jews thought of them as freedom fighters. They hated being ruled by foreigners, and believed their only king was God or somebody God would appoint. They seem to have begun in AD6, when a man called Judas of Galilee led a revolt against the Romans.

The Zealots were an underground movement: when you met people in the street you could not tell whether or not they were Zealots. Some of them were also Pharisees. They were waiting for the Messiah to lead them (see Unit 4). Simon (not to be confused with Simon Peter), one of Jesus' closest followers, was a Zealot. Mark mentions two other important people who may also have been Zealots:
● Judas Iscariot, one of Jesus' followers
● Barabbas, who was released by Pontius Pilate before Jesus was crucified.

The Essenes

The Essenes were like monks. Some lived in the towns, but most lived in the desert in Judea. People like them wrote the Dead Sea Scrolls, a collection of books which were discovered at Qumran in 1948. They believed all the other Jews had gone away from what God wanted, and that they alone were the true people of God. Because of this, their rules were very strict. Many did not marry; when they did it was simply to produce children. The Dead Sea Scrolls say that it took two years of hard training to become a member of the community at Qumran. After that, they gave up their possessions and shared all they had with the other members of the group.

Most Jews were not members of these four groups. However, the ordinary people in Jesus' time probably looked to one of the groups to guide them.

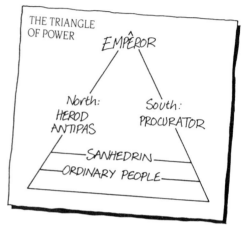

THE TRIANGLE OF POWER

EMPEROR

North: HEROD ANTIPAS

South: PROCURATOR

SANHEDRIN

ORDINARY PEOPLE

The Romans did allow the Jews a little power to run some of their own affairs. The *Sanhedrin*, the Jewish council, existed to control religious matters, and it had some authority to act as a criminal court. Its seventy members were made up from:
● Sadducees
● Pharisees
● Teachers of the Law or scribes (we shall be finding out more about these in Unit 7).

The Temple High Priest, who acted as the chairman, was an automatic member. He brought the total membership up to seventy-one.

Mark records that Jesus appeared before the Sanhedrin when he was on trial for his life.

We shall be finding out much more about these things as we continue our study of Mark's Gospel.

◤FOLLOW UP◥

1. Draw the map shown in this unit. It will help if you colour code it, so that the area ruled by Herod Antipas is in one colour, and the area ruled by the procurator is in another.

2. Look up the first five books of the Old Testament in a Bible.
What are their names in English?
Why are they important?

3. Why were
● the synagogues
● the Temple
important?

4. Write a paragraph on
● the Pharisees
● the Sadducees
● the Zealots
● the Essenes.
Who were they, what were they like, and what did they believe?

5. What was the Sanhedrin?

6. If you live in or near an old Roman town, you may have a museum near you which shows what life was like in Roman times. Try to visit it, to find out more about life in the Roman Empire.

How is Mark used by Christians Today?

Mark's Gospel is about Jesus, and Jesus is central to Christianity. Christians believe that there is one God, who exists in three ways (as *Trinity* or tri-unity). God is Father, Son and Holy Spirit. God the Son became a man in Jesus. Jesus showed God's love for people in his birth, his teaching, and in his suffering, death and resurrection. Jesus' death frees people from their sins, and takes away the barrier between God and the world. (This is a very complicated idea, and we will be finding out more about it later on.)

Christians want to know what Jesus did in Israel nearly 2,000 years ago. There are four main written sources of information for this. These are the four Gospels of Matthew, Mark, Luke and John in the New Testament. What we say about how Christians use Mark is also true for the other three. Each Gospel presents Jesus in a slightly different way from the others and so has its own special value. Mark's is the shortest, but many people think that he is the best story-teller. As we shall see, his Gospel is also important because it was almost certainly the first to be written.

Christians today study the Bible – particularly the accounts of Jesus' life – informally in groups, and on their own.

66 *So what part does Mark play in Christian life today?* **99**

Worship

Christians worship God in private and in public, and B*ible reading* plays an important part in both. This includes readings from Mark's Gospel.

Probably the most important sort of Bible reading for Christians is reading from the Gospels. This happens at many services, including the E*ucharist* (see Unit 49), which celebrates what happened at Jesus' Last Supper with his disciples and is the most important act of worship in most churches. (We will be looking at the Eucharist in detail later on.) In Roman Catholic, Orthodox, and most Anglican churches, the Gospel is read by one of the clergy. This shows the deep respect people have for what the Gospels say. In Protestant Free churches, any member of the congregation may read aloud from the Gospels, while the others listen carefully or follow the readings in their own copies of the Bible.

Sometimes the readings from the Gospel will be very long. During H*oly Week*, for instance, Christians remember Jesus' suffering and death, and the whole of that story is read. Sometimes it will be taken from the version in Mark (chapters 14 and 15).

Nearly all Christians have a *sermon* as part of their public worship. This will usually take up ideas from the Bible readings and explain what they mean, and what Christians should do about them.

In *private worship* Christians read the Bible on their own, and think and pray about what it says. They will often choose to read one of the Gospels. And if they are in a difficult situation they might look at something Jesus said or did to help them. For example, if they wanted to know what to do about someone who had hurt them, they might look up Mark 11:25. Or if they needed courage, they might want to read about Jesus' courage when he faced death in Mark chapters 14–15.

Sometimes Christians use words from the Gospels when they pray. Two prayers from Mark which Christians have found helpful are: 'I do have faith, but not enough. Help me to have more!' (9:24; the words of a father seeking healing for his son) and the words Jesus prayed just before his trial and death: 'Not what I want, but what you want' (14:36).

Study

Christians have always thought that it is very important to study the Bible. Mark and the other Gospels are studied because they say what Jesus did and said. Sometimes Christians will join Bible study groups, where they will meet to read the Bible together and work out what it means for them. Bible study groups are often organized by churches or by Christian Unions in schools, universities and places of work.

Some people study the Bible full time in universities, polytechnics and colleges. Their work will be very important for us as we look at Mark, because we will be considering things which they have said. A biblical scholar working on Mark would try to answer questions like these:

Who wrote it?

Did Jesus actually do or say these things? What is the evidence?

What was Mark trying to say to his readers?

Where did he get his information from?

What happened to the stories about Jesus before they were written down?

> Does this passage mean anything for people today?

Scholars do not always agree with one another's answers to these questions, as we shall see. But they do try hard to find the truth. Many are themselves Christians, and would say that their work is important for the church. After all, if people are going to follow what the Bible says, it is important to work out what it really means. And all of them would agree that the Gospels are extremely important historical documents which deserve close study, no matter what religion people are.

However, some Christians do not think that biblical scholars should question the Bible in the way they do. They say that the Bible is God's Word to men and women, and therefore it can never be wrong in anything it says. The vast majority of Christians agree that God speaks to his people in the Bible, but would say that it was written by human beings who could sometimes get things wrong. They would say that it is best to think of it as a unique record of God's action in history, especially in the person of Jesus, and people's response. The Bible is *words about God's Word*.

We shall be finding out much more about what Mark means to Christians today as we study the Gospel.

In Christian churches today, the Gospels are read aloud to the congregation.

FOLLOW UP

Draw a spray diagram of 'How Mark is Used by Christians Today'. (If you are not sure what a spray diagram is, there is one in Unit 34.)

Mark:
Who, What, Why, Where and When?

What is a Gospel?

The word 'gospel' comes from Anglo-Saxon. It is a translation of a Greek word which means *good news*. The earliest Christians believed that the story of Jesus' life, death and resurrection was a powerful message which God had given them to spread all over the world. It was good news for people who accepted it, because it promised them a new sort of life on earth, and the hope of heaven after death. The first meaning of 'gospel' is the *message about Jesus*.

For about thirty years or so after Jesus' crucifixion the gospel was not written down. Most of Jesus' first followers were still alive, and they spread the good news about him by their teaching. At most they had notebooks to remind their helpers of the things Jesus had said, and the order of events which led up to his death. As time went on, however, what we know as the four *Gospels* of the New Testament came to be written – Matthew, Mark, Luke and John. There were three main reasons why this happened:

● The earliest disciples of Jesus began to die off. There was a need to write down their teaching about Jesus before it got lost.

● Christianity was growing very fast among people who had all sorts of religious backgrounds. The Gospel writers thought there was a danger that some of them might bring wrong ideas with them into the church. The Gospels were written to stop this from happening.

● Christians were being persecuted by the authorities. Some were arrested and killed. The Gospel writers wanted:

– to show that there was nothing dangerous about Christianity

– to encourage Christians to carry on believing in what they thought God had done in Jesus.

You can see that the Gospels are much more than lives of Jesus. All four of them contain a lot of stories about what he said and did – and these were very important for the early Christians, because they believed that God had worked in him in an absolutely unique way. But the Gospels are not dry modern biographies. They were written to help people understand the

The reign of the Emperor Nero was a time of persecution for the early Christians. This statue of the cruel emperor stands in Rome.

Christian message about Jesus, and the *meaning of his life*. The early Christians believed that message was the most important thing in the world – and so do Christians today. The Gospels are part of their Scriptures, the holy books through which they believe God still speaks to men and women. So, as we read Mark's Gospel, we will be asking three sorts of questions:
- What does it tell us about Jesus' life?
- What does it tell us about what the first Christians thought about Jesus?
- What do Christians think about it now?

 Mark thinks that the message about Jesus is so important that he leaves out a lot of information which a modern biographer would find interesting. He tells us nothing about Jesus' childhood and education, for instance, and very little about his family.

Who was Mark?

This is a much more difficult question than it might seem at first sight. Christian tradition says that he was the same Mark (or 'John Mark') who appears in stories and letters in other parts of the New Testament. If this is right, then we know that his home was in Jerusalem, that his mother's name was Mary, and that he set out with Paul (one of the great missionaries of the early church) on his first missionary journey (Acts 12:12; 13:1–5). There must have been some sort of quarrel, because Mark left the expedition early and went home. For a while Paul would have nothing more to do with him (Acts 15:37–40), but eventually they patched it up, and Paul talked about him in his later letters (Colossians 4:10; Philemon 24).

Tradition also links Mark with *Peter*, Jesus' closest disciple. An early Christian bishop called Papias was writing just under 100 years after Jesus' crucifixion. He said that an earlier Christian leader told him that although Mark had not been one of Jesus' original followers, he was later Peter's helper. According to Papias, Mark wrote down the stories Peter told about Jesus while he was preaching. In the New Testament, the First Letter of Peter talks

about 'my son Mark' (1 Peter 5:13).

What do modern scholars make of the Christian tradition about who Mark was? There seem to be three main points to think about:

- 'Mark' was one of the commonest men's names in the Roman Empire. There is no hard and fast evidence that the 'John Mark' of Acts is the same person as the 'Mark' in Paul's letters or the other 'Mark' in 1 Peter. There must have been lots of Marks in the early church.

- Our Mark often does not seem to know exactly where places in Judea and Galilee are: he gets his geography wrong when he writes his Gospel. This seems very strange if he was John Mark, whose home was in Jerusalem. (See the map in Unit 1.)

- But a lot of the stories in the Gospel *are told from Peter's point of view*, and at least one story could really have come only from him, because he was the only follower of Jesus present at the time (14:66–72).

So it seems that Christian tradition is right when it talks about a connection between Mark and Peter, but it is much less certain that he was the 'John Mark' of Acts.

When and where was Mark written?

In AD64 the Roman Emperor Nero was killing Christians in Rome. Two things point to this as the time when Mark was writing:
- Peter died under Nero.
- A lot of the stories in Mark seem to have been written to encourage Christians who were suffering persecution (see especially 13:9–13, Unit 44).

In any case, we know that it could not have been very much later than this. Matthew and Luke both used Mark when they were writing their Gospels, and we think that they were written in about AD84–85.

So Mark was almost certainly written in about AD64–65, some thirty years after

Jesus' death and resurrection. *That makes it the earliest of the four Gospels. Therefore Mark is our most important source for the life of Jesus.*

Nero's persecution of the early Christians happened in *Rome*, and so did Peter's death. It seems very likely that Mark was written there too. Two things seem to confirm this:

● Mark explains to his readers Jewish ways of doing things. This would have been necessary only if large numbers of them were Gentiles. The Christians at Rome were mainly Gentile.

● Mark sometimes uses Latin words written in Greek letters, instead of proper Greek ones. (This is not quite such a strong argument as the first one. Using Latin words may, after all, have been quite common throughout the Roman Empire.)

The Synoptic Problem

The first three Gospels – Matthew, Mark and Luke – are very similar in places, and look at the life and teaching of Jesus from the same point of view. For that reason they are called the '*Synoptic*' Gospels (Synoptic is Greek for 'looking together').

Scholars have realized for a very long time that they are dependent on one another in some way, but working out exactly how is extremely difficult. This is called the *Synoptic Problem*.

Church tradition used to say that Matthew was the earliest Gospel, and for a while some people tried to defend that position. Now, however, nearly everyone agrees that Mark was written first and that Matthew and Luke used his Gospel when they wrote their own.

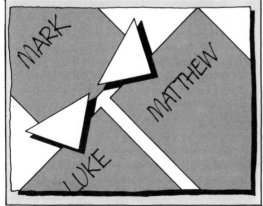

Where did Mark get his information from?

We have already seen that there is a strong connection between Mark's Gospel and Peter, and that some of the stories Mark tells may well have originally come from him. But where did the rest come from?

● The early Christians thought that the most important part of the story about Jesus was the series of events which led up to his death. (We shall be looking at this in detail later on.) This was almost certainly the first part of the Gospel to be written down. Most scholars think that Mark had one of these written accounts in front of him when he was working on his own retelling of the last week of Jesus' life. (He may also have had one for the 'Little Apocalypse' of Mark 13.)

● Jesus spoke Aramaic, a language related to Hebrew. Papias talks about an early collection of 'sayings' of Jesus 'in the Hebrew language, which every person translated as best he could'. Notebooks like this may well have been common in the early church. They would have helped preachers. Now, Mark's Greek is not very good. Our translation irons it out but the Gospel as he wrote it moves in a very breathless, jerky kind of way, almost as a child would write.

Greek was the international language of the Roman Empire, but it might not have been what Mark usually spoke. Some scholars have pointed out that he often writes as if he has translated something from Aramaic, and just occasionally he gives us actual Aramaic words. Perhaps behind some of Mark's Gospel there are written stories in Aramaic. This was Peter's language too.

● The sayings of Jesus would have been handed down by word of mouth and remembered. This was the normal way of learning in Mark's time, when books were very expensive.

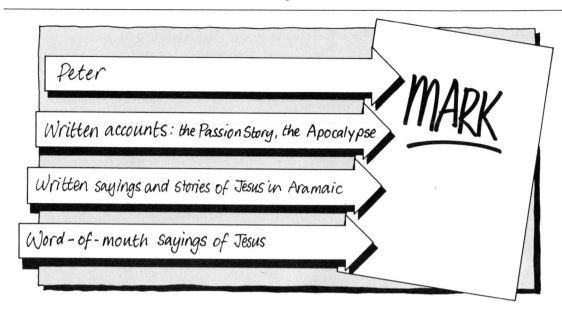

Peter

Written accounts: the Passion Story, the Apocalypse

Written sayings and stories of Jesus in Aramaic

Word - of - mouth sayings of Jesus

MARK

In writing his Gospel Mark probably drew on a number of sources, as the diagram shows.

How accurate was all this information? Opinions vary. Many Christians would want to say that God the Holy Spirit has always guided the church, and would not have let Mark and the other Gospel writers get things too mixed up. People who do not believe in God, however, would not find this a very satisfactory answer – and it is only fair that they should be answered on their own grounds.

Here are some things we can say.

● Thirty years is a long time. That is the gap between Jesus' death and the writing of Mark.

BUT it is not a ridiculously long time. Some of Jesus' original disciples were still alive. For Mark to write about Jesus is not like us writing about King Arthur.

● The stories about Jesus were originally handed on by word of mouth – even the ones which were already written down when Mark used them. They could easily have been altered if people wanted to. There are some places in the Gospels where almost everybody agrees that the early Christians added something to the words of Jesus in order to help people understand them better. We will be seeing some of these in Mark. (A whole branch of New Testament scholarship is concerned with this. It is called *Form Criticism*.)

BUT people in Mark's time were much more used to having to remember things than we are today. It is important not to get carried away. Some of the sayings of Jesus may have been altered and added to. But it is extremely unlikely that all of them were completely altered or wholly made up.

Finally, our own verdict on whether some of the stories Mark tells are historically accurate or not depends on what sort of a world we think we are living in. Perhaps we could all one day agree about what Jesus taught. But our view on whether he healed the sick, or fed people properly with tiny amounts of food, or was raised from the dead, depends first on whether we think those things are possible at all.

▲FOLLOW☞UP▲

1. Why is Mark so important as a source for the life of Jesus?

2. What does 'Gospel' mean? Why were the four Gospels written?

3. What are the problems with saying that Mark is the same person as the John Mark of Acts?

4. When do most people think Mark was written? Give two reasons for this.

5. Which of the early disciples of Jesus is closely linked to Mark?
What other sources of information did Mark have about Jesus?

6. 'The Gospels are all made up.' Either *defend* or *give the arguments against* this statement.

Jesus' Message:
The Kingdom of God

Suppose you lived in a country ruled by foreign invaders who did not care about you or your countrymen, and thought of you as little more than slaves.

How would you feel? It is the sort of thing which is happening in some parts of the world today. And it was the situation the Jews faced at the time of Jesus. They were sick to death of it.

There were nationalist guerrilla forces in first-century Palestine, as there are in the world today. But Jesus rejected the methods of the freedom-fighting Zealots. His Kingdom would not come by force

Time and time again, other countries had taken the Jews' freedom away from them. So they started looking forward to an age when they would have it back. They waited for the time when God would be in charge – a time when he would save them from their enemies, just as once long before he had saved them from the Egyptians (Exodus 12–14). And this time it would be final. *Instead of just another human kingdom, the Kingdom of God would arrive.* (Thinking about the future in this way is called *eschatology.*)

Titles of Jesus

1. The Messiah or Christ

'Messiah' and 'Christ' mean exactly the same thing. They are just in different languages. Messiah is the Hebrew word. (Hebrew is the ancient language of the Jews. The Old Testament was written in it.) Christ is the same word translated into Greek, the language of the New Testament.

Both Messiah and Christ mean 'a person who has been anointed'. In other words, someone who has had oil poured over his head. This seems rather strange at first sight. But the ancient kings of Israel were anointed with oil at their coronations (see 1 Samuel 16:1–13, where David is anointed king). The kings of Israel were therefore all called 'messiahs' (although English Old Testaments translate the word simply as 'king' or 'the anointed' when it is used about them:

see 1 Samuel 24:10).

The kings of Israel were not always as good as the people would have liked, so they began to look for a *new and better King* whom God would send – *the* Messiah. This hope for a new Messiah became very strong when the Jews were exiled in Babylon, and the last true king to be descended from David had died. The prophets wrote poems about the new Messiah's arrival (see for example Isaiah 11:1–9 and Zechariah 9:9–10).

By the time of Jesus there were a number of ideas about what the Messiah would do when he came. People thought that God would send him to start his Kingdom going. But how would he do this? And what would he be like?

● Many Jews – especially the Zealots – thought the Messiah

would be a great warrior who would lead a new Jewish army and throw the Romans out of Israel.

● The Essenes seem to have expected two, or even three Messiahs. One of these would be a Jewish warlord. Another would be a priest. (Priests as well as kings were anointed in the Old Testament – see Exodus 28:41.)

Mark says that Jesus was the Messiah. But he also says that he introduced his close followers to a very shocking idea. This was that the Messiah's job was not to win a war, but to suffer and die for others. We shall be looking at these ideas in detail later on.

Christians today believe that Jesus is the Messiah, too. That is why he is usually called 'Jesus Christ' or sometimes just 'Christ'.

The Jews' ideas about the Kingdom of God first grew up over 500 years before Jesus' birth, when Israel was at war with a country called Babylonia – a war Israel could not win. In 587BC a huge Babylonian army rampaged through Judah, and the holy city of Jerusalem with its Temple was captured and partly destroyed. Hundreds of people were killed. Those who survived were taken prisoner and exiled in Babylon. The prophecies from these times contrast the people's sufferings with a better time to come.

Prophecies were the messages spoken by prophets. Prophets were men and women who claimed to hear what God said, and who passed his message on to the people.

Eventually the Jews were allowed to return home to Israel. But they were not really free. The Babylonians' rule was followed first by the Persians, then the

Greeks, and finally the Romans.

Over all this time the people still hoped for the coming of God's Kingdom, and their hopes grew. During Jesus' life and just before it, most Jews thought that God was going to help them soon – that the Kingdom of God was on its way. One of the main ideas they had about the Kingdom was that God would send someone called the *Messiah*. This was one of the names or titles given to Jesus by his followers.

People at the time of Jesus had different ideas about the Messiah. But they also had different ideas about what the Kingdom of God was going to be like. God was going to be in charge, but what would this mean?

● The Zealots thought that it meant that the Jews would govern their own country according to God's laws after all the Romans had been thrown out.

● The Essenes believed that the Kingdom would begin with a kind of heavenly war against all evil powers and all evil people.

When that war was won, everything that was wrong with the world would be destroyed. A paradise would follow – the Kingdom of God.

Mark says that Jesus taught that the Kingdom was arriving. But he did not think like either the Essenes or the Zealots.

Jesus' view of the Kingdom in Mark

● **God will bring it about.** Jesus disagreed with the Zealots when they said that the Kingdom could be brought near by fighting for it. He thought that people could not bring in the new age – only God could. The Kingdom was like a seed growing into a plant (Mark 4:26–29). God makes the seed grow, and he makes the Kingdom come.

● **But it will still be a struggle.** If God is going to rule, then evil must be stopped. People's lives will be changed. Mark shows

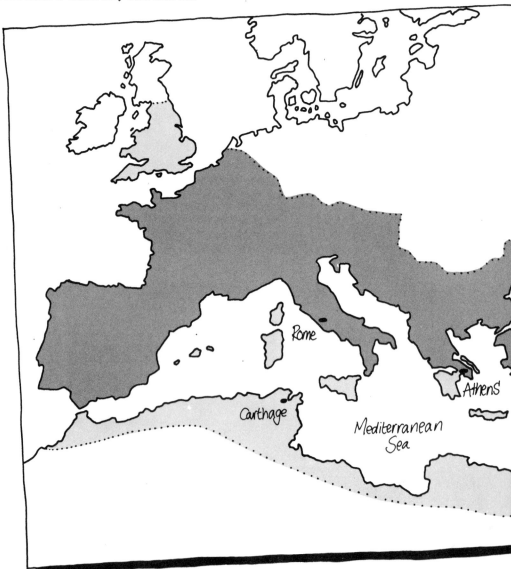

how he thought Jesus acted as though this struggle has already begun:

    – The Kingdom brings a struggle against sin, which Jesus forgives.

    – It brings a struggle against illness, which Jesus heals.

    – It brings a struggle against demons, which the Jews (and Mark) believed could possess people, and which Jesus overcomes.

● **A new society will be born.** The Kingdom of God did not just mean the rule of God. It was also *the people in the Kingdom*. The Jews were God's chosen people. But Mark shows how Jesus taught that anybody could get into the Kingdom – including sinners, outcasts, and Gentiles. And their relationship with God would not be for this life only. After death they would be happy with him for ever. Christians still believe this today.

Like all Christians, Mark believed that Jesus was raised from the dead. He believed this showed that what Jesus had said about the Kingdom was true. By following Christ, Christians look forward to sharing a future with Jesus which will survive death. This will be the full and final arrival of the Kingdom.

THE ROMAN EMPIRE
from 146BC to its extent by AD117

Black Sea

Antioch

Alexandria • Jerusalem

Jesus' eschatology

It is quite difficult to work out Jesus' eschatology, and there has been a lot of discussion about it over the past 100 years. One reason for this is because, although the Gospels sometimes show him talking about the Kingdom of God *as though it had already arrived with his preaching*, at other times he spoke about it as though it was *still somehow in the future*. (You can compare Mark 9:1 with 12:34 as examples of each idea.)

A few people think that Jesus really expected God to end the world and remake the universe. They say that he thought this would happen very quickly – perhaps within the lifetime of his own followers. If this is right, then he thought of his work not as bringing in the Kingdom, but as preparing people for its arrival.

Others disagree with this. They say that Jesus taught that the Kingdom had *begun in his preaching and teaching*, but that at some time in the future it would be fulfilled. This is the view taken by this book.

▲FOLLOW▲UP▲

1. When the Kingdom of God came, the Jews thought, foreign rule of Israel would be replaced by God's rule.
● What do we call this kind of thinking about the future?
● How did the Zealots think they could bring about the Kingdom's arrival?
● What did the Essenes think about the Kingdom?

2. ● What does *Messiah* mean?
● What does *Christ* mean?
● What did most people (like the Zealots) think the Messiah's job would be?
● How did Jesus' teaching differ from this, according to Mark?

3. Summarize what you have learned so far about Jesus' teaching on the Kingdom of God.

4. Christians say the Lord's Prayer very often. It is printed below in a modern version.

Our Father in heaven,
hallowed be your name,
your kingdom come,
your will be done,
on earth as in heaven.
Give us today our daily bread.
Forgive us our sins
as we forgive those who sin against us.
Lead us not into temptation
but deliver us from evil.
For the kingdom, the power, and the glory are yours
now and for ever. Amen.

Discuss this prayer in class. What do you think it shows about Christian belief in the coming of the Kingdom of God?

5. Try to interview some Christians. Ask them what they understand by 'the Kingdom of God'. (It might help if you use a tape recorder.) Do they have different ideas? This exercise would be made more interesting if you interview Christians who attend different sorts of churches.

UNIT 5

Mark Begins his Gospel

Books did not have proper titles when Mark was writing his Gospel. Instead they were called by their first words, which told their readers what they were about. Mark's Gospel is like this. (People only began to call it 'The Gospel According to St Mark' much later.) Look at the first verse of the text. What does Mark say his book is?

 READ MARK 1:1–8

The work of John the Baptist

Mark begins by saying that his book is 'Good News about Jesus' – and then he immediately starts talking about John the Baptist! This seems a bit strange. Why does he do it?

John died while Jesus was still teaching and preaching, but he was still an important person for the first Christians. Mark tells us some more stories about him later on in the Gospel, so he seems to know quite a lot about him. What did he think about him?

Look again at verses 2–3. Mark introduces John with a quotation from the Old Testament prophets. This talks about a mysterious *messenger* God will send to prepare the way for the coming of the Messiah. Mark has already called Jesus *Christ* (the Greek word for Messiah), and he thinks that John is the messenger the prophets had promised.

Imagine you were going to have somebody very special to stay at your home. What would you do?

One of the first things would be to clean up! Just as we would clean up our homes before the arrival of a guest, so Mark shows John preparing the people for the coming of the Messiah by getting them to 'clean up their lives'. He tells them to *turn away from their sins* – that is, to stop doing the things which they knew God had said were wrong. Lots of Jewish teachers told people that it was wrong to sin, but Mark thinks what John says is special. The Messiah is coming soon! There isn't much time!

Mark tells his readers that John *baptized* people in the River Jordan. This literally means that he dipped them in it, but the meaning of this washing is symbolic. John's baptism was a sign that the people were washed clean of their sins and were ready to welcome the Messiah when he arrived. Here again we know that other Jewish teachers sometimes 'washed' or baptized their followers, but Mark wants to make it clear that John did it *because the Messiah was coming*.

Read verses 7 and 8 again. Mark tells his readers that John said somebody was coming who was much greater than he was. Mark thinks that this person was Jesus. A slave would undo his master's sandals every day, but in Mark's story John says that he is not worthy (good enough) even to do that for him.

Mark thinks that John prepared the way for Jesus, but that does not mean Mark didn't think much of John. *For Mark, John is a great prophet*. We can tell this by looking again at verse 6, where Mark tells his readers what John wore. This is very like the description of the prophet Elijah in the Old Testament (2 Kings 1:8).

Many Jews thought that Elijah was the greatest of all the prophets, and that he would return before the Messiah came. Like John, Elijah spent a great deal of time in the desert. By describing John in the way he does, Mark is trying to tell his readers something about him. He is a great prophet – perhaps he was even the 'Elijah' who was expected to return. (Later on in the Gospel, Jesus talks about John like this: 9:13.) And if 'Elijah' has returned, the Messiah must be coming soon.

We have seen that Mark thinks that John is the messenger the prophets had promised, and that he is a great prophet like Elijah. Both of these things point towards the coming of Jesus as the Messiah. But what does Mark say John thought Jesus was going to do?

We get a clue to this in verse 8, where John says that the man coming after him will baptize people 'with the Holy Spirit'. These are difficult words to understand, but what they probably mean is that Jesus is going to bring people in touch with God in a new way. John was just preparing people for God to act – Jesus will bring the real thing. This verse would have had a special meaning for Mark's first readers. When they became Christians they would have been baptized. This was a sign that they shared in the new relationship with God which Jesus brought, and they would have seen it as the baptism in the Holy Spirit which John talked about.

In the desert, John the Baptist lived off the land – eating honey from wild bees, and locusts fat from green crops. He seems a wild and eccentric figure, yet he was following in the footsteps of the Old Testament prophets, as the people were quick to recognize.

Notes

1:1: Some old versions of Mark leave out the words *Son of God* here, but we should keep them in. The Greek expression Mark uses is a peculiar one which nobody else would have copied. He uses it again at the end of the Gospel (15:39). For 'Christ', see Unit 4.

1:2: Mark says that this prophecy is from Isaiah, but in fact it is a mixture of Isaiah 40:3 and Malachi 3:1. These two texts may have been combined by the early church for use in preaching before Mark used them here.

1:4: The Greek word for 'turning away from your sins' is *metanoia*, which literally means 'changing your mind'. Do you think that this helps us to understand what John meant?

FOLLOW UP

1. Give short answers to these questions:
- In which river did John baptize people?
- Whom was John dressed like?
- What did John eat?

2. Fill in the missing words:
'The man who _____ _____ after me is _____ _____ than I am. I am not good enough even to _____ _____ and _____ his sandals.' Who is John talking about?

3. Give two ways in which Mark thinks that John is important.

4. Why did John tell the people to turn away from their sins?

5. How does the beginning of Mark's Gospel prepare the reader for the arrival of the Messiah?

The Messiah Arrives

Mark has told his readers how John prepared the people for the coming of the Messiah. Now the real drama is about to start.

READ MARK 1:9–15

The baptism of Jesus
(verses 9–11)

Mark has no stories about Jesus' birth or his childhood. He appears on the scene for the first time in this story, and is baptized by John. At once, three things happen:

Jesus sees the heavens open.

This modern baptism in Bolivia helps us to picture Jesus' baptism. Although the style of baptism varies, outdoor or indoor, adult or child, it remains an important part of Christian faith. The believer is saying goodbye to the old life and starting a new one, washed clean of past sins.

He sees the Spirit of God descending on him.

He hears a voice from heaven.

What are we to make of all this? It is interesting to wonder what Jesus might have felt like, but Mark does not tell us. He is much more interested in what the story means for his readers. Each part contains some 'good news' for them.

● **The Kingdom of God is about to arrive.** In Unit 4 we saw that the Jews of Jesus' time were waiting for the Kingdom of God. In Jewish writings which looked

forward to its arrival we often find the idea that God is suddenly going to open heaven. For instance, one of the last prophets had asked him, 'Why don't you tear the sky apart and come down?' (Isaiah 64:1). This is just what Mark says happened at Jesus' baptism. The Kingdom of God is almost here: everything the Jews had longed for over the years is about to come true.

● **The Holy Spirit has returned.** The Jews of Jesus' time thought that the Spirit of God was the 'part' of God which had spoken to the Old Testament prophets a long time ago. Since the last of the prophets the Spirit had been very quiet – but many people believed that he would come back with the Messiah. In Mark's story of Jesus' baptism this is what happens. The Holy Spirit descends on Jesus like a dove, proving that he is the Messiah.

● **Jesus is the Son of God.** For Mark, this is the best news of all. It is announced by God himself speaking from heaven. The words used here are very like some from one of the Old Testament psalms. They were originally meant for the coronation of one of Israel's kings:

'You are my son: today I have become your father' (Psalm 2:7).

However, the story has a darker side as well. The words of the voice from heaven are not just about being a king. They would also have reminded Mark's readers of a passage in the book of Isaiah, which talks about the mysterious *Suffering Servant* of God:

'Here is my servant, whom I strengthen – the one I have chosen, with whom I am pleased' (Isaiah 42:1).

We do not know who the writer of these words thought the Suffering Servant was, but he talks about him dying for the people. Some Christians say that the prophet was looking into the future and thinking about Jesus himself. By echoing his words, the voice from heaven is preparing Mark's readers for the death of Jesus.

Titles of Jesus

2. Son of God
One of the most important titles Mark uses for Jesus is 'Son of God'. In the sections we have just been looking at, the title appears in the first verse of the Gospel, and the voice from heaven says that Jesus is 'my own dear Son'.

The Jews of Jesus' time thought that the Messiah was going to be a new King. In the Old Testament the king of Israel was sometimes called God's 'Son'. We have already seen that words from one of the king's coronation psalms are very like what the voice from heaven says: 'You are my Son.' The title 'Son of

God' therefore carries with it the idea of a *kingly Messiah*.

As we read the Gospel through, however, we will notice that Jesus hardly ever uses this title about himself. He does not deny *being* the Son of God, but it is only *other people* who call him that.

Why is this?

One probable reason is that Jesus did not want people to get the wrong idea about what sort of a Messiah he was going to be. Jews like the Zealots were expecting the Messiah to be a warrior king (see Unit 1), but Jesus thought of his path as one of suffering.

After Jesus' death and resurrection, however, the early Christians felt able to call Jesus the 'Son of God' quite openly. There was no longer any danger that the title would be misunderstood, or that Jesus would be made the leader of a rebellion against the Romans. Instead, the early Christians began to understand that Jesus was a kingly Messiah and the Son of God in a quite different way: he was God himself, made man. For this reason the title 'Son of God' became one of the most important ways they had of speaking about him.

The temptation of Jesus
(verses 12–13)

Mark says that the Spirit 'made Jesus go into the desert' after his baptism. There he was tempted by Satan for forty days. He tells this story very briefly.

What does 'temptation' mean? When we say we are tempted to do something, it usually means we are considering doing something we shouldn't. Sometimes the temptation can be very strong, so that we feel almost helpless. It is a great struggle not to give in – but if we do manage to resist, we feel better about ourselves afterwards. It is as though we have gone through a sort of test, and come out winners.

Go on – take one! No one's looking!

Ever since the very early days of Christianity, Christians have believed that Jesus' temptation somehow helps them when they are being tested. One early Christian writer wrote about it like this:

'(Jesus) is not one who cannot feel sympathy for our weaknesses. On the contrary, we have a great High Priest who was tempted in every way that we are, but did not sin' (Hebrews 4:15).

Notes

1:9: John is baptizing in the River Jordan. The River Jordan was the last river the Jews had to cross before they reached the Promised Land in the ancient stories of the Old Testament. In those days they were led by Joshua the son of Nun. The name 'Joshua' is the same as 'Jesus' in Hebrew. Perhaps we can think of Jesus as the new 'Joshua' who is leading the people of God to a new 'promised land' – the Kingdom of God!

1:10: The Holy Spirit descends on Jesus 'like a dove'. Perhaps this is an echo of the story of creation in Genesis 1, where God's Spirit hovers over the unmade world – or perhaps we could think of the dove which brought the olive branch to Noah, to show him that the flood was over (Genesis 8:11). Today doves are often used as symbols of peace. Because of Mark's story, Christians sometimes use a dove as a symbol for the Holy Spirit himself. Lots of people have tried to work out why Mark uses this picture language, but nobody really knows.

1:13: Jesus is with the *wild animals*. Although the translation makes it sound as though the angels are protecting Jesus from the animals, this part of the story could have another meaning.

Some of the Old Testament prophecies looked forward to a time when God's rule would come and even wild beasts would be tamed: 'At that time I will make a covenant with all the wild animals and birds, so that they will not harm my people' (Hosea 2:18).

Perhaps the wild beasts in this story have been tamed by the presence of Jesus – a further proof that the Kingdom is coming. The word translated 'but' here can equally well mean 'and'.

The *angels* minister to Jesus. This is like some more words from the Psalms about those who trust God: 'God will put his angels in charge of you to protect you wherever you go' (Psalm 91:11).

1:14: Mark says that Jesus started preaching 'after John had been put in prison'. Later on in the Gospel Mark tells the story of John's arrest and execution (6:14–29).

This is certainly one of the reasons why Mark tells the story of Jesus' temptation. It is to give encouragement to his readers, who may themselves be facing temptation. It is as though the story is saying to them, 'Don't worry! Jesus has been through it all too!'

But there is another reason as well. Jesus' temptation shows him defeating Satan. The Jews of Jesus' time believed that when the Kingdom of God arrived, there would be a huge battle between God and the devil, between the forces of good and the forces of evil. Jesus is beginning this battle in his temptation. It continues throughout the Gospel in all the stories which show Jesus casting out evil spirits. Like John the Baptist's prophet's clothing and the descent of the Holy Spirit at Jesus' baptism, the temptations of Jesus are a sign that the Kingdom is coming.

Jesus proclaims the coming of the Kingdom (verses 14–15)

Everything Mark has written so far has been like an introduction. Now Jesus himself begins to preach:

'The Kingdom of God is near! Turn away from your sins and believe the Good News!' (1:15).

These words are Mark's *summary of the whole of Jesus' message*. We should certainly not think that Jesus only spoke like this once, and then went on to talk about other things. Mark has chosen these words and placed them at the beginning of Jesus' preaching so that his readers know what to expect in the rest of the Gospel. Jesus' message is about the Kingdom of God, and what people should do about it.

But what did Jesus mean when he talked about the Kingdom of God? Read again the information in Unit 4.

FOLLOW UP

1. Mark says that three things happened to Jesus at his baptism. What were they?

2. ● What does the voice from heaven say to Jesus in this story?
● These words would have reminded Mark's readers of two passages from the Old Testament. What two ways of understanding Jesus do they bring out? Say why.

3. What does the title *Son of God* mean? Answer as fully as you can.

4. How does Mark summarize the message of Jesus?

5. Some Christians think that Jesus' temptations are a help to them when they are tempted. Explain this as best you can.

The Authority of Jesus

Which of these people do you think has authority, and why?
  □ A policeman/woman
  □ A schoolteacher
  □ A judge
  □ The Archbishop of Canterbury
  □ The Prime Minister

What does 'authority' mean?
  How does Mark show Jesus' authority in these two stories?

READ MARK 1:16–28

Here, Jesus shows his authority in three ways:
- He tells people to follow him
- He teaches people new things
- He heals people.

The call of the disciples

Just before this story, Jesus has said, 'The right time has come, and the Kingdom of God is near! Turn away from your sins and believe the Good News!' (Mark 1:15). Now he starts to choose people to follow him. In Jesus' time, many Jewish teachers had followers who were called *disciples*, which means 'people who learn'. They would listen to their master's teaching and try to learn it by heart. Why do you think this was?

Jesus was different from most Jewish teachers, though:

● A Jewish teacher would wait until people decided to follow him, but Jesus *tells* the four fishermen to be his disciples. The Kingdom of God is near, and there is no time to waste.

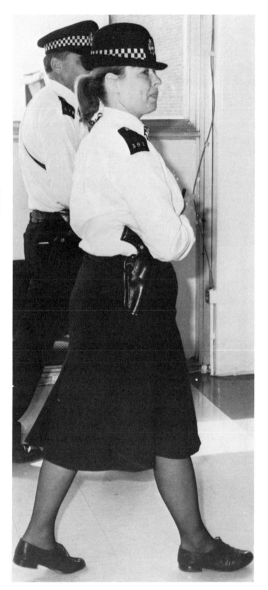

Some people have authority because of the position which society has given them. Others have authority through the strength and magnetism of their characters. Which type of authority do you think Jesus had?

33

● Most Jewish teachers' disciples were well educated. Jesus chooses ordinary people. Why do you think he did this?

We have seen that the four men – Simon, Andrew, James and John – were fishermen.

 Simon was also called Peter or Simon Peter.

They worked in the north of Israel in an area called Galilee. Lake Galilee was in the east of this region. The fishing industry was very important for the people who lived there – most people in Jesus' time ate meat once a week at the most, and an important part of their normal diet was fish. The Jewish historian Josephus says that there were 330 fishing boats on the Lake in the first century. When Jesus tells the four men to follow him, they do not hang about, but drop everything and hurry to start their new life. They will no longer catch fish; they will catch 'men' (people)! Their job will be to get people to follow Jesus – to draw them into the 'net' of the Kingdom of God.

Think what kind of person could make you want to give up everything to do as they said.

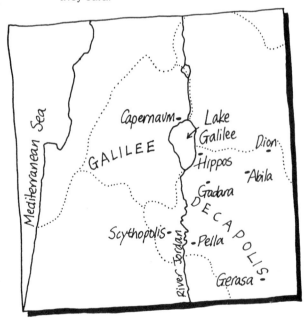

Why did the disciples follow Jesus? Here are three answers for you to think about:

66 They had heard Jesus teach before and liked what he said. **99**

66 They had been followers of John the Baptist, and he had pointed them to Jesus. John's Gospel says this is what happened – see John 1:35–51. **99**

66 Some people have what we call a magnetic personality. Perhaps you can think of someone you know or have seen on television who would only have to walk into a room to make you sit up and take notice. There is just something about them. Perhaps Jesus had this quality (which we also call *charisma*) and the fishermen recognized it. **99**

So, do you think the men followed Jesus because of what he said, because of who he is, or both?

The man with an evil spirit

This story begins Mark's 'Day in the Life of Jesus'. Jesus travels to the town of Capernaum and goes to preach in the synagogue on the Sabbath.

A synagogue is a Jewish place of worship, and there was at least one in every town. (There had to be at least ten Jewish men to form a synagogue.) There was a service on some weekdays and on the Sabbath. The Sabbath is the Jewish holy day. It starts at sundown on Friday and finishes at sundown on Saturday.

The Sabbath service consists of prayers, a blessing, readings from the Jewish scriptures (the Tenakh, which Christians call the Old Testament), and a sermon. The sermon explained the readings, and any adult male could be invited to preach, especially if he was skilled in explaining the Torah or Law (see Unit 1). So Jesus began to teach. Mark does not tell us here what Jesus said (he does so later in his Gospel). What he does say is that 'the people who heard him were amazed at the way he taught, for he wasn't like the teachers of the

Law; instead, he taught with authority'
(Mark 1:22).

The *Teachers of the Law* or *scribes* spent
their time studying the Torah. The Torah
was believed to be God's guide to how to
live. So the scribes tried to make sure
God's Law was not broken. They did this by
adding a number of new rules – the *Oral
Law*. For example, the Torah said people
should not work on the Sabbath. The
scribes wanted to know whether this meant
that only some work was forbidden, or *any*
work. Many said it meant any work,
including writing or setting broken bones.
Most scribes were also Pharisees. If
someone asked a question about the Law,
the scribes would usually reply, 'There is
a teaching that says . . .' so and so.
They would back up what they said by
remembering what someone else had
said, rather like lawyers do today. Jesus
did not do this. His teaching was 'new'. He
spoke 'with authority'. *His authority did not
come from saying the same thing as other respected
people. It came from himself.*

Jesus showed his authority, too, by
casting out evil spirits. The Jews believed
that God had made the world, and that it
was good (see Genesis 1:1–2:4). But they
also knew there was a lot of suffering.
They believed that illness – especially
mental illness – was caused by evil spirits.
Some said there were over seven million
demons in the world, and they were very
dangerous. They liked to live in tombs
and places where there was no water,
although they could be anywhere. They
were most active at night and in the heat of
midday, and were particularly dangerous to
travellers, women giving birth, and children
who were out after dark.

There were three main ideas about
where they came from:

● Some said they were the spirits of evil
people who had died.

● Some said they had been around for a
very long time, and had fought God when
he created the world. They had lost that
battle, but did not give up and still carried
on their sinister work.

● Some said that when the world was
young, two angels came down to earth
because they realized women were
beautiful. (This story was based on Genesis
6:1–4.) One of them returned to God, but
the other did not: he stayed to have
children. Those children were the demons.

The man with an evil spirit may have had a
mental illness. It was believed that this was
caused by the demon getting inside him in
some way. Many people in the first century
said they could get rid of evil spirits (*exorcize*
them), but they did it through spells and
magic. *Jesus does not use magic: he simply orders
the spirit to leave, and it does.*

Some Jews thought that when the
Messiah came, he would destroy the
demons. It was part of bringing in the
Kingdom of God. In this story, the demon
also knows this. In Matthew's Gospel, Jesus
says, 'It is . . . God's Spirit who gives me the
power to drive out demons, which proves
that the Kingdom of God has already come
upon you' (Matthew 12:28).

So, Jesus shows his authority. He
calls people to follow him. He teaches
something new. He cares about people. He
casts out evil spirits. And the news about
him spread like wildfire.

►FOLLOW ✋UP◄

1. Quick Quiz:

Answer a), b), c), or d) to the following questions:

● Jesus called his first disciples at
  a) the Dead Sea
  b) Lake Galilee
  c) the River Jordan
  d) the English Channel

● The first disciples were called
  a) Matthew, Mark, Luke and John
  b) Levi, Thomas, Judas and Zebedee
  c) Simon, Andrew, James and John
  d) John, Paul, George and Ringo

● A 'disciple' means
  a) someone who learns
  b) someone who follows
  c) a fisherman
  d) a Pharisee

● Jesus tells them they will catch
  a) men
  b) fish
  c) a cold
  d) bigger fish

● Jesus taught in the synagogue in
  a) Galilee
  b) Lake Galilee
  c) Nazareth
  d) Capernaum

● Someone came into the synagogue. He was
  a) the rabbi
  b) a man with an evil spirit
  c) John the Baptist
  d) a demon

● Jesus said to the spirit
  a) 'Who are you?'
  b) 'I have authority over you.'
  c) 'Be quiet, and come out of the man!'
  d) 'Leave here!'

2. Draw the diagram of the synagogue in Unit 12 and label it. Write a paragraph underneath saying what happened in synagogues. Why were they important?

3. Explain
  a) Who were the scribes?
  b) What was the Oral Law?
  c) How was Jesus' teaching different from that of the scribes?

4. You were present in the synagogue when Jesus taught and exorcized the evil spirit. Write a letter to a friend saying what happened, and how you felt.

5. Did Jesus believe in demons? Do demons exist? Here are some possible answers:

● Jesus did believe in demons because they exist. They can still attack people today, and cause a lot of suffering.
● Jesus did believe in demons, but they do not exist. We know today how illness is caused, but people in the first century did not. Jesus lived in the first century, and so he would have believed in demons. Even if Jesus is the Son of God, he was also a human being and had many of the ideas of other human beings of his time.
● Jesus did not believe in demons. He was the Son of God and so would know they did not exist. He acted as though they existed because other people thought they did. If he had healed people without saying he was casting out demons, they would not have understood.

In small groups, discuss whether demons exist, and whether Jesus believed in them. Give your reasons. When you have finished discussing this, appoint someone from your group to tell the rest of the class what your group thought. (It would be helpful to tape record your group's discussions.)

6. Write an essay on the following topic:
'How effectively could the stories of the call of the disciples and the man with an evil spirit be used in proclaiming the Christian message today?'

Jesus the Healer

Mark now tells two stories about Jesus healing people. These are followed by Jesus' decision to leave the area of Capernaum, where he had been staying.

READ MARK 1:29–39

Jesus heals Simon Peter's mother-in-law (verses 29–31)

It is interesting that this miracle takes place in a private house. There was no crowd around to tell people what happened. So where did Mark get his information from? Some people who study the New Testament think Mark got the story straight from Peter himself. After all, it is about Peter's mother-in-law!

Fever was common in Galilee, and it caused a great deal of suffering. Doctors at the time could not always help. The Talmud includes a magical formula which people could say to try to get rid of fever. This formula may have been in use in the time of Jesus. But, once again, Jesus does not use magic: his power to heal comes from his own authority.

The Talmud was – and is – a very important book which contains a vast amount of Jewish rabbis' teaching.

The cure of Peter's mother-in-law is rather different from the cure of the man with an evil spirit (see the last unit):

● Mark does not mention that Jesus said anything here. He simply touches the woman. (Look at verse 31, and compare it with 1:25.)

● There is no mention of a demon. If Mark thought the fever was caused by an evil spirit, he does not say so. So, Jesus can deal with all forms of illness, not just those caused by demons.

The story says two things to Mark's first readers and to Christians today:

● Jesus' miracles are not done for show. He does not have to have large crowds in order to heal people. He heals them because he cares about them.

● After she is cured, Peter's mother-in-law 'began to wait on them (Jesus and his disciples)'. Mark may be hinting that, just as she served Jesus at table, so Christians should serve Jesus in their lives.

The healing of many people (verses 32–34)

The people of the town gathered 'in front of the house' (probably Simon and Andrew's home). They brought with them people who were ill, so that Jesus would cure them. This happened in the evening, when the Sabbath was over: it ended at sundown. Carrying things or people was not allowed on the Sabbath by Jewish Law (see Jeremiah 17:24) so the people waited until evening to bring those who were ill to Jesus.

Mark sees this short story as the sort of thing that often happened in Jesus' work. There are two other passages where he says that Jesus healed a large number of people (see 3:7–12 and 6:53–56). Mark wanted his readers to know that Jesus did not just cure a few people. The miracles show two things:

● that the Kingdom is coming

● that Jesus is the Messiah, even if only the demons realize it (verse 34). (See the next unit to find out why Jesus would not let the demons say anything.)

A preaching tour (verses 35–39)

Jesus gets up early next morning and goes off to a lonely place (or desert) to pray.

Some Christians have problems with the idea of Jesus praying. Christians believe that Jesus is God. If Jesus is God, why does he need to pray?

This need not really be a problem. Christians believe that Jesus is God, but they also believe that he was a human being. So they would say it was as a human that Jesus prayed. Jesus was also a Jew, and it was Jewish practice to pray in the early morning. We can see this from Psalm 5:2–3:

'I pray to you, O Lord;
you hear my voice in the morning.'

(See also Psalm 88:13.)

Some people who study the New Testament say that Mark tells us Jesus prays in times of stress (see Mark 6:46 and 14:32–42). They say that Jesus may have needed God's help here for two reasons:

● Jesus had performed a lot of miracles, and he was exhausted. He needed strength to carry on his work, and he gets that strength through prayer.

● People have been amazed by Jesus' work so far. This reaction is good, but it is not enough. People have not yet realized what kind of a Messiah Jesus is, or what his Kingdom really means. Jesus wants them to understand both.

Do you think these ideas help us understand why Jesus prays here?

Jesus' prayers are interrupted when Simon Peter and 'his companions' (probably the other disciples) find him.

Following Jesus' example of healing the sick, many Christians have taken a lead in health care – setting up hospitals and hospices, fighting leprosy, and meeting basic needs for food, clothing and shelter.

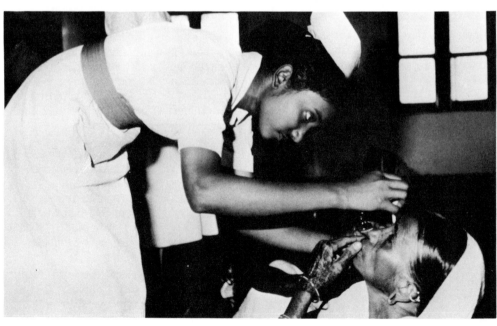

Everyone is looking for Jesus. This is not surprising. Suppose someone you knew was very ill, or even dying. If a man came to your town who could work miracles, wouldn't you try to find him?

Jesus does care about people, and he does heal them, but he does not want to be known simply as a wonder-worker. Jesus and his message mean much more than that.

Look again at verses 36–38, where the disciples find Jesus and he tells them they are all going to move on to the other villages in Galilee. Below the surface meaning of what the disciples say and what Jesus says there is a hidden meaning:

The disciples say
Everyone is looking for you.

surface meaning	hidden meaning
The people in Capernaum are trying to find Jesus.	In Jesus' time and today, everyone is looking for Jesus. People need him even if they do not realize it.

Jesus says
'We must go on to the other villages . . . because that is why I came.'

surface meaning	hidden meaning
Jesus is saying that is why he came out of Capernaum.	Jesus is saying he must spread the Good News of the Kingdom, because that is why he came from God.

Mark would have expected his readers – both in his time, and today – to pick up these hidden meanings.

The section finishes with verse 39: 'So he travelled all over Galilee, preaching in the synagogues and driving out demons.'

This preaching tour is dealt with in just one verse, but it may well have taken months to carry out. 'Preaching' and 'driving out demons' are two sides of one coin. They are both the work of the Messiah who brings in the Kingdom of God.

FOLLOW UP

1. The sentences below have been jumbled up. Match the first half of the sentences with the correct second half to give the story.

Simon Peter's mother-in-law	went out to pray.
Jesus took her	because they knew who he was.
That evening, people brought	the demons.
Jesus healed	preached and cast out demons.
Jesus drove out	is looking for you.'
Jesus did not let the demons speak	all go to the other villages.
Early next morning, Jesus	found him.
Simon Peter and his companions	was ill with a fever.
They said, "Everyone	by the hand and cured her.
Jesus told them they would	them from their diseases.
They travelled through the villages, and Jesus	the sick to Jesus.

2. Look at the section 'Jesus heals Simon Peter's mother-in-law.'
● Where may Mark have got the story from?
● In what two important ways is this story different from the cure of the man with an evil spirit?
● What does the story say to Mark's first readers and to Christians today?

3. Why does Mark record that Jesus healed a large number of people?

4. What may the preaching tour story mean to Mark's readers and to Christians today?

5. Write the following essay:
'Christians believe that Jesus is God, yet Mark shows him praying. What is the problem with this? How might a) a Christian, and b) a non-Christian explain this problem? Which explanation do you think is right, and why?'

UNIT 9

Jesus Heals a Leper

In the work we have done so far, we have seen how Mark tells his readers about Jesus' authority over demons and over disease. In this new story, Mark continues this theme.

READ MARK 1:40–45

Our translation says that the man Jesus healed was suffering from 'a dreaded skin disease'. The Greek word Mark uses for him is simply *leper*.

Leprosy is a horrible disease, and at the time of Jesus it was incurable. The skin of a person with leprosy became covered in terrible sores. The muscles wasted away, so that his or her appearance was completely changed. The disease lasted until the sufferer died – which was anything from nine to thirty years.

The man in Mark's story may have had this sort of leprosy. It was fairly common at the time. However, the Jews also called other severe skin diseases 'leprosy', and people suffering from them 'lepers'. All 'lepers' (whatever the actual disease) were treated in the same way. The Law of Moses had special rules about how they were to behave (Leviticus 13–14), and people thought that they were outside God's chosen people. If you touched a leper it made you religiously unclean – unfit to worship God for a while. For this reason, and perhaps also because people were afraid of catching the disease, lepers had to live alone. As they walked about they had to shout the warning 'Unclean! Unclean!' to passers-by.

Look at the story again. We can say four things about it straight away.

● **The leper breaks the rules.** He does not approach Jesus in the right way. He seems to go straight up to him without any warning. This is very surprising, and even shocking behaviour. It is as though the leper's *desperation* about his disease, and his *faith* that Jesus can cure him, have driven him to forget how he should behave.

● **Jesus touches the leper.** If the leper's behaviour is strange, then what Jesus does is really shocking! People in Jesus' time thought that you could catch leprosy very easily – and we have already seen that touching a leper made you religiously unclean. But Jesus does not seem to care about any of this. He is so moved by the leper's faith and by his terrible condition that he does not think of himself at all.

● **It takes only a word from Jesus to make the leprosy go away.** This would have been very important to Mark's readers. They were used to stories about Greek wonder-workers, who claimed to be able to heal people by magic spells and with complicated rituals. The story of the leper would have shown them that Jesus is not just another of these wonder-workers. His healings were not magic, and he does not need any 'props'. One word from the Messiah is enough!

● **Jesus tells the man to show himself to the priest.** In this way Jesus insists that the man is obedient to the Law of Moses. As part of the rules about how lepers had to behave, this laid down special sacrifices which a leper had to offer once a priest had checked that he was cured. In this way he or she could be welcomed back into the company of ordinary people. Here Mark wants his readers to see that Jesus' care for the man did not stop once he had cured him. He wants what is best for him afterwards as well.

However, Mark has another reason for emphasizing this part of the tale. In the stories which follow, Jesus is going to be accused of breaking all sorts of religious rules. The story of the leper shows that Jesus obeyed the Law of Moses, and expected other people to obey it too.

Lepers were outcasts from society. As we read through the Gospel we see how Jesus welcomed other outcasts into the Kingdom of God.

The Messianic secret

Look again at verses 43 and 44. Here Mark says that Jesus 'spoke sternly' to the cured leper and told him: 'don't tell anyone about this.' Now look at verse 45. We see that the man completely ignored what Jesus had said. Instead of keeping quiet, he 'began to spread the news everywhere'.

This is not the only place in Mark's Gospel where something like this happens. In the last unit we saw that Mark says Jesus

A rabbi holds the precious scrolls of the Law: for the Jews regard the Law as God's commands for his people. This was Jesus' belief too.

Notes

1:41: The Good News Bible says that 'Jesus was filled with pity', but the original word Mark used was one which means 'filled with anger'. Jesus was angry that the leper had suffered so much.

'would not allow the demons to say anything, because they knew who he was' (1:34), and in the synagogue at Capernaum Jesus ordered the demon to 'be quiet!' after the demon called him 'God's holy messenger' (1:24). At least nine times in Mark's Gospel, Jesus forbids people to spread news about him, or say who he is. It is as though the fact that he is the Messiah is a secret Jesus wants to keep, but which always leaks out. People who study Mark's Gospel call this 'the Messianic secret'.

Why should Jesus have wanted to keep the fact that he was the Messiah secret? After all, Mark thinks that the story of Jesus is good news – and isn't good news worth spreading around?

By the time Mark was writing for his Christian readers in about AD64 things had changed. People had the whole story – they knew what kind of Messiah Jesus was. But when Jesus was still preaching, people had very different ideas about what the Messiah would be like. Remember that the Zealots thought he would be a warrior-king who would drive the Romans out of Israel (see Unit 4). At the time of Jesus, there was a very real danger that people would get the wrong idea about the sort of Messiah he was going to be. By keeping his Messiahship secret, Jesus was trying to avoid people getting the wrong ideas about him.

But this is not the whole answer to our question. We have already seen, in the story of the leper, that the news about Jesus got around despite what he said about keeping it quiet. So why did Jesus go on telling people to be quiet about him? Why didn't he just give up?

The idea of a *secret* was a very important part of Jewish thinking at the time of Jesus. Their writings often describe *God's plan for his Kingdom* as a 'secret' shared only with a very few people, and at very special times. The Messianic secret in Mark is a special secret like this. As we read the Gospel we shall see how Jesus shared it with his closest disciples (8:29, 9:2–9). The demons know about it too, because they are spirits. But for most of the time Jesus' Messiahship is hidden, and people guess at it. The time when the secret is finally revealed for everyone to see is in the story of Jesus' death and resurrection, right at the end of Mark.

FOLLOW UP

1. ● What is leprosy?
● Was the man in the story definitely suffering from this? Explain your answer.

2. What was surprising about the behaviour of
● the leper?
● Jesus?

3. How were 'lepers' treated at the time of Jesus? How do you think they might have felt about this?

4. Do you think there are people today who are treated as outcasts from society? Discuss this with your teacher, or in small groups. What do you think this story might have to say to Christians about how they should behave towards such people?

5. Jesus told the cured leper to show himself to the priest. Write a play script of the conversation they might have had.

6. What do you understand by the Messianic secret in Mark's Gospel? In your answer, you must give at least *two* examples of places in the Gospel when Jesus forbids somebody to spread the news about him, or to say who he is.

Jesus Heals a Paralysed Man

In the last unit we saw how quickly the news about Jesus began to spread. In this new story Mark gives us the first hint that Jesus got into trouble as he got more and more famous. The authorities in Jerusalem send their spies to find out about him.

READ MARK 2:1–12

The idea of making a hole in a roof and lowering somebody through it seems very strange to us, but it would have been quite easy in Palestine at the time of Jesus. Houses there had flat roofs made from beams, with branches between, plastered over with mud. The stairs were on the outside of the house. All that the men in the story had to do was go up the stairs and break through the mud plaster. The damage to the house would have been very slight and easily repaired. Even so, the house didn't belong to them. They must have been very determined to see Jesus.

Jesus' first words to the paralysed man are even more strange:

'My son, your sins are forgiven.'

Imagine a doctor telling you your sins were forgiven if you went to him for a check-up! So why does Jesus speak like this?

We have already seen that Jewish people at the time of Jesus thought that disease was often caused by demons. Another idea was that *sin* sometimes caused illness. One Jewish teacher at the time of Jesus said that 'there is no sick man healed of his sickness until all his sins have been forgiven him'.

The paralysed man in Mark's story may have thought like this. It is even possible that he thought he was ill because God was angry with him, and this made his illness worse. Jesus is trying to reassure him by telling him his sins are forgiven. It is as though he had said:

'Cheer up! Don't be afraid – God isn't angry with you.'

The coming of the Kingdom brings forgiveness and healing.

The opposition starts

Mark tells his readers that Jesus' words shocked some teachers of the Law (scribes, see Unit 7) who were sitting there. This is not surprising. The Jews believed that only God could forgive sins. By claiming to be able to forgive sins, Jesus was insulting God (blasphemy).

The teachers of the Law in this story are almost certainly the agents of the ruling Sadducee party in Jerusalem which controlled the supreme court or *Sanhedrin* (see Unit 1). One of the jobs of the Sanhedrin was to make sure that the people were obeying the traditions of ancient Judaism laid down in the Torah.

Jesus understands why the teachers of the Law are worried. He tries to show them that what he has said to the paralysed man really is true. 'Look,' he says to them, 'is it easier to say, "Your sins are forgiven", or to say, "Get up, pick up your mat and walk"?' (Remember that to the Jews these meant more or less the same thing.) To make sure that the teachers of the Law have got the point – that Jesus has authority to forgive sins – he repeats these words to the paralysed man, and he gets up and walks!

Why did Mark use this story?

● It shows Jesus doing something which the Jews thought only God could do.
● It shows his readers that Jesus was not just a wonder-worker who cured people's bodies. He made people whole by healing them *and* forgiving their sins.
● It introduces the conflict which will eventually lead to his death.

▲FOLLOW UP▲

1. The following sentences give the story of the healing of the paralysed man, but they are in the wrong order. Put them right:
● The teachers of the Law thought Jesus was blaspheming.
● The four men went onto the roof.
● Jesus was preaching at Capernaum.
● The people watched the man leave and were amazed.
● Four men came to Jesus carrying a paralysed man, but could not get to him because of the crowd.
● Jesus told the man his sins were forgiven.
● Jesus told the man to pick up his mat and go home.
● The four men made an opening in the roof and lowered down the paralysed man.
● Jesus knew what the teachers of the Law thought and said the Son of Man had authority to forgive sins.

2. Complete the following sentence:
'I will prove to you, then, that . . .'
● Who was the Son of Man?
● What does *Son of Man* mean here?

Notes

2:5: Mark emphasizes that Jesus performs the miracle because of the *faith* of the paralysed man and his friends. This faith forms a kind of friendship with Jesus, and all the miracles in Mark's Gospel come about *because faith already exists.* Although in this story the teachers of the Law are allowed to see the healing of the paralysed man as proof of Jesus' authority, it is the faith of the man and his friends to which Jesus responds. Later in the Gospel, Jesus refuses to do a miracle for some Pharisees who, far from having faith, are simply out to trap him (8:11–12).

2:10: Jesus calls himself the 'Son of Man' here. This was a common expression meaning 'I' or 'this man here', and it is the usual way Jesus talks about himself in Mark. But it sometimes has another, hidden meaning as well, and we will explore this later on.

2:12: Mark frequently ends his stories by noting the astonishment of the crowds at what Jesus had said or done. Perhaps the people here included some of the teachers of the Law who were convinced by the miracle they had seen, but Mark does not say so.

3. Give *three* reasons why Mark tells this story.

4. People in Jesus' time thought that illness was sometimes caused by sin.
● Why do you think they held this view? Discuss this with your teacher and other members of the class before writing your answer.
● Do you think they were right? Explain your answer.

The Messiah's Banquet

Jesus' problems with the Jewish religious leaders continue in the two stories in this section: the calling of Levi and the question about fasting.

READ MARK 2:13–22

Many Jewish teachers (rabbis) would teach their followers while they were on a journey, and this is what Jesus does. When he comes across Levi, a tax collector, he calls him to become one of his disciples.

We do not know who Alphaeus, Levi's father, was, but we do know something about Levi. It is very likely that he was also called Matthew. His job was to collect taxes for the Roman authorities. Galilee was an important place for trade, as merchants travelling from Africa to Europe usually made their way through the area. The government charged them a fee to use the roads, and Levi may have collected this money.

Tax collectors were hated for a number of reasons. No one likes the taxman! And in this case the tax collectors often took more money than the government wanted, and kept the rest for themselves. Many became extremely rich at the expense of their fellow-Jews. They were thought to be outside God's chosen people because of their reputation, and because they had dealings with Gentiles (non-Jews) and often worked on the Sabbath. This made them unfit to worship God (ritually unclean).

So Jesus' call of Levi was very shocking. Jesus did not condemn him or avoid him: he wanted Levi as a disciple! Like the four fishermen in Mark chapter 1, Levi does what Jesus says right away. He cannot return to his old job: he has decided he wants to follow Jesus and to enter the Kingdom.

Jesus not only calls Levi to be a disciple, he has a meal with him and 'other outcasts'. Most Jews thought that these men and women, like Levi, were not good enough to be the people of God. They may have been 'bad characters' – people who did very wrong things, such as tax collectors and prostitutes. Or they may have been what the Pharisees called 'the people of the land' – people who lived in Palestine but did not keep the Jewish Law. One reason why Law-abiding Jews could not eat with these outcasts was because they did not prepare food in the way set down in the Law of Moses. However, Jesus shows that there is room for them in the Kingdom.

Look again at verse 16. Some 'teachers of the Law, who were Pharisees' did not like the idea of Jesus eating with 'such people'.

Pharisees *were* interested in getting people to repent – to change their minds and join God's people. But they had to

The Messianic banquet

A special meal with family or friends is one of the good things in life. That is why people in Jesus' time sometimes said that the Kingdom of God would be like a celebration meal. They did not really think everyone would eat together at an enormous table. The idea was a great get-together of people all enjoying each other's company – they would be like a big family or group of friends. So another name for the Kingdom of God was the *Messianic banquet* (the Messiah's feast).

Mark's readers, and the people who knew Jesus, would have heard about the idea of the Messianic banquet. So when Jesus ate with 'tax collectors and other outcasts', they would have realized that his action had a hidden as well as a surface meaning. They would have thought like this:

Jesus eats with 'tax collectors and other outcasts'

surface meaning	hidden meaning
They had a meal together.	Jesus is inviting them to the Messianic banquet, or the Kingdom of God.

We have seen that Christians believe that people who are members of the Kingdom of God are part of God's family not just in this life. After death, they will live with God for ever. Here, and in other parts of his Gospel, Mark shows that Jesus' invitation includes 'bad characters' like the tax collectors and outcasts. The Kingdom of God is for them too.

The idea of the Messianic banquet lies behind two special meals which the early Christians ate together:

● The **agape** (say it 'aggapay') was a meal, with prayers, that Christians shared with each other. Some Christians today still eat this 'fellowship meal' together, although most do not.

● The **Eucharist** (Holy Communion/Mass), has been very important for Christians right from the beginning. It looks back to the Last Supper which Jesus had with his disciples. We shall find out more about it in Units 48 and 49.

keep the rules first. Jesus went straight to the outcasts. The Pharisees did not. Jesus treated the outcasts with the same kindness he showed to everybody else. The invitation to the Kingdom of God was for everyone.

The story ends with one of Jesus' most famous sayings:

'People who are well do not need a doctor, but only those who are sick. I have not come to call respectable people, but outcasts.'

What do you think he meant?

The question about fasting

(verses 18–22)

Mark says (verse 18) that 'some people' (probably some Pharisees) asked Jesus why he and his disciples were not fasting. Fasting means going without food for a time. Religious people fast because they see it as a duty to God.

The Bible says: 'Man must not depend on bread alone to sustain him, but on everything the LORD says' (Deuteronomy 8:3).

Food is important to keep us alive, but it

is not everything. The idea of fasting is to remember that we do not just need food: we need God as well.

The Jews all fasted (as they still do) once a year on the Day of Atonement. On this day, Jews remember their sins. They fast to show they are serious about asking for God's forgiveness. Very strict Jews in Jesus' time also fasted every Monday and Thursday from 6 a.m. to 6 p.m. This may well be what the 'followers of John the Baptist and the Pharisees' were doing.

Why wasn't Jesus joining in?

Look again at verses 19 and 20. Jesus was not against fasting; he was simply saying that it was not the right time. The Messiah was with them: the Kingdom was here! It was a time to be happy, like a wedding feast. No one wanted to miss a Jewish wedding feast. The couple who got married did not go away on a honeymoon: they stayed at home for the celebrations. They invited their close friends to a party that went on for a week! It was no time to be unhappy, and no one fasted if there was

The time when Jesus was there with his disciples was not a time for fasting. It was more like a wedding, when everyone celebrates and is happy.

a wedding on. One Jewish teacher (rabbi) from about Jesus' time said that the coming of the Messiah would be like a wedding. And Mark's readers would be thinking, again, of the Messianic banquet.

The wedding celebrations stopped when the bridegroom went away. When he talks about the bridegroom, Jesus means himself. The bridegroom will be taken away from his friends, and then they will fast. Here Jesus is saying four things:

● **He is talking about who he is.** In the Old Testament, God is sometimes called the 'bridegroom' or 'husband' of the people of Israel (see Isaiah 54:5 and 62:5). God's relationship with his people is like a marriage. Jesus may be calling himself 'the bridegroom' because it hints at who he really is.

● **He is talking about what he does.** In the Old Testament, the 'marriage' between God and his people is not stable. The people keep breaking their side of the agreement (covenant). The book of Hosea says that things are so bad that there has been a divorce. But Hosea also says there will be a new 'marriage' between God and human beings. Jesus is the 'bridegroom' in this new 'marriage'.

● **He is saying what will happen to him.** The bridegroom will be taken away. In other words, he will be killed. In coded language, Jesus is talking about his death.

● **He is saying what will happen to the bridegroom's friends.** The bridegroom's friends – the Christians – will fast after Jesus' death. The first Christians did this often. A large number of Christians still fast today. For example, many Roman Catholics fast on the special days of Ash Wednesday and Good Friday. Some Roman Catholics also fast every Friday (the day on which Jesus was crucified), and for an hour before going to Mass. Christians generally may fast to prepare for special work, or to free themselves for an uninterrupted time of prayer.

Verses 21 and 22 seem a little hard to understand at first. Read them again. Both verses mean the same thing:

It is no good putting new wine into used wineskins. In Jesus' time, people did not usually use bottles. Wine was kept in bags made from animal skins. After a time, these skins became old and brittle. When grape juice is fermenting to become wine, gas is produced. If you put new wine, which is still fermenting, into old wineskins which cannot stretch, the gas will burst them. New wine must be poured into fresh, flexible wineskins.

If you have an old coat, it is no good patching it with new cloth. In Jesus' time, 'new cloth' meant cloth that had not shrunk. So the new patch would shrink and pull away from the coat making an even bigger hole.

Notes

2:15: The Good News Bible says, 'Jesus was having a meal in Levi's house.' This may be right, but the Greek says 'he was having a meal in *his* house.' Mark *may* be talking about Jesus' house, not Levi's.

2:16: The Good News Bible says that 'some teachers of the Law, who were Pharisees' saw where Jesus was eating. We can translate this verse in this way, meaning that some of the scribes ('teachers of the Law') were also Pharisees. However, some Greek copies of Mark say 'the scribes *and* the Pharisees', and this may be what Mark wrote.

What did Jesus mean?

Jesus is not telling people how to patch their clothes, or how to make wine. What he means is that old and new things do not really mix. He is saying that the new thing – the Kingdom – does not really mix with the old things – the ways the Jews have been living up until now. He is not saying that the old ways are stupid and useless. He was a Jew himself and he kept the Law. He is simply saying that, now the Kingdom has come, the old must make way for the new.

When Jesus called Levi to follow him, people were shocked. He had chosen, not just respectable people, but the 'outcasts' – those society had no time for.

1. You are reporting for the *Galilee Star*. Write a newspaper article with the title:

PREACHER IN TROUBLE: ROW OVER DINNER WITH TAXMAN

2. Who were the 'tax collectors and other outcasts' Jesus met and ate with? What did they do? Why do you think they were attracted to Jesus? (Answer as fully as you can.)

● If you can, talk to one or more Christians, and ask them: Do they think it is important that Jesus mixed with outcasts? Why? Who would he have mixed with today? What do they think this means for the way they live their lives? (It will help if you can tape record the conversation.) If you interview more than one person, it would be interesting to see if there are any differences in their views.

If you cannot do the interviews, discuss with your group why you think it might be important to Christians today that Jesus mixed with outcasts. Write down your group's views. Some Christians have made it their life's work to help people society rejects. Does the group know of any?

3. Jesus said, 'I have not come to call respectable people, but outcasts.' 'Respectable people' really means 'righteous people' – those who are thought to be all right with God. People disagree about what Jesus meant when he said 'I have not come to call righteous people'. Does he mean:

● those who are already all right with God, and so do not need Jesus to call them?

● or is it that he cannot call 'self-righteous' people – those who think they are so good that they do not need anything done for them?

What do you think Jesus meant? Why do you think this?

4. ● What was the Messianic banquet? Answer in as much detail as you can.

● How does this passage in Mark bring out the idea of the Messianic banquet?

● What do Christians today do to show that being the people of God is like taking part in a meal?

● How effective is it to talk about the Kingdom of God as a meal or feast?

5. ● What is fasting? Why do religious people fast?

● Why wasn't Jesus fasting?

● What did Jesus mean when he talked about a wedding?

● What did Jesus mean when he talked about himself as 'the bridegroom', and said the bridegroom would be taken away from his friends?

6. What did Jesus say when he talked about a piece of new cloth and wineskins? What did he mean?

Rules, Regulations and Religion

So far, Mark has told three stories about the conflict between Jesus and the religious authorities:

- The paralysed man (2:1–12)
- The calling of Levi (2:13–17)
- The quesion about fasting (2:18–22)

You can see that these stories come after one another: they are in a series. Many people who study the New Testament think that Mark often grouped together stories because they deal with the same theme and not necessarily because they happened in that order in the life of Jesus. This may be what has happened here.

In this unit we look at two more stories which round off the section on conflict:

- The Sabbath corn
- The man with the paralysed hand

READ MARK 2:23–3:6

The Sabbath corn

One of the ways the Law of Moses protected poor people was to allow them to pick food from growing fields or vineyards. But they must not use tools or carry large quantities away with them (Deuteronomy 23:24). So Jesus' disciples were not stealing by picking the corn. But they made the Pharisees angry because they were doing it on the Sabbath (see Unit 1).

The Pharisees believed that the most important thing in life was to obey God's Law, the Torah. So they were very careful to avoid anything which might infringe the Law, even in the smallest way. And they expected others to do the same. They had their own ways of interpreting the Old Testament which helped them to obey God's Law, and they often added rules of

their own, to prevent them breaking the Law by accident. They called this 'putting a fence around the Law'. In this way they hoped to please God.

The Pharisees in Mark's story probably thought that by picking corn Jesus' disciples were breaking the part of the Law which said that you should not *reap* on the Sabbath, even during harvest time (Exodus 34:21). 'Look,' they say to Jesus, 'it is against our Law for your disciples to do that!'

Jesus' answer shows a different way of thinking altogether. He did not want to do away with the Law (Mark made this clear in Jesus' conversation with the leper in 1:44). But as far as Jesus is concerned people come first: the Law is given to help them. That is why Jesus reminds the Pharisees of the Old Testament story about King David. He broke the Law when he was hungry, just like the disciples.

The Pharisees were used to this kind of argument. Jewish teachers always tried to back up what they had to say with a story from Scripture. Jesus uses David as an example, not just because his 'crime' was like the disciples', but because he was a great religious hero and man of God. Even David ate the bread which was meant for the priests – so pleasing God is not just a matter of rules and regulations, but about meeting people's needs.

Finally, Jesus drops a bombshell. 'The Sabbath,' he says, 'was made for the good of man; man was not made for the Sabbath.' The Pharisees thought exactly the opposite, and Jesus' words undermined their whole religious tradition. When we understand this we can begin to see why they became so hostile to Jesus.

By putting human need above all

religious laws, he was asking them to accept a completely new way of thinking. They would have been outraged. What right had Jesus to do this? In the next verse (28) Mark answers that unspoken question: Jesus is the Messiah, the *Son of Man*.

The story of the Sabbath corn would have had a special relevance for many of Mark's first readers. These were Gentile Christians, who would not have kept the Jewish Sabbath. We know that in the early days of the church, Gentile Christians were often criticized for not keeping the Law of Moses. This story would have comforted them. Since the Son of Man is Lord of the Sabbath, what matters is not whether you keep every detail of the Law, but being close to Jesus.

THE SYNAGOGUE

It was Jesus' custom to go to the synagogue on the Sabbath. It was the centre for worship, and for teaching, in each community. The drawing gives an idea of what a synagogue looked like in Jesus' time. It is based on the ruins of a synagogue at Capernaum – though many would have been simpler.

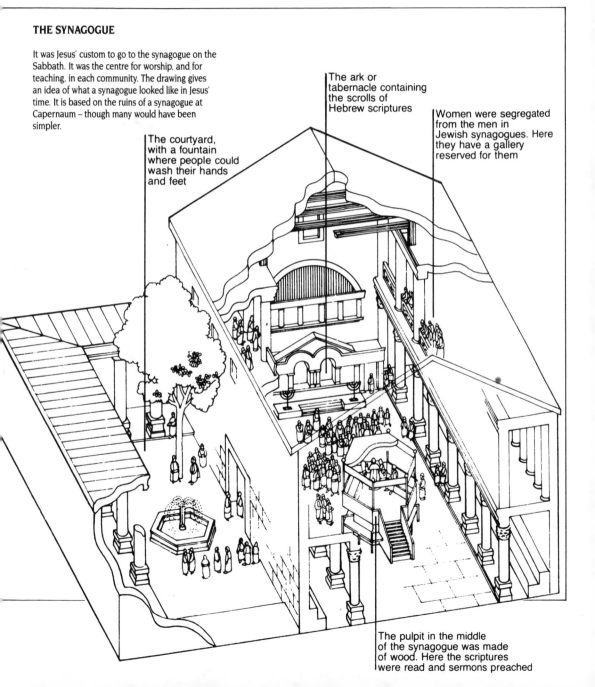

The ark or tabernacle containing the scrolls of Hebrew scriptures

Women were segregated from the men in Jewish synagogues. Here they have a gallery reserved for them

The courtyard, with a fountain where people could wash their hands and feet

The pulpit in the middle of the synagogue was made of wood. Here the scriptures were read and sermons preached

The man with the paralysed hand

This last story in the series continues the themes of the Sabbath Law and of the growing threat to Jesus from the authorities. Read 3:1–6 again.

Mark makes it clear that by this time everyone was agreed that Jesus could perform miracles. Nobody in this story seems surprised that the man is healed. Look back and compare this with the reaction of the crowd in the story of the paralysed man (2:12, Unit 10). The big question now is not whether Jesus can heal people, but whether he does it on the

Sabbath, in front of the Pharisees who are out to get him.

The 'people . . . who wanted to accuse Jesus of doing wrong' (verse 2) are the same as the Pharisees who left the synagogue at the end of the story (verse 6). They were probably members of the Sanhedrin, important people. They would have had special seats right at the front of the synagogue, with a good view of everything that was going on. Despite this, Jesus tells the man to come up, and he heals him in front of them all.

The Herodians

Mark says that the Pharisees 'met at once with some members of Herod's party'. It seems likely that they were the supporters of Herod Antipas, the ruler of Galilee, but we know nothing more about them. Mark is pointing out that there were a number of different groups of people who were against Jesus. The Pharisees did not think very much of Herod – if they were willing to do a deal with his followers, they must have been getting very anxious.

This was a deliberate challenge to the Pharisees, and must have taken a lot of courage. The Jewish laws about healing on the Sabbath were very clear. It was allowed only if somebody's life was in danger. But *the life of the man in the story is not threatened.* It may be unpleasant to have a withered arm,

The drawing shows a Pharisee wearing on his forehead the small box (phylactery) which contained key passages from the Law.

Notes

2:26: Mark's version of Jesus' words says that *Abiathar* was the High Priest at the time of the story about David, but here he seems to have made a mistake. The original story is in 1 Samuel 21:1–6: the priest there is Abiathar's father, *Ahimelech*. The regulations about the 'bread offered to God' (it is usually called the *showbread*) are in Exodus 25:30 and Leviticus 24:9.

3:4: Jesus is making a general point about the Sabbath here – but perhaps Mark wants us to think about the Pharisees' attitude. By plotting to kill Jesus, they are in some sense guilty of *destroying life* on the Sabbath.

but it does not kill you. Jesus could easily have avoided upsetting the Pharisees by waiting until the next day before healing him. In that way, he would not have broken the Law.

Why didn't Jesus do this? Look again at verse 4. Here Jesus is once more putting human need above religious rules, just as he did in the story of the Sabbath corn. But there is more to it than that.

Mark wants us to understand that the coming of the Kingdom of God has started to change the rules. The stubborn Pharisees refuse to see this (verse 5). They are clinging to the old ways of thinking. But the Kingdom has come: God's salvation is here. Even when a man is healed in front of them, the Pharisees only worry about rules. It is this refusal to accept the arrival of the Kingdom that leads them first to hate, and finally to plot to kill, Jesus (verse 6).

▲FOLLOW✋UP▲

Answer these questions as fully as you can:

1. ● Why are the Pharisees angry with the disciples in the story of the Sabbath corn?
● What story does Jesus use in his argument with them?

2. Explain how Jesus' attitude to the Sabbath was different from that of the Pharisees.

3. How does the story of the man with the paralysed hand show Mark's readers the courage of Jesus?

4. Should Christians always try to avoid an argument? How would these stories help them to answer this question?

5. You are a Pharisee who was present at the synagogue. Write a letter to your friend Hilkiah ben Machir about your reactions to Jesus' behaviour.

6. Some Christians say that Sunday should be kept special and that no shops should be open. Using these stories argue *either* for *or* against this view.

The New Israel

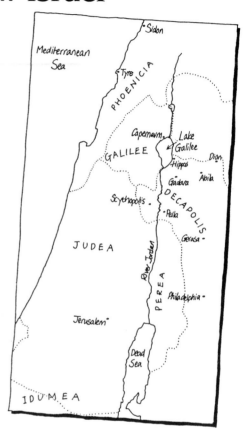

READ MARK 3:7–19

The crowd by the Lake
(verses 7–12)

Mark says Jesus went away to Lake Galilee. This may be because of the threat from the Pharisees and the members of Herod's party. We then have Mark's second story of Jesus healing many people (the first was 1:32–34 and the third is 6:53–56). Notice two things:

● If you look at the map, you will see that people came to Jesus from all over Israel. Although, once again, people seem to go to Jesus just to be healed, Mark may be saying that, in some way, people throughout Israel want to be included in the Kingdom of God: the new people of God, or the *new Israel*. The idea of the new Israel is important for the section of Mark we are covering in this unit.

● People also come from Tyre and Sidon. These were non-Jewish (Gentile) towns, and Mark shows that Jesus and the Kingdom are not just for the Jews: they are for the Gentiles, too.

(To find out why Jesus did not allow the evil spirits to say who he was, see the section 'The Messianic Secret', Unit 9.)

The map shows the places mentioned by Mark in this section: the focus is Galilee.

Jesus chooses the twelve
(verses 13–19)

Jesus picks twelve people to help him in his work. They are often called disciples, but they are called 'apostles' here. 'Apostles' means 'people who are sent' to do something. They are to do three things:

Later Christian leaders

After Jesus' death, a vast number of Christian leaders were appointed. The number of *twelve* leaders stopped being so important, partly because of the size of the church, and because many Gentiles were now Christians. Gentiles would not have thought the number twelve was as important as Jewish Christians did.

Eventually, the leaders of the church became known as bishops, priests, and deacons. We do not know exactly when this happened. The bishop was in charge of the church in his area, and the priests and deacons were his assistants, who lead the local Christian communities. Roman Catholic, Eastern Orthodox and Anglican Christians still have bishops, priests and deacons, and they believe the bishops are the successors of the twelve. You might want to find out more about bishops in the churches today by reading about them in books on modern Christianity.

● **be with Jesus.** They are his close friends, and listen to what he says. Mark's readers – both in his time and today – know that this is what all Christians have to do.

● **preach.** They are to spread the good news about the Kingdom of God. Christians today see telling others about Jesus as a vital part of their work.

● **drive out demons.** They share Jesus' authority to heal people. The Acts of the Apostles shows them performing miracles (see, for example, Acts 3:1–9). Many Christians believe that this power to heal continues today.

Why did Jesus choose *twelve* people? The answer is that the Kingdom of God

'Disciples' means 'people who learn'. Jesus' disciples learn from him. There were many disciples of Jesus who were not members of the 'inner circle' of the twelve, including a large number of women.

is the new people of God. The Jews were divided into *twelve* tribes, named after the sons of Jacob (whose story is recorded in Genesis). The new Israel (the new people of God) does not have twelve tribes, but it does have twelve apostles – a number which had special significance for Jewish believers.

We know very little about some of the twelve. This is what we do know:

● The group included people who were frowned on by the Jewish leaders:

Fishing the Lake was one of the main trades in Galilee in Jesus' day, and fishermen still make a living there. At least four of the 'apostles' were fishermen, and the area around the Lake was Jesus' base for much of his ministry.

– Matthew was probably Levi, the tax collector

– Simon the Patriot (or Simon the Canaanite) was a Zealot, a member of the guerilla group who wanted to throw the Romans out of Palestine.

● Some of them were ordinary, working people: at least four (Andrew, Peter, James and John) were fishermen.

● Their leader, next to Jesus, seems to have been Simon Peter. 'Peter' comes from the Greek word *petros*, which means 'rock', and Jesus gave Simon this new name. It may mean that Peter had a firm, solid character which people could rely on. (See Unit 29.) In AD65 Peter was executed for his faith. The same thing happened to James, and may well have happened to other members of the twelve. They followed Jesus to the death.

● They certainly were not perfect. There was jealousy, and some may have had quick tempers. This may be why Jesus calls James and John 'Boanerges' or 'Men of Thunder' (see the story in Luke 9:51–55, where they wanted to call down fire from heaven on a village that would not accept Jesus). And one – Judas – was apparently dishonest.

● The early Christians believed that members of the twelve wrote many of the books and letters that we now have in the New Testament:

– Peter was supposed to have written the letters called 1 and 2 Peter.

– John was supposed to have written John's Gospel.

Notes

3:14: Some Greek copies of Mark leave out the words 'whom he named apostles'. Mark probably did not write them: they were added later. Mark's special name for the group may simply have been 'the twelve'. However, the word 'apostles' does sum up their job very well.

– Matthew was supposed to have written Matthew's Gospel.

(Many people who study the New Testament today are doubtful that these books and letters were actually written by the apostles. But it is possible that some of the writers drew their information from what the apostles themselves wrote or said.)

● One of the twelve was Judas Iscariot, the man who betrayed Jesus to the Jewish authorities. We shall find out more about him later in Mark.

FOLLOW UP

1. Find the names of the twelve in this wordsearch. They could be written across, down, or diagonally, and could be written either forwards or backwards.

```
J A Z A I B P A J C E I T O N P H N
A G F H Y C K A D L O K N H L R B I
M B L U J M M Z L F M M O J O E M T
E T O I R A C S I S A D U J G M Z P
S X H K Y E A J W M T N H V G U A G
S R A D Y T T C P M T Y U K W E S S
O Y G N J Z Q E L V H R S N N X U L
N F E J D N S X P G E O N D F F E L
O K U V R R X T M N W H I J T N A L
F X B J A M E S I A O H L I I O D S
A Z A V W E N W I J Q M E M R J D Q
L T B Q L W R G D N K H I F O S A T
P H I L I P Q Z I Q O L E S R C H O
H S C C R F U P S O N I S R K E T R
A W V N V S D Y H A B P Z N B Q N J
E T B A R T H O L E M E W H F Q R P
U E L D W Y R X C O P Z D A E L L O
S I M O N T H E P A T R I O T G I R
```

2. What two things should we notice about Mark's story of the crowd by the Lake?

3. ● What does Jesus say the twelve have to to?
● Which of these things are important for Christians today, and why?
● Why does Jesus choose *twelve* people?
● Look again at the list of things we know about the twelve. Pick at least one of them, and say how you think this point would be important for Christians today.
● Most Christians today think the twelve have successors. What are these successors called?

What is Wrong with Jesus?

READ MARK 3:20–35

Here Mark gives his readers two quite separate stories about Jesus, which he has combined. The first story is about Jesus and his family. It starts in verses 20–21, and is finished off in verses 31–35. The second story interrupts the first one, and is in verses 22–30. It is about Jesus and the teachers of the Law. In both stories the main characters think that there is something wrong with Jesus.

Jesus and his family
(verses 20–21 and 31–35)
Look again at verse 20. Mark tells his readers that the crowds kept Jesus and his disciples so busy that they did not even have time to eat. Because of this, Jesus' family got worried about him; people were starting to say that he was 'beside himself' (our translation says 'He's gone mad', but this is a bit too strong for the expression Mark uses). Jesus' family set out to make sure that he was all right.

Mark wants his readers to see that, although Jesus' relatives show the normal sort of concern which we often find in families, they do not really understand him yet. Perhaps they are embarrassed about the reputation he is getting!

Mark never tells us whether Jesus' family succeeded in seeing him, and in verses 31–32 we have a rather sad picture of them, standing on the fringes of the crowd and having to send him a message. What really interests Mark is what Jesus says next. It's surprising, even a little shocking (verses 33–35). *Their love for Jesus is not something which only they can have.* Anybody who 'does the will of God' is a member of Jesus' family. The coming of the Kingdom of God means that everyone who wants to can become one of the family of God.

Jesus, Beelzebul and the teachers of the Law
(verses 22–30)
In the second story, the idea that Jesus is beside himself appears again in a much more unpleasant form. The teachers of the Law suggest that he is possessed by a demon: this is what gives him the power to perform exorcisms (verse 22).

Jesus gives two answers to this accusation (verses 23–26 and verse 27).

Down the ages, and still today, Christians have exorcised evil spirits in the name of Jesus.

The first is to point out how silly it is. If Jesus drove out devils by the Devil's power, the forces of evil would be fighting among themselves, and God would still be winning.

His second answer (verse 27) is more difficult to understand. The teachers of the Law think that Jesus is possessed by an evil spirit *because they see that he is so successful at exorcisms*. Only a power as great as Satan's could produce results like this. But they have got it all wrong. Jesus' miracles do not prove that he is possessed. They are signs that Satan, the 'strong man', is being overthrown. The Kingdom of God is coming.

In the five conflict stories of chapters 2 and 3 (see Units 10–12) we saw how Mark emphasizes the stubbornness of the Jewish authorities at the time of Jesus. Here the teachers of the Law are *so blind* to the Kingdom of God that they see what Jesus is doing as the work of the Devil. This is why Mark introduces the idea of a sin which is unforgivable – a sin against the Holy Spirit. Read verses 28–30 again.

What does Mark mean? It is very important to understand these verses in *context* – that is, the place they have in the Gospel stories. The teachers of the Law have refused to see Jesus' miracles as signs of the Kingdom of God, and have accused him of being possessed by a devil. This comes very close to saying that something which God himself (the Holy Spirit) has done is evil – *that goodness is not goodness at all.* This sort of blindness makes forgiveness impossible. To a person as stubborn as this evil seems like good, and good like evil. How then can they turn to God and find forgiveness?

Notes

3:20: Mark says that Jesus 'went home'. But his family have to travel to see him, so Mark probably means Capernaum, not Nazareth.

3:21: The Good News Bible says that it was other people who were saying that Jesus had gone mad, but the Greek could equally well mean that it was the family themselves.

One of the strangest things about Mark's Gospel is his lack of interest in the family of Jesus. He does not tell the story of Jesus' birth, and here, Jesus' mother is not even named.

Some people have suggested this may be because Mark was for some reason hostile towards the church in Jerusalem, which was run by James the brother of Jesus (see Acts 15:13 and Galatians 1:19). They think this may even be why he has chosen to put a story about Jesus' family next to one about the teachers of the Law. We cannot be sure about this.

3:22: See the explanation of what the Jews thought about devils in Unit 7. 'Beelzebul' or 'Beelzebub' appears as the name of a god of the Philistines (ancient enemies of the Jews) in the Old Testament (2 Kings 1:2). It means 'Lord of the Flies'. By the time Mark was writing, it was probably just another name for Satan.

3:23: Jesus begins to talk in parables. We will be finding out more about these in our next unit.

3:26: This story also appears in the Gospels of Matthew and Luke, but they have an additional saying of Jesus which makes its connection with the coming of the Kingdom even clearer. In their version Jesus says: 'it is not Beelzebul, but God's Spirit, who gives me the power to drive out demons, which proves that the Kingdom of God has already come upon you.' (Remember that the Jews thought that the Kingdom of God would come *after* the defeat of Satan and his demons.)

3:27: In Jesus' saying the Devil is a 'strong man' who needs to be tied up – presumably by somebody even stronger. The Greek word John the Baptist used about Jesus when he called him 'one who is greater than I' (1:7) is really 'one who is stronger' – the Messiah who is going to destroy Satan.

The Good News Bible talks about Jesus' 'brothers', but the Greek word used here can often mean other close relatives, such as cousins. Many Christians believe the tradition that Mary remained a virgin all her life. It could be argued either way from this passage.

3:35: Only Jesus' *mother* and his *brothers* go to see Jesus, but he says that people can be his *sisters* as well. (The word 'sisters' in our translation of verse 32 is almost certainly a mistake and should not be there.) The Kingdom of God is open to men and women alike.

Mark tells us that Jesus proved his power over evil by casting out demons. The medieval drawing shows a monk standing between the Devil and a man whose soul he claims.

▲FOLLOW UP▲

1. Write a letter from Jesus' 'brother' Jude to his other 'brother' Simon about why Jesus is making the family worry so much.

2. Who does Jesus say are his brothers, sisters and mother? What do you think he meant?

3. What did the teachers of the Law say about Jesus, and what were his answers?

4. What do you understand by the 'unforgivable sin' in Mark's Gospel?

5. Read the section on Jewish beliefs about demons in Unit 7. From this and from what you have learnt in this unit, answer the following question in essay form and as fully as you can: 'Why are the exorcisms Jesus performed such an important part of Mark's understanding of the Kingdom of God?'

6. Can it ever be right for Christians to put their families second? How would Mark's Gospel help them to answer this question?

UNIT 15

The Parables
of the Kingdom

Mark does not often give his readers a lot of Jesus' teaching all at once. Usually he mixes it up with stories about things that happened to Jesus, or miracles he performed. However, in the next two units, we look at a section of Mark which breaks this rule. It is a collection of Jesus' teaching and of the stories he told. These stories are called the 'Parables of the Kingdom'. They begin with the parable of the sower.

 READ MARK 4:1–20

Mark has already told us once that Jesus spoke *in parables*. What does this mean?

Parables were stories used by teachers at the time of Jesus. They got the point across by comparing one thing with another. Teachers helped their listeners to understand a difficult idea by saying it was like something they were used to in their everyday lives. Sometimes parables were very short, but they could also be quite long stories. The rabbis were very fond of them, and we still have some examples of Jewish parables from around the time of Jesus.

In many ways, Jesus' parables are similar to the parables of other teachers of his time. Most of the people who followed him were from the countryside or from small towns. They were surrounded by the sights and sounds of farming. Through the year they saw the seeds being sown, crops beginning to grow and then ripen, and finally the harvest. Even Jerusalem, the capital, was a small town by our standards, and the people who lived there knew all about country life. So, when Jesus taught in parables he nearly always used picture language from farming to help his listeners understand what he was saying. Many

other Jewish teachers did this too – but what makes Jesus' parables different is their message: they are all about the Kingdom of God.

Mark makes it clear to his readers that this is not the only way in which the parables of Jesus are unusual. For some people they are riddles which are impossible to understand (the Greek word for 'parable' can also mean 'riddle'). In the last unit we saw how Mark emphasizes the stubbornness of the religious authorities who refused to accept the coming of the Kingdom. In the same way, some people have minds so closed to the Kingdom that they cannot understand the parables.

This is what verses 10–11 are about. Look at them again. Jesus says that the disciples 'have been given the secret of the Kingdom of God', but others are *outside* the Kingdom. To describe these outsiders he quotes some words from the prophet Isaiah (6:9–10) about the people of his time. No matter what Isaiah did, they would not listen to him, and could not accept what God was offering to them. Jesus is saying that some people are 'tuned in' to the Kingdom and will understand the parables (even if they have to have them explained to them), but others are so stubborn that not even the parables will help them. So people's response to the parables is the same as their response to the Kingdom of God. Some people will simply not accept it: their hearts and minds are closed.

The parable of the sower

The story in verses 3–8 is called the parable of the sower. It is one of the most famous stories Jesus ever told. It is explained in verses 13–20. Read both these sections again.

The parable of the sower is one of Jesus' most famous stories. The seed was sown 'broadcast' – that is scattered by hand from a bag slung across the farmer's shoulders.

● Some of the *words* used in these verses are different from the ones Jesus usually uses. For instance, Jesus does not talk about 'God's message' in this way anywhere else. But we do find this expression in the writings of later Christian teachers.

● A parable usually makes *only one point*, but here we have a series of pictures about different things which can happen to different types of people. Would anybody listening to Jesus telling this story have been able to understand all of them at once?

● Some of the things mentioned in the explanation (like 'trouble and persecution', verse 17) seem very like the sort of things which were happening to Christians at the time Mark was writing.

● The original story seems to have been embroidered so that there is some confusion about whether the seed is God's message (verse 14) or those who hear it (verse 18).

The explanation of the parable that Mark says Jesus gave seems a very good one. We all know people who lose their enthusiasm for something after a while, and who drop whatever it is they have begun. Perhaps we have occasionally done something like this ourselves! And we know people who, once they are convinced about a cause, go steadily on.

Many people who study the New Testament say that these verses did not really come from Jesus at all. They think that the explanations were added later, to help Christians who were going through hard times. Reasons given are:

If verses 14–20 were added to Jesus' words by Mark or the early church, what was the original meaning of the parable of the sower? The basic message of the story is clear. Jesus is saying the Kingdom will certainly come, despite its small beginnings in his own ministry and all the difficulties ahead. God is like a farmer sowing his seed. He scatters it about everywhere. Some finds good soil. Some falls on stony ground and some is choked by weeds. But he knows the harvest will come. The followers of Jesus should not despair when things seem to be going wrong: the Kingdom is coming. (We shall see in the next unit that this is very like the meaning of some of the other parables of the Kingdom.)

Some Christians find it very hard to accept that the early Christians may have added things to what Jesus said. Was it right for them to do this? This is a very complicated question, but we *can* be sure that if the Gospel writers did do it, they saw nothing wrong in it. They were not trying to deceive anyone. They believed that God was guiding them through the Holy Spirit as Jesus had promised. And they were simply helping people understand their faith and to live a Christian life.

Notes

4:13: Although the twelve disciples are closest to Jesus and have the secret of the Kingdom (verse 11), not even they understand things fully yet. Mark thinks that it was only after the resurrection of Jesus that the disciples fully grasped the meaning of the Kingdom.

►FOLLOW UP◄

1. ● Explain what a parable is.
● Write a parable of your own. You might want to begin it with the words, 'Life is like . . .'

2. What sort of language did Jesus use in his parables? Why do you think he did this?

3. Divide a piece of paper into two columns. In the left-hand column put the text of the parable of the sower, and in the right-hand column put the part of the interpretation (verses 13–20) which goes with each bit of it, like this:

Once there was a man who went out to sow corn.	The sower sows God's message.

Finish off the whole parable.

4. Why do people say that the interpretation of the parable of the sower was not part of Jesus' original teaching? Give *three* reasons. Do you agree with them? Why?

5. A very early parable was told to King David by the prophet Nathan. We usually call it the story of Nathan's lamb. Read about it in 2 Samuel 12:1–13.

More Parables

In chapter 4:21–34, Mark seems to have collected together some short parables which Jesus probably told at different times.

A lamp under a bowl

READ MARK 4:21–23

People use lamps to light a room, not to stick under a bowl or a bed. Jesus is saying that whatever is hidden will be brought out into the open. This general meaning applies to two things:

The Kingdom
Even if the Kingdom is difficult to see at the moment, Jesus' followers will see it. The disciples may have thought Jesus' message had not converted as many people as it should. Even so, the Kingdom is on its way.

The people in the Kingdom
The truth about Jesus and the Kingdom should not be hidden away. Those who believe in Jesus should not hide away the Good News. They should spread it. This would be true even if they are being persecuted for their faith. (This may have been happening to Christians in Mark's church.) If someone is a member of the Kingdom, they're not going to keep quiet about it!

'The person who has something will be given more'

READ MARK 4:24–25

These two verses are very hard to understand. It is easiest to deal with them one by one.

Verse 24 The Good News Bible tries to make sense of something that looks very odd in the Greek. What Mark actually wrote was this:

'And he said to them, "See and understand. The measure you measure out will be measured out to you, and more will be given to you."'

This could mean any one of three things:

● After their death, God will judge people in the same way that they have judged others. This is how the Good News Bible understands it, and Matthew and Luke have similar sayings which are talking about judgement (Matthew 7:2; Luke 6:38).

● It could just be saying something about life. We get out what we put in. If we put in a great deal, we may find we get even more from it than we expected.

● The most likely explanation seems to be that, once again, Jesus is talking about the Kingdom. If people are 'tuned in' to the Kingdom – if it really matters to them – their understanding of Jesus' message and their care for other people will increase. They will grow in their faith.

Verse 25 Again, it is not very clear what this means. Jesus seems to be saying that if you are alive to God the parables will make you understand things even better. If you close your mind to the Kingdom, the parables will just confuse you and make you worse off than you were in the first place. This might well apply to the Pharisees: they start off by not listening to what Jesus says, and end up by plotting to kill him.

The growing seed

READ MARK 4:26–29

Jesus again uses pictures drawn from farming to talk about the Kingdom. This is the second of the *parables of growth*: the first was the sower, and the next is the mustard seed.

Scholars used to think that these parables showed that the coming of the Kingdom happened gradually: it takes time for a seed to develop into a plant, and it takes time for the Kingdom finally to arrive. However, this really misses the point. The important thing is that plants (which represent the Kingdom) do appear – how long they take does not really matter.

In this parable, the farmer leaves the seed alone once he has planted it. There are two possible ways of understanding this:

● **The farmer represents God.** The farmer leaves the seed alone and gets on with his normal life. God lets the world run on, and then brings in the Kingdom (the harvest). There are two problems with this idea:
– Many scholars think that when Jesus uses parables of growth, the plant, not the harvest, represents the Kingdom. The harvest represents the Day of Judgement, when people will have to answer to God for the way they have lived.
– The Jews of Jesus' time did not believe that God 'lets the world run on'. They thought God was very active in what happened on earth.

A better idea seems to be:

● **The farmer represents Jesus' followers.** The farmer's job is to sow the seed, then it is left to the soil. The disciples spread the message, but they should leave it to God to bring in the Kingdom. People like the Zealots thought they could force it to arrive by fighting the Romans. Once more, Jesus shows that God's actions, not people's, make the Kingdom come.

The mustard seed

READ MARK 4:30–32

Once again, the Kingdom is compared to a plant. In Palestine, mustard plants could be as much as ten feet (three metres) high, even though they started life as a tiny seed. Jesus' work may seem to have little effect at the moment, but the Kingdom will come as surely as a mustard seed grows into a mustard plant.

In the Old Testament, world empires were sometimes described as trees which provide shelter for birds. The birds represented foreign nations who were part of the empire (Daniel 4:10–12). Here, God's empire – the Kingdom – is a tree, and birds make their nests in it. Here, too, the birds represent foreigners. Hebrew and Greek use the same word for 'foreigners' and for

'Gentiles'. So, Gentiles will be included in the Kingdom. Mark's early readers, many of whom were Gentiles, would have understood this.

The mustard seed was not really 'the smallest seed in the world'; this was a figure of speech used by people of Jesus' day.
  Mark actually says that the mustard plant is the biggest of all garden shrubs, not the biggest of all plants.

Why Jesus used parables

READ MARK 4:33–34

These two verses round off Mark's section of Jesus' parables. He mentions 'other parables' which he has left out. Some of these are found in the other Gospels. Mark says Jesus 'told them as much as they could understand'. Like any good teacher, Jesus made sure his pupils could understand what he said.
  In 4:10–12 Mark has already given us some idea of why Jesus used parables. These verses mean much the same thing, so it is worth reading that passage and the notes on it again (see Unit 15).

Lamps are meant to give light, Jesus said, not to be hidden. He made an obvious point, but his words have a deeper meaning. Lamps like the one in the picture, with a wick, and using olive oil, were in common use in Bible times.

FOLLOW UP

1. Draw a picture strip of the parable of the growing seed.

2. In the following sentences the words have been jumbled up. Put them in the correct order:
a) No bed or a bowl puts a one under a lamp.
b) Put a lampstand on it you!
c) A seed Kingdom is like the mustard of God.
d) The mustard in the seed is the smallest world.
e) Of all the biggest it grows to be plants.
f) Branches make their birds in its nests.

3. Fill in the gaps in the following sentences:
● Whatever is _____ away will be brought out into the open, and whatever is _____ up will be _____ .
● The same _____ you use to _____ others will be used by God to _____ you, but with even greater

_____ .

● The person who has _____ will be given _____ , and the person who has _____ will have _____ from him even what he _____ .

4. Copy the table below. Be careful to include the headings of the lines across and the columns down.

The table is about the meaning of Jesus' teaching in Mark 4:21–34. Fill in the boxes using these symbols:

  ✓ = yes, I think this piece of teaching means what this column says

  ⋰⋰ = I think this piece of teaching *might* mean what this column says.

(It is best not to use crosses, as these will clutter up the table too much.)

Examples

– If you think the growing seed means that the Good News should be spread, put ✓ in the box.
– If you think the growing seed *might* mean that the Good News should be spread, put ⋰⋰ in the box.
– If you do not think the growing seed means that the Good News should be spread, leave the box blank.

THE TEACHING IS OR SAYS . . .	PIECE OF TEACHING				
	A lamp under a bushel	'The person who has something will be given more' (verses 24 and 25)	The growing seed	The mustard seed	The summary of why Jesus used parables
Gentiles will be included in the Kingdom.					
God lets the world run on normally, then brings in the Kingdom.					
It is up to God, not to human beings, to bring in the Kingdom.					
The coming of the Kingdom happens gradually.					
The parables help people who are 'tuned in' to the Kingdom to understand better, but they confuse other people.					
We get out of life what we put into it.					
God will judge people.					
The Good News should be spread.					
The Kingdom may be hard to see at the moment, but it will come.					
People might think Jesus' message does not seem to have converted as many people as it should.					
It is about the Kingdom.					
It is a parable of growth.					
It is a parable.					

5. Mark 4:25 reads:

'The person who has something will be given more, and the person who has nothing will have taken away from him even what he has.'

It has sometimes been said that this means God will make people richer if they are good at making money, and will make people poor if they are not. Do you think this is what Jesus meant? Why?

6. Read Mark 4:1–34 again, together with the notes in this unit and Unit 15. Write the following essay:

'Why do people think Jesus taught in parables? What do you think is the best explanation, and why?'

Jesus Calms a Storm

Mark has told miracle stories before, but they have all been healings. There are two things we can say about this new story:
● It begins a new section of miracle stories in the Gospel.
● It is the first of the nature miracles.

What do we mean by nature? The Jews believed that God could control things like the weather. Read the text.

READ MARK 4:35–41

In what way does Mark show Jesus behaving like God?

Mark must have known lots of stories about Jesus. What was special about this story for him? People who study the New Testament have come up with three main answers to this question:
● It is exciting.
● It shows who Mark thinks Jesus really is.
● It hints at how Mark thinks his readers should live.

An exciting story

During the day, Jesus had been teaching people about the Kingdom. In the evening, he and his disciples left by boat for the other side of Lake Galilee.
　　Lake Galilee has always been stormy. Sudden, violent winds funnel between the hills, whipping up the waves and threatening fishermen's lives. The storms are over as quickly as they began. Some of Jesus' disciples were fishermen and would have seen this very often. Mark's description of the weather is just right for the area.

Who is this man?

Look again at verse 41. The whole story leads up to the disciples' question. No wonder they asked it! How would you feel if your best friend spoke to a storm – and it stopped? Mark wants his readers to think about this, but he also wants them to *answer* the question for themselves. 'Who is this man?' *Jesus is the Son of God.* The story contains two sorts of important clues to help them. Both come from the Old Testament.

1. Clues about water
● Before creating the world in the book of Genesis, God's Spirit 'was moving over the water' (Genesis 1:2).
● When God brought the Jews out of Egypt, he parted the waters of the Red Sea to allow them to walk through (Exodus 14:21–32).
● In the Psalms, it says that sailors in trouble

'called to the LORD
and he saved them from their distress.
He calmed the raging storm
and the waves became quiet'
(Psalm 107:28–29).

Mark's readers would have known these stories – we have already said that the Jews believed God could control the weather. Here, Jesus is shown to control the weather, and this could only mean one thing. *Jesus is behaving as though he were God.*

2. Clues about fear
The disciples were frightened when Jesus calmed the storm. In the Old Testament, when God did something spectacular, people were often frightened. For

Mark tells how Jesus calmed a fierce storm on Lake Galilee. The picture reminds us of the enormous forces of nature, over which Jesus many times demonstrated his control.

example, when God gave Moses the Ten Commandments, the people 'trembled with fear' at the signs of God appearing on the mountain (Exodus 20:1–21). *The disciples were afraid because they were seeing God at work.*

How to live

Mark's first readers were Christians, and he tells this story to strengthen their belief that Jesus is the Son of God. We have seen that he is shown to be this by his power over nature, which is the same as God's power in the Old Testament.

Many people think the storm is also a symbol. It stands for the many troubles a Christian may come across in life. What do you think these might be? In this story, Christians in trouble are urged to trust Jesus. Jesus helped his disciples in the storm. Christians should trust Jesus to help them.

Many scholars have held that Mark's Church was among the persecuted Christians in Rome. (See Unit 3.) If this is so, or if his readers were members of some other persecuted Christian community, it may be that Mark had them especially in mind in choosing this story. Like the

Notes

4:37–38 Mark is very fond of including little details in his stories, so he mentions that there were 'other boats' nearby, and that Jesus was 'sleeping with his head on a pillow.' These details make his writing seem very real and some people have suggested that they look like the recollections of an eyewitness, perhaps Peter (see Unit 3). Note too how Mark is not afraid to show the disciples in a rather bad light: they seem to be angry with Jesus for letting things get out of hand – and being able to sleep through it all!

4:39 Jesus commanded the wind and waves with the same words he used to the man possessed by an evil spirit in Capernaum (1:25): 'Be still!' His authority to heal and to calm is the same in both stories.

disciples, their lives were threatened, but they should trust Jesus, whose power can save them.

But faith is not just for the bad times. True faith focusses steadily on God, in good times and bad. It is like the faith of Jesus, which allows him to sleep in the storm, safe in the knowledge of God's love. Here again he is fulfilling the words of the Psalms: 'I go to sleep in peace; you alone, O Lord, keep me perfectly safe' (Psalm 4:8).

FOLLOW UP

1. What do the nature miracles show?

2. What did Jesus say to calm a) the wind, and b) the storm?

3. ● In the story, how did the disciples show their lack of faith?
● Do you think this lack of faith was understandable? Say why in as much detail as you can.

4. Is Lake Galilee a common place for storms today?

5. ● In the Old Testament, who controlled water and storms?

● Give the two Old Testament quotations which show this.
● Mark says Jesus has these powers. What does this tell us about his view of Jesus?

6. In groups, prepare a mime based on this story. See if you can find some appropriate music to use.

7. Write an essay on the following topic:
'The story of the stilling of the storm is said to be helpful to Christians in trouble. In what cases might this be true today?'

The Madman in the Tombs

 READ MARK 5:1–20

This is one of the most brilliantly told stories in Mark's Gospel. It is so vivid that some scholars think Mark got it straight from Peter.

We can imagine the disciples, still frightened by what had happened on the Lake, putting in to land.

The shore is deserted. For some reason, nobody is about. Why does no one else come here? And then they hear the answer in the distance: something bellows like a wild animal. It roars again and again, and they realize the horrible truth that it is a human voice.

Then a man leaps onto a rock on the horizon. He is dressed in rags soaked in his own blood. A few links of broken chains grip the powerful sinews on his arms. He catches sight of them, shrieks, and charges . . .

Once more, Mark has packed his story full of meaning. It follows the stilling of the storm, and the two stories echo Psalm 65:7:

'You (God) calm the roar of the seas,
and the noise of the waves.
You calm the uproar of the peoples.'

But in Mark, it is Jesus who does both things. So, who does Mark think Jesus really is?

This is the first time Jesus has been out of Palestine. On the far side of the Lake he is in the area of the Ten Towns (Decapolis) – independent Greek city-states. His mission extends to non-Jews in Gentile areas like this one. Jesus cares for everybody, and the Kingdom is open to Gentiles as well as Jews, both of whom were included in the early church (as Mark's readers knew).

There is a problem, though. If you look at Gerasa on the map, it is not on the shore of Lake Galilee, but over thirty miles away. So some Greek copies of Mark have 'Gadara' instead of 'Gerasa' – Gadara was only six miles from the Lake. The area around Gadara would seem the best place for the story to have happened. There were caves in the rock wall on the shore there which were used as tombs.

It may be that Mark wrote 'Gerasa' because his knowledge of Palestinian geography was not very good. When his original book was copied, someone saw the problem and changed it to Gadara.

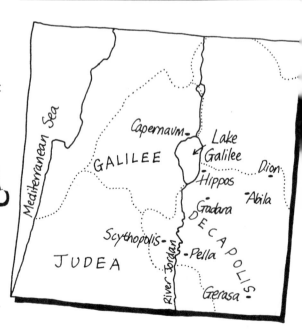

The madman in the tombs seems to have been a very violent lunatic – the most dangerous maniac Jesus has met so far. People did not want him around (would you have done?), and so they made him live in a burial ground. Remember that people believed demons lived in places like this: they probably thought it was the only place he belonged.

The man was beyond all human help: the only attention he got was when they chained him up. It was not clear whether this was to stop him hurting himself, or to stop him attacking other people. (What do you think?) But Jesus' care for human beings is so great that he has compassion on someone whom everyone else has rejected.

When the man sees Jesus, he runs towards him. Perhaps he was enraged by the sight of him, or part of him realized that Jesus could help. There are several things to notice about the conversation he has with Jesus:

● He calls Jesus 'Son of the Most High God'. Again, the demons realize who Jesus is, and what the Son of God does to demons. There was an ancient idea that demons could gain power over an exorcist simply by saying his name, and this may be in Mark's mind. It is interesting that demons living in a Gentile area call God by a Gentile name: in the Old Testament, it was non-Jews who used the title 'the Most High God' (Daniel 3:26).

● Jesus asks 'What is your name?' Mark thinks he is asking the demon what its name is, not the man himself. If a demon could gain power over an exorcist by saying his name, an exorcist could cast out a demon more easily if he knew what it was called.

It turns out that the man is possessed by many demons, not just one (as in the earlier exorcisms in Mark). The Good News Bible uses the name 'Mob'. In the Greek, the word is *Legion*. The idea is that the man has as many demons as there are soldiers in a Roman legion (army division): which was up to 6,000! Roman legions were often very violent and brutal, so the name would conjure up the idea of a huge, savage power that could destroy and cause death.

● The spirits ask Jesus not to send them out of the area. People thought demons would sometimes ask a favour in return for leaving someone, and that they preferred to stay in one place.

Mark says the demons went into a herd of pigs, who stampeded over a cliff and were drowned. (It is not clear whether he thought the demons were killed as well.) Jewish food laws forbade them to eat pigs, but Gentiles kept them. People believed that when demons were cast out they often did some mischief. The Jewish historian Josephus talks about a demon upsetting jugs of water, and the Greek writer Philostrates mentions a demon who pushed a statue over. Mark sees what happened to the pigs as evidence that the demons really were cast out of the man.

We have already looked at whether demons exist (see Unit 7). But scholars have come up with different ideas about what Mark says happened to the pigs.

see over

The local people came to see what had happened, and were extremely frightened. They all knew about the shrieking lunatic in the caves. What was this great power that could change him into a sane human being? It might be dangerous. So they begged Jesus to leave. But it was more than simple fear. We have already seen that Mark always uses the word 'frightened' to mean 'frightened in a religious way' (see Unit 17). Something outside their control – something so incredible that it could not be fully understood – had happened. They were Gentiles, but the power of the Jews' God had touched their lives. Mark may well have thought they later became Gentile members of the church.

The man wanted to stay with the person who had set him free from his terrible suffering. He wanted to be a disciple. This was the right way to respond to a miracle of Jesus. A Gentile madman does what the Jewish leaders refused to do. But Jesus did not let the man stay with him. There was something better for him to do. The apostles must preach to the Jews, but he is to preach to the Gentiles in the Ten Towns about Jesus (see map). He starts the process of bringing the Gentiles into the Kingdom and into the church.

Notes

In verses 2, 7 and 8, the man seems to have *one* demon, not many. This may be because he sometimes spoke as though he had one demon, and sometimes as though he had many. When Peter retold the story, he reproduced the man's confusion. An alternative view is that different versions of the story have been combined: one said that the man had a single demon, another that he had a legion of them.

If you re-read verses 19 and 20, you may notice that Mark again hints at who Jesus really is. Verse 19 says, 'tell them how much *the Lord* has done for you' (the Lord means God). Verse 20 says 'telling what Jesus had done for him'. Mark shows that what God does and what Jesus does are the same thing.

People have said . . .

An old folk story about some pigs has been mixed up with the exorcism story. Wouldn't Jesus care for animals as well as people? Or are 2,000 pigs less important than a human being?

Mark is reporting the facts: the demons entered the pigs and made them stampede.

Jesus made the pigs stampede because this was the only way he could convince the man that he was cured. The man believed he had demons, and needed proof that he was free of them.

To the Jews, pigs were unclean. Jesus was a Jew, and so he got rid of them. (This is very unlikely. Jesus does not seem to have thought in this way, which would be very anti-Gentile.)

The pigs stampeded in fright when the man had a violent fit (possibly when Jesus cured him).

FOLLOW UP

1. You are a television journalist for 'Ten Towns TV at Ten News'. Write a report for the viewers about the healing of the madman. You might want to include an interview with one of the people who looked after the pigs.

2. Read Mark's version of the story again. Then read Matthew's and Luke's versions of it (Matthew 8:28–34, Luke 8:26–39. Matthew has two madmen cured, not one). Which Gospel writer do you think tells the story best, and why?

3. Why did the men say, 'My name is "Mob" (Legion) — there are so many of us!'?

4. Look again at people's ideas about why we have pigs in this story. Which idea do you think is the best explanation, and why?

5. ● How does Mark show that this story happened in a Gentile area?
● Why is this important?

6. How does Mark show Jesus behaving like God in this story?

7. The man in the tombs was clearly mentally disturbed, whatever the cause.

EITHER: In small groups, discuss how we *should* treat people who are mentally ill today.

OR: Do some research on how the mentally ill are *actually* treated in Britain today. (It would be well worth asking a psychiatric nurse to come to speak to the class, if you can arrange it.)

Jairus' Daughter and the Woman who Touched Jesus' Cloak

READ MARK 5:21–43

Jesus goes back across the Lake, and a crowd of people flock to see him. The two miracles he performs in this passage have some things in common:

● Both are about faith: Jairus and the woman trust in Jesus.

● Both are about people who are beyond medical help.

● Both are about females. In Jesus' time, women were thought of as second-class citizens. Girls were not as important as boys. Jesus does not share this attitude. If someone is suffering, he or she must be helped. It makes no difference whether they are male or female.

The story about Jairus' daughter is interrupted by the healing of the woman who touched Jesus' cloak. It may have happened just as Mark reports it. But some people argue that this may be another instance of Mark's fondness for breaking up one story with another, even though the events took place at different times. (We have come across this 'sandwich' arrangement elsewhere.) In any event, it is easiest for us to deal with each miracle in turn.

The woman who touched Jesus' cloak (verses 25–34)

The woman suffered from a menstrual problem, or some kind of infection that produced similar symptoms. The bleeding had become a constant haemorrhage, making her weak and exhausted. It also made her ritually unclean according to Jewish Law – an 'untouchable', not allowed to worship as one of God's chosen people (see Leviticus 15:25). This had been going on for twelve years, and the doctors had been no help at all. But she has been told about Jesus' power to heal, and she believes it: 'If I just touch his clothes, I will get well.'

Jesus somehow knew that 'power had gone out of him', and he wanted to know who had touched him. (The disciples, slow on the uptake again, think someone's barged into him!) The woman is clearly frightened now – is Jesus going to punish her for bothering him? But Jesus' reply is reassuring. In Greek, verse 34 says:

'Daughter, your faith has *saved* you.'

Jesus cares not only for her physical health but for her spiritual wellbeing too. She can go in peace. Her faith in Jesus not only made her well, it saved her. She is now one of the family – a 'daughter' of Jesus – and a member of the Kingdom of God.

Jairus' daughter (verses 21–24 and 35–43)

Jairus was an official or 'ruler' of the local synagogue: he made all the arrangements for worship. He was an important person in the local community. So here we have an example of a Jewish leader who was not against Jesus, but wanted his help. Like the woman who touched Jesus' cloak, he has complete faith in Jesus' power, even though his daughter is dying.

Jesus takes with him Peter, James and John: the three disciples who were often with him on important occasions (at the Transfiguration, for instance, in Mark 9:2 and in Gethsemane, Mark 14:33, which we shall look at later). By the time they reach Jairus' house, the girl is dead, and the Jewish mourning ceremonies have started (verse 38). Even though he knows this, Jesus tells Jairus to 'believe' – to have faith. And then something absolutely incredible happens.

Jesus brings the dead girl back to life. This is the only example recorded in Mark, and the people who saw it were 'completely amazed'. Not surprising! If your daughter had just died and then came back to life, how would you feel? And she was not a ghost or an illusion: she was walking around, and they gave her something to eat.

This story is very important for Mark's readers:

● Only God has power over death. In the Old Testament, God brought the dead back to life (Ezekiel 37:1–14). In 1 Kings 17:17–24 the prophet Elijah prays that God will bring a boy back to life, and he does. Mark does not mention Jesus saying a prayer: he himself brings the girl back from the dead. Once more, Jesus is behaving as though he were God.

● Someone else comes back from the dead at the end of Mark. Like all Christians, Mark believed in Jesus' resurrection. And in a way this story is a shadow of what is to come. (There is a big difference, though. Jairus' daughter was brought back to *normal* life, and would die again. Jesus was raised

to a new kind of life, and would never die. Christians believe that he is alive for ever.)

● Jesus has power over death. The little girl was raised to life: Jesus will save people from death. Christians believe they are members of the Kingdom of God, and that their relationship with Jesus will carry on after death.

Of course people take different views about what happened. It's important to realize that what any of us thinks depends not only on the actual evidence available, but on what we believe is possible (our 'presuppositions').

Some people say nothing happened. The whole story was made up to get across the important points we have just looked at.

Many people believe that Mark is writing the truth. It really happened. Jesus raised the girl from the dead.

Some people say the girl looked as though she was dead, but was not. Jesus said 'the child is not dead — only sleeping'. Perhaps the girl was asleep and Jesus simply woke her up. Or she was in a deep coma, and Jesus brought her out of it. The problem with this idea is that people in Jesus' time often said someone was 'sleeping' when they were actually dead. This is certainly how Mark understood Jesus' words: Jesus prefers to say she is 'sleeping' rather than 'dead', because his action of raising her from the dead is like waking someone who has fallen asleep.

Notes

Mark reports Jesus' words in verse 41 as 'Talitha koum'. This is not Greek, but Aramaic (the language spoken by people in Jesus' time). Mark's Gentile readers may not have known Aramaic, so he explains what the words mean. Mark may have got this detail from Peter, who remembered Jesus' original words. Some people think he keeps the words in so that Christian healers could use them. Origen, an early Christian writer, says that words like this lose their power if they are translated.

Like the other miracle stories, the two in this unit show Jesus' power and compassion. But the miracles are connected to the Kingdom. And here Mark shows the power of Jesus over death. Membership of the Kingdom of God continues beyond the grave.

Notes

'Don't tell anyone . . .': There is another reference to the Messianic secret (see Unit 9) in verse 43. After such a dramatic miracle, it seems rather out of place. However, the command to silence may be simply because, if too many people knew Jesus could raise the dead, they might follow him simply as a wonder worker.

A group of Middle Eastern women stop to chat in the street. In Jesus' time women were very much second-class citizens. His attitude to women, as described in the Gospels, is very different from that of his contemporaries.

FOLLOW UP

1. Summarize Mark 5:21–43.

2. What religious lessons might Mark's readers – in his own time and today – be expected to draw from these stories?

3. ● What are the Aramaic words Jesus uses?
● What do they mean?
● Why does Mark include them?

4. In these stories, how does Mark show Jesus behaving as though he were God?

5. Look again at the different views about the raising of Jairus' daughter. What do you think happened, and why?

6. There are two other stories of Jesus raising people from the dead in the other Gospels: the raising of the widow's son at Nain in Luke 7:11–17, and the raising of Lazarus in John 11:1–44.
● Read the stories.
● How does John's story of the raising of Lazarus help us to understand Mark's story of Jairus' daughter?

Rejection at Nazareth

Mark has now told four miracle stories in a row, and we have been looking at them in the last three units. They are:
- The calming of the storm (4:35–41)
- The madman in the tombs (5:1–20)
- Jairus' daughter, and the woman with a haemorrhage (5:21–43)

In these stories Mark has shown that the right way to respond to Jesus is with *faith*:

Nazareth, in the hills of Galilee, was Jesus' home town.

In the calming of the storm Jesus asks the disciples, 'Have you . . . no faith?' (4:40)

The madman wants to become a disciple of Jesus once he is cured (5:18).

Jairus and the woman have faith that Jesus can help them (5:23 and 28).

In this new story, Mark continues the theme of faith, but he does it in a surprising way. Jesus goes to his home town – and is rejected there.

READ MARK 6:1–6a

Mark tells the story well. It is exactly the way people tend to behave. Try to put yourself in the position of the people at Nazareth. They had known Jesus all their lives. He had been the village carpenter, and they were neighbours of his relatives. They were used to seeing him around.

Then, all of a sudden, he leaves home and starts wandering about, preaching and healing people. Rumours about him reach Nazareth – but surely, they should have been the first to know about all this! It can't really be true that the boy whom they had seen playing with his friends and talked with in their homes had grown into somebody so special!

Then Jesus arrives home with his followers. The village people go to the synagogue. They are curious to find out about Jesus for themselves, and some of them perhaps resent all the attention he has been getting. Jesus starts teaching them – but he isn't even a proper rabbi.

> Who does he think he is? He's only a carpenter!

He may have been able to pull the wool over the eyes of the people in Capernaum, but he can't fool them, his own townsfolk (verses 2–3)!

We have already seen that the question 'Who is Jesus?' is a central theme in Mark's Gospel (see 4:41, Unit 17). The people at Nazareth are asking the right sort of questions in verses 2–3, but they get the answer wrong. Their familiarity with Jesus has blinded them to the real answer. Jesus seems to have been aware that this might

happen, and he quotes a well known proverb to them (verse 4): 'A prophet is respected everywhere except in his own home town and by his relatives and his family.'

So, if things went wrong at Nazareth, what does Mark think should have happened? Look again at verses 2–3 and at verses 5–6. Mark says, the people should have had *faith*.

Faith has always been very important for Christians. The miracle stories we have already looked at, and our story here, all talk about it. So what is faith?

One of the problems faced by the early church was to explain why the majority of Jesus' own people, the Jews, refused to accept him as the Messiah. By telling this story Mark is trying to answer this problem. The people at Nazareth represent all the Jews who did not become Christians. Just as the people in the story could not accept Jesus because he was only a carpenter, so Mark thinks that the Jews did not accept Jesus as the Messiah because they had a different understanding of what the Messiah would be like (see Unit 4).

Faith does *not* mean believing that impossible things are true. For Mark, and for all Christians, faith is a loving trust in what God is doing through Jesus, and an openness to the Kingdom of God. The woman with the haemorrhage in the last story had this sort of faith, and Jesus calls her his 'daughter' (5:34) – her trust in him has brought her healing and has made her a member of the Kingdom of God. But the people at Nazareth do not have this sort of loving trust. They do not welcome the Kingdom. For this reason Mark says that Jesus 'was not able to perform any miracles there,' except for a few healings. God can come to people in Jesus, he can invite them into his Kingdom, but he can do nothing if they do not welcome and accept him. He does not force himself upon people against their will.

Notes

6:3: The Good News Bible calls Jesus the 'son of Mary'. This is very peculiar, because Jewish men were always called by their father's names, not their mother's. It could be that the people are insulting Jesus – by calling him the son of Mary they are implying that he is illegitimate. But some Greek versions of Mark say 'the son of the carpenter and of Mary' here, and it is much more likely that this is what Mark actually wrote. (Later Christians may have changed some of the manuscripts of Mark to read 'son of Mary' because they believed that Jesus had no human father.)

For Jesus' family, see the notes on the story in 3:31–35 (Unit 14).

6:6a: The Good News Bible says that Jesus was 'surprised' that the people did not have faith. Although the Greek word Mark uses can mean this, it does not fit in very well with what has just gone before (verse 4). Mark really means that Jesus was amazed at how deep their unbelief was – not that he was not expecting it.

FOLLOW UP

1. ● Fill in the missing words:
'A _____ is respected everywhere except _____ and by his _____ and his _____ .'
● Why did Jesus say this?

2. Why do you think the people at Nazareth rejected Jesus?

3. You are a reporter on the Nazareth Morning Post. Under the title 'No Miracles Here: local boy fails to impress' write an account of Jesus' visit to his home town.

4. What does faith mean in Mark's Gospel? In your answer you must discuss this story and at least one of the miracle stories you have studied.

5. Why do you think Mark told this story?

Jesus Sends Out
the Twelve

READ MARK 6:6b–13

In this story Jesus sends out the twelve disciples to preach. This section links up with a part of the Gospel we have already studied: the choosing of the twelve apostles in 3:13–15 (see Unit 13). If we put the first part of each story in columns side by side, we can see this very clearly:

3:13	**6:7**
Then Jesus went up a hill and *called to himself the men he wanted*. They came to him, and *he chose twelve,*	*He called the twelve disciples* together
whom he named apostles. 'I have chosen you to be with me,' he told them. 'I will also *send you out* to preach,	and *sent them out* two by two.
and *you will have authority to drive out demons.'*	*He gave them authority over the evil spirits.*

Our second story has the same shape as the first one, and very similar content. They are very close *parallels*.

Mark tells his readers that the apostles did three things on their journey:
● They preached that people should turn away from their sins.
● They drove out demons.
● They healed the sick.

What does this mean? So far in Mark, we have already seen:
● that Jesus preached that the Kingdom of God was near and that people should turn away from their sins (1:15, see Unit 6)
● that Jesus drove out demons (1:23–27)

● that Jesus healed sick people (e.g. 3:10–11, etc.)

Now the twelve apostles are joining in with this work. *They are helping to bring in the Kingdom of God by sharing in what Jesus does.* This is very important for Mark because he thinks of the apostles as the beginnings of the church (see Unit 13), the new people of God. Like all other Christians, Mark believed that the church is intended to carry on the work of Jesus in the world: to preach, to heal the sick, and to overcome the powers of evil.

Look at verses 8–11. Here Jesus gives instructions to the apostles about their journey. They are to travel in the simplest way they can: with sandals and a stick, but without money, a beggar's bowl, food or extra clothes. They must not stay anywhere

What not to take...

1. Money
2. Begging bowl
3. Food
4. Space clothes

too long, or waste time on people who will not listen to them. What are Mark's readers meant to understand by all this? Here are some things for you to think about.

The apostles are travelling light. They are completely dependent on God.

● The apostles must be honest. At the time of Jesus, wandering preachers sometimes got money from people dishonestly. For this reason Jesus forbids them to carry a begging-bowl.

● The journey is very urgent and very important. Jesus tells the apostles that if they are not welcomed into a town they must shake its dust off their feet when they leave it (verse 11). This is interesting, because it is what the Jews did when they returned to Palestine after being in a Gentile country. They shook off the dust of a place which was *unclean* to make sure that they did not defile God's people when they went back to them. But the people the apostles are going to visit are *Jews*! Mark wants his readers to understand that times have changed with the journey of the apostles. What matters now is not whether or not you are a Jew, but whether you accept the teaching of the apostles, who bring with them the news about God's Kingdom. By shaking the dust off their feet the apostles are to *warn* people that they could be left outside it (verse 11). Mark's readers can be glad that they have heard and received the apostles' teaching, passed on to them.

Notes

Oil was very commonly used by healers at the time of Jesus. We know that the early church used it too (see James 5:14). It is still used by Catholic Christians today in the Sacrament of Holy Unction (the Anointing of the Sick) and in the healing ministry of other churches.

FOLLOW UP

1. What were the instructions Jesus gave to the apostles for their journey?

2. Why did Jesus say that the apostles should not take a begging-bowl with them?

3. What did the apostles have to do if a town did not welcome them? Why?

4. Why did Mark think it was important that the apostles had authority to drive out demons?

5. In what ways do you think this story might help the Christian church to understand its mission to the world today? In what ways might it be unhelpful?

6. St Francis of Assisi (like many others) was inspired by this story to live a life of poverty and preaching. Try to find out something about him.

The Death
of John the Baptist

We have already noticed that Mark often interrupts one story with another. Here he fills the interval between the sending of the apostles and their return with an account of the death of John the Baptist. Read the notes in Unit 5 to remind you of why John was so important to Mark.

READ MARK 6:14–29

If you look at this story carefully you will see that it has two parts. The first part is in verses 14–16, where people are arguing about who Jesus is.

Who is Jesus?

Mark tells us that Jesus' reputation as a miracle worker had spread everywhere, and finally reached Herod. People were trying to work out who Jesus was, and Mark says that they had three favourite theories about him (verses 14–16):

> He was John the Baptist, come back to life.

> He was Elijah.

> He was a prophet.

Mark wants his readers to understand that the people have not yet realized the truth about Jesus. But they *are* beginning to think along the right lines. There is something special about him, something to do with God. We will look at each idea in turn.

● **The John the Baptist theory.** John was an extremely important person in his day, and we know that in many ways he was very like Jesus. Mark himself tells us that the crowds listened to John when he preached to them, and that he had disciples (2:18). Jesus had been baptized by him, and people thought they were very close. (Look at the story of the question about fasting in 2:18–22. The Pharisees expect Jesus' disciples to behave like John's.) We should not be surprised that people sometimes muddled up Jesus and John.

Mark tells us that Jesus started teaching and performing miracles at around the time John was arrested (1:14). This may be why people thought Jesus was John risen from the dead (6:14). People were puzzled by Jesus' healing powers, and this idea provided them with one possible explanation. Only something as spectacular as a man returning from the dead could account for the things Jesus was doing!

● **The Elijah theory.** We have already seen that the Jews believed that Elijah was going to return before the Messiah came to bring in the Kingdom of God (see Unit 5). The Old Testament stories about Elijah say that he performed miracles (e.g. 1 Kings 17:8–24), and so Mark tells us that some people thought that perhaps Jesus was Elijah, at last returned.

Here Mark thinks that people are getting warm – but they haven't got it right yet. (See the notes on 1:6 and 9:13: Mark thinks that John was the 'Elijah' who was to return.)

● **The prophet theory.** There had been no prophets in Israel for a very long time (see Unit 6), and people at the time of Jesus were well aware of this. They believed that prophecy would start again with the coming of the Kingdom of God. In the book of Deuteronomy in the Old Testament there is a passage which talks about a mysterious *prophet like Moses* who was to come. It goes like this:

'I will send them a prophet like you (Moses) from among their own people; I will tell him what to say, and he will tell the people everything I command' (Deuteronomy 18:18).

We know that people like the Essenes (see Unit 1) remembered this passage and looked forward to the prophet's arrival. It seems very likely that the people in Mark's story were thinking along the same lines. Perhaps Jesus was the 'prophet like Moses' who was going to begin the revival of prophecy before the coming of the Kingdom of God.

However, even this is not enough for Mark. The answer to the question 'Who is Jesus?' is not going to be reached in this story. Mark is building up suspense for his readers. Later on, Peter will get the answer right (8:29). We shall be looking at this in another unit.

Herod and John the Baptist

Mark has given his readers three of the ideas people had about Jesus. Look again at verse 16. Mark says that Herod thought Jesus was John the Baptist returned to life. In verses 17–29 Mark tells us why. Herod had had John killed, and he was afraid that he had come back to haunt him. The story of John's death is a very interesting one, and Mark tells it well. But his version is not the only one we have. In about AD93 the Jewish historian Josephus wrote a book about the history of the Jews which he called *Antiquities*. He also tells his readers about the death of John. Read Mark's version again.

The Herod of this story is Herod Antipas, the ruler of Galilee. Mark calls him a king, which may have been what Herod encouraged people to say. But in fact he was really only a puppet of the Romans, who gave him the title *tetrarch* (ruler). They later banished him to Gaul for asking to be made a king! The Herod family was very large and had a reputation for all kinds of cruelty and immorality. Mark's story fits in well with this. When Mark says that Herodias' daughter danced before Herod, he means the kind of dance which would usually be performed by a prostitute.

Some people who study the New Testament have suggested that there were people at the time of Jesus who thought that John was the Messiah. This is not as unlikely as it sounds. There were quite a lot of people who were said to be the Messiah. If this is true, then perhaps it explains why Mark and the other early Christian writers spend so much time on John. They were trying to correct what they thought was a wrong idea about him.

John the Baptist was beheaded at Machaerus, one of King Herod's fortresses. The picture shows its position, but not its magnificent furnishings.

There is one more thing which we can add. We know that Mark thought John was the Elijah who would return before the Messiah came. In the Old Testament there is a series of stories about Elijah's troubles with King Ahab of Israel and his evil wife Jezebel (1 Kings 18–19). In these stories, Jezebel encourages Ahab to behave badly, just as Herodias leads Herod astray in Mark. It seems very likely that Mark thought that history was repeating itself in this story of the new 'Elijah', a wicked king, and his wife.

Notes

6:17: This is a very confusing verse. Marrying your brother's wife was forbidden by the Law of Moses (see Leviticus 18:16 and 20:21). But it is not clear who Mark means by Herod's brother *Philip*. Herod had a half-brother called Philip, but he married Salome (Herodias' daughter). Herodias had been married to a different brother who lived in Rome before she married Herod. If Mark has made a mistake, it is not surprising. The Herod family had a habit of marrying one another's wives, and often had very similar names.

6:19: Queen Jezebel wanted to kill Elijah, too (see 1 Kings 19:2).

6:22: Tradition says that the girl who danced before Herod was Herodias' daughter by her previous husband. Her name was Salome. The Good News Bible agrees with this. However, some old copies of Mark say that it was Herod's daughter, or even 'his daughter Herodias', as though she was named after her mother.

◤FOLLOW◢UP◤

Quick answer questions

1. The Jews believed that somebody was to come before the Messiah came. Who?

2. Mark says that people had three ideas about who Jesus might be. What were they?

3. Who did Herod think Jesus was? Why?

Things to do

1. Using the story in Mark, write a play about the death of John the Baptist. Your characters should include:
   – John
   – Herod Antipas
   – Herodias
   – Salome
   – Joachim, a captain of the guard
   – Soldiers
   – Herod's friends

You might like to practise your plays in groups and perform them to the class.

2. Read 1 Kings 16:29–33 and the stories about Elijah in 1 Kings 18:1—19:14. Here are some things for you to think about as you do so:
● What was Jezebel like?
● Why was she annoyed with Elijah?
● In what ways do you think Elijah was like John the Baptist?

You might like to discuss those ideas with your teacher.

3. Try to get a copy of Josephus' *Antiquities* from the library. Read the story of John's death in *Antiquities* xviii.5.2. In what ways is it different from Mark's version?

4. Answer this question as fully as you can in an essay: 'What are Mark's reasons for telling his readers about the death of John the Baptist?'

The Feeding of the 5,000

 READ MARK 6:30–44

Marks tells us very little about what the twelve had 'done and taught' on their mission. They return to Jesus, and go off for a rest.

The feeding of the 5,000 is another of the *nature miracles* (see Unit 17). Jesus' action again shows his compassion on the tired, hungry crowd, and that he has power over nature. But it means much more than this. Mark even has a very similar story in 8:1–10 – the feeding of the 4,000, which we shall look at later. So it was obviously very important for Mark's readers. Why was this?

There are two main reasons:
● It shows who Jesus is.
● It looks forward to the Last Supper and to the Messianic banquet.

Let's look at these in turn.

The miracle shows who Jesus is

In around 1300BC the Jewish people were slaves in Egypt. God appointed Moses to lead them out to a land of their own. They eventually arrived in Israel, but before that they wandered in the desert (wilderness) to the south-west of Israel. At that time God gave them his Law (the Torah). And he also made sure they had enough to eat: every morning, food called manna appeared on the ground.

Here Jesus miraculously gives people food, as, long before, God had given his people food in the desert. (In verse 32, 'lonely place' can also mean 'desert place' or 'wilderness'.) Once more, Jesus behaves as though he were God.

Jesus is also shown to be like Moses.

One rabbi had said, 'The first redeemer (Moses) made food come down from heaven. The last redeemer (the Messiah) will too.' Through Moses, God spoke to the people and told them how to live. In Jesus, Mark believes, God speaks to the people in a new and even greater way.

In 2 Kings 4:42–44, the prophet Elisha fed 100 men with twenty small loaves. Elisha was the successor of Elijah, the great prophet whom people thought would return before the Messiah arrived. It is as though the Old Testament – the Law represented by Moses, and the Prophets represented by Elisha – is fulfilled in Jesus.

The miracle looks forward to the Last Supper and to the Messianic banquet

The loaves were small rolls, and the fish were about the size of sardines. But it doesn't really matter what the food was.

Mark tells how Jesus made five loaves and two fish enough to feed 5,000 men! A mosaic in the Church of the Multiplication, in Galilee, commemorates the event.

The point is that the Messiah hands out the food to a large number of people. There will be many people at the Messianic banquet (see Unit 11).

At the end of his life, Jesus and his disciples had the Last Supper together. He gave them bread and wine, which he said were his body and blood. We shall find out more about this later. But the feeding of the 5,000 is in a way a shadow of what is to come. Here Jesus gives bread to the crowd. Soon he will give the bread (his body, sacrificed in death) to his followers at the Last Supper. And the church will repeat his actions. This would have happened in Mark's church too. So Mark's readers – the first Christians and Christians today – immediately think of the Last Supper when they read this story.

People hold different views about this story. Many believe that Mark has got his facts right. Jesus actually fed 5,000 people with just five loaves and two fish. Others say:

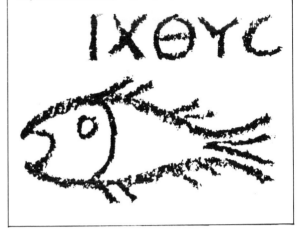

The early Christians used the fish as a secret sign – a sort of code by which they could recognize each other. In Greek, the first letters of the words 'Jesus Christ, God's Son, Saviour' makes another word – *ichthus*, a fish. Mark's first readers might well have thought of this when they read about Jesus giving the people fish.

● The people only really got a tiny scrap of bread each.

● The people in the crowd saw that Jesus was willing to share his food with them, and they felt guilty. They shared their packed food with each other, and somebody mistook this for a miracle.

● Jesus met a band of Zealots in the desert. Zealots would sometimes form 'groups of a hundred and groups of fifty' as part of their drill.

● The whole story has been made up to get across the important ideas we have just looked at.

● Mark has exaggerated the numbers: there were far fewer than 5,000.

Some people think Mark tells the same story later in a different form (the feeding of the 4,000). We shall look at this idea soon. For the moment, here are two more things for you to think about:

● If the number of people has been exaggerated, or everyone only got a tiny scrap of food, how could anyone have thought it was a miracle? The same goes for the idea that they shared their food. If you shared a packed lunch with some friends, would you think this was a miracle? People were no more stupid in Jesus' day than they are now.

● There is no real evidence that the crowd was a band of Zealots. If they were, what was Jesus doing with them? His ideas about the Messiah were quite different from Zealot ones.

Notes

6:39: Mark says the grass was *green*. Some scholars think this is a detail he got from an eyewitness, as Peter would have been. The grass is green in Palestine only in the spring.

6:41: Jesus is acting as a typical Jewish host at a meal, thanking God for the food before handing it out. He 'looked up to heaven' as a sign of giving thanks, not as a piece of mumbo-jumbo to make the miracle work.

FOLLOW UP

1. ● In this story, how does Jesus act like
– Moses?
– Elisha?
– God?
● Why is this important?
● In John's version of this story, the people wanted to make Jesus king (John 6:1–15). Why, do you think?

2. ● Write out Mark 6:41 and Mark 14:22 (part of the story of the Last Supper).
● How and why are these verses similar?
● Why is this important?
● Why is the idea of the Messianic banquet important here?

3. Read the story of the manna in Exodus 16.

4. Look again at the ideas people have put forward about what happened. Write some notes on your findings.

Jesus Walks on the Water

The story of Jesus walking on the water is one of the most famous in Mark's Gospel. It is his third *nature miracle* (the first two were the calming of the storm and the feeding of the 5,000). Mark puts another of his summaries of Jesus' healing work at the end.

📖 READ MARK 6:45–56

This story is very like the calming of the storm in 4:35–41. Both stories take place on Lake Galilee, with the disciples in a boat. This is not very surprising. We know that some of Jesus' closest disciples were fishermen and that he spent a lot of time in the villages and towns around the Lake, where a boat was a sensible way of getting about.

However, look again at verse 52. Mark says that the disciples were astonished at Jesus walking on the water 'because they had not understood the real meaning of the feeding of the five thousand'. At first glance this seems very odd. What has Jesus walking on the water got to do with a miracle about bread?

We studied the feeding of the 5,000 in the last unit. There we saw that the best way to understand the story was to look at

It was here, on Lake Galilee, Mark says, that Jesus came to his disciples walking on the water.

some ideas from the Old Testament. The same thing was true with our work on the calming of the storm (Unit 17). Mark wrote these nature miracle stories with these ideas in his mind. When he says that the disciples were astonished because they had not understood the feeding of the 5,000, he is giving his readers a clue about how they should understand all the nature miracles. Each says something about Jesus, using ideas which come from the Old Testament. So what Old Testament ideas lie behind the story of Jesus walking on the water?

Old Testament ideas in the walking on the water

● This story and the calming of the storm have two things in common: *water* itself and the disciples' fear. Look back to Unit 17 to remind yourself what these mean.

● The Old Testament often pictures God as walking over the sea. Psalm 77:19 says:

> 'You walked through the waves;
> You crossed the deep sea.'

Sometimes the sea is used as a symbol for death or desperate danger (Psalm 18:15–17). Jesus, walking on the water, is behaving like God in the picture-language of the Old Testament.

● Verse 48 says that Jesus was going to 'pass by' the disciples. This does not seem to mean very much at first sight. But Mark is thinking about the occasions in the Old Testament when God appears, and the writers talk of him 'passing by'. Here are some examples:
– The 'dazzling light of God's presence' *passed by* Moses (Exodus 33:19–23).
– God *passed by* the mountain top where Elijah was camped (1 Kings 19:11–12).
– Job says in despair, 'God *passes by*, but I cannot see him' (Job 9:11).

● Jesus says to the disciples, 'It is I. Don't be afraid!' (verse 50). The Greek words Mark uses for 'It is I' are simply 'I AM'. This is what God calls himself in Exodus 3:14.

We can see that the story of the walking on the water is packed with Old Testament ideas. Most of Mark's readers would probably have recognized and understood them easily. Look at them again. They all point to one conclusion: that when Jesus walked on the water, it was like the appearances of God long ago. Mark thinks that this is the real heart and meaning of the story.

Many people who study the New Testament say that there is a second reason why Mark tells this story. According to them, the disciples represent the people in Mark's church. We think that they suffered from all sorts of troubles, like persecution. They may have felt like the disciples, struggling against the waves which seemed to threaten their lives. But Mark is saying that Jesus will help them, even at the darkest times (verse 48), and Christians should have a loving trust in him. This is very like one of the meanings of the calming of the storm: see Unit 17.

Clearly Mark tells the story because he thinks it has important things to say about Jesus. But what did go on that night?

Here are some of the ideas people have put forward:

● Jesus was not really walking on the water at all. He had a raft, or was walking on a hidden reef.

● Jesus was walking near the water, not on it. (The Greek word which Mark uses can mean 'close by' as well as 'on'.) The disciples made a mistake.

● Mark made the whole thing up, using the Old Testament, because he wanted to say things about Jesus which he felt were important.

● The miracle happened as Mark says it did, and as most Christians have always believed.

The first and second ideas here are really rather silly. It seems very unlikely that Jesus would have built himself a raft in the middle of the night, or that the disciples would have thought that they had seen a ghost just because someone was walking along the sea-shore, or a reef. Some people think it doesn't really matter what actually happened. They argue that even if Jesus did not walk on the water, it is still possible to believe that the inner meaning of the story is true. What do you think?

Jesus heals the sick in Gennesaret (verses 53–56)

Mark now goes on to give one of his summaries of Jesus' healings. These take place at Gennesaret, where Mark says the disciples and Jesus landed (verse 53). This is rather surprising, because they set out for Bethsaida (verse 45)! (See the map in Unit 13.) They may have been driven off course by the *wind* (verse 48). But some people think that originally these verses were separate from the story of the walking on the water, and Mark has added them on rather clumsily. We have noticed before that his geography is not very good.

FOLLOW UP

Quick answer questions
- What is the name of the Lake in this story?
- What do a) the disciples and b) Jesus say in this story?
- What time of day does Mark say it was when Jesus walked on the water?

Longer questions:
1. EITHER

How are ideas from the Old Testament useful in helping us to understand the walking on the water? (You must give at least three examples in your answer.)

OR

What do you think Mark thought was the inner meaning of this miracle, and why?

2. Mark says that the disciples 'had not understood the real meaning of the feeding of the five thousand'. Find three other places in Mark where the disciples are said not to understand something.

Notes

6:49: The fact that the disciples say 'It is a ghost!' has led some people to suggest that this was originally a story about Jesus after he had risen from the dead (a resurrection appearance). Mark certainly does not think so, however, and neither do Matthew or John, who also tell this story (Matthew 14:22–33; John 6:16–21). In any case, the early church was very careful to say that the risen Jesus was *not* a ghost. For these reasons, this idea seems very unlikely to be true.

6:48a and 51a: 'He saw that his disciples were straining at the oars, because they were rowing against the wind . . . Then he got into the boat with them, and the wind died down.' These verses are so like the details in the story of the calming of the storm (4:37 and 39) that some people have said Mark has muddled the two stories. This seems quite possible: the idea of a strong wind does not appear to add anything to a miracle about walking on the water.

6:52: The Good News Bible is very weak here. In fact Mark's Greek says that the disciples' *hearts were hardened*. Mark thinks that the miracles are like the parables (see Unit 15). They do not produce faith automatically. You have to be tuned in to understand them – and the disciples are not. We shall look at this idea in more detail later on.

The slowness of the disciples is a constant theme in Mark.

6:56: Every Jew had to wear a tassel on the edge of his robe (Deuteronomy 22:12). This seems to be what Mark has in mind here. The woman with the haemorrhage has already touched Jesus' cloak and been made well (see Unit 19). Mark wants to emphasize that Jesus' power was so great that even his clothes were charged with it.

In Acts 19:12 Luke says that Paul's handkerchiefs and aprons had similar healing powers. Throughout the history of Christianity people have treasured the clothing and personal belongings of holy men and women for the same reason. Quite often, they have kept parts of their dead bodies as well! These are called *relics*.

What Makes a Person Unclean?

In this unit, we look at Mark's second long collection of Jesus' teaching (the first was the parables of the Kingdom in 4:1–34). For the time being, it rounds off the theme of the authorities' hostility towards Jesus.

One of the ideas in Judaism is that God has said that some things are *unclean*, while other things are *clean*. We have already come across this briefly in the story of Jesus and the leper in 1:40–45. Unclean things barred you from public worship for a while. People steered clear of anything that might make them unclean, in order to please God. Clean things were safe to use. This idea went back to the Law of Moses, which laid down rules about which things were which. There were unclean foods, such as pork, unclean diseases such as leprosy, and unclean actions such as touching a dead body. Originally a lot of these rules seem to have had to do with simple hygiene. Even so, a good Jew saw them as part of God's commandments; the way God intended people to live.

By the time of Jesus a lot of traditional laws had grown up alongside the Torah, which were supposed to help people to keep it. In our story Mark calls these traditions 'the teaching handed down by our ancestors' (verses 2, 3). The Pharisees (see Unit 1) thought that these traditions were almost as important as the Law itself. However, not everyone agreed with them. The Sadducees (see Unit 1) said that the Torah was enough on its own.

Mark's story shows his readers where Jesus stood in this argument. As we have come to expect by now, his attitude towards the whole business is a very radical one. Like the story of the Sabbath corn (2:23–28), it begins with the disciples annoying the Pharisees.

READ MARK 7:1–23

Look again at verse 5. The Pharisees are angry because Jesus' disciples have not been washing their hands in the traditional way before eating. This was not a matter of good table manners, as we would think today. At the time of Jesus there were complicated religious rules about washing. Because of the way Mark has arranged the story, Jesus' answer does not come straight away. But when it does (verse 15) it is a real bombshell.

'There is nothing that goes into a person from the outside which can make him ritually unclean. Rather, it is what comes out of a person that makes him unclean.'

As usual, at first the disciples do not understand what Jesus is saying. Mark says that Jesus explained things for them (verses 17–23). True religion is not a matter of rules and regulations. God is not really bothered about how people wash their hands. For Jesus, the things that really matter are the things which 'come out of a person' (as we would say, what is in our hearts). What matters is not dirty hands, but the sins people have inside them. The Pharisees have got it all wrong. They have been looking only at the surface. God's interest goes deeper.

In the rest of the story, Mark has been trying to show how dangerous it is to forget this. In theory, the Pharisees understood that loving God and loving your neighbour were more important than rules about

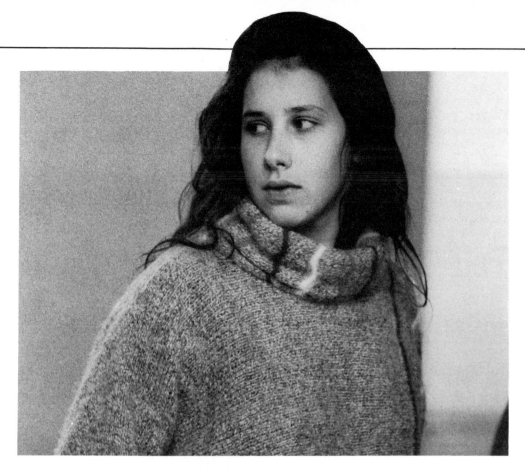

It's what comes from inside us – wrong motives, dark thoughts, jealousy . . . – that spoils our lives, Jesus says.

washing hands or not eating pork. The trouble was that they concentrated so hard on keeping every last rule that they sometimes lost sight of the most important things.

In verses 6–13 Mark gives his readers an example. The traditions of the Pharisees said that if you made a solemn oath that something belonged to God (was 'Corban'), it could not be used for anything else – even to help somebody. So although God's commandments said that people were to respect their parents, if someone had money they needed, but did not want to give it to them, he had only to say it was Corban – and they couldn't get at it! It was a perfect example of how religious rules could be used to let people off doing what God really wanted.

Jesus says that people who behave like

this are hypocrites (verse 6) who 'put aside the commandments of God and obey the teachings of men' (verse 8). They are like the people in the time of Isaiah (verses 6–7) who honoured God with their words, but were far away from him in their hearts.

Jesus, Christians and the Law of Moses

Jesus does not seem to have much time for the traditional teachings which the Pharisees thought were so important. However, in the story of the healing of the leper (1:40–45) Mark was careful to show that Jesus respected and obeyed the Law of Moses.

Jesus and his first disciples were all Jews. Many later Christians were Gentiles. One of the biggest issues in the early church was to decide whether these Gentile Christians should keep all the religious laws in the Torah. Some Jewish Christians thought they should, but others disagreed. (This is one of the major themes in another New Testament book, the Acts of the Apostles.) From verse 19 of our story it seems that this argument was still going on when Mark was writing his Gospel. Mark has added his own comment to Jesus' words – something he hardly ever does: 'In saying this, Jesus declared that all foods are fit to be eaten.' Mark thinks that Jesus was more interested in the *purpose* of the Law than simply obeying it on the surface. So Christians are free to eat what they like: what matters is what is going on in their minds and hearts. In the end this view won the day. Christians were not required to keep the Jewish food laws.

Notes

7:1,2: Jewish writings say that only priests had to wash their hands in this way. The Pharisees at the time of Jesus seem to have behaved as if they were priests, as an extra expression of their devotion to God. They expect Jesus' disciples to do the same. In the next two verses Mark explains Jewish customs for his readers. Many of them were Gentiles, and might otherwise have missed the point.

7:11–12: Jesus may have been thinking of an actual case. It is a terrible example of religious corruption. The rabbis themselves later banned this kind of misuse of solemn oaths.

7:21–23: Lists of faults like this one are very common in literature from around Mark's time. There is another one in Romans 1:29–32. Some people have suggested that Mark has expanded Jesus' words in a conventional way, to make a sort of commentary on verse 20.

FOLLOW UP

Quick answer questions
● What annoyed the Pharisees about the behaviour of Jesus' disciples?
● What did the Law of Moses say about parents?
● What does 'Corban' mean?
● What does Jesus say makes a person unclean?

Longer questions
1. Look at the stories of the question about fasting (2:18–22) and the Sabbath corn (2:23–28).
● In what ways are they similar to 7:1–23?
● Why do you think this might be?

2. 'You put aside God's commands and obey the teachings of men' (verse 8). What example did Jesus give of behaviour like this? Explain it fully.

3. Why does Mark say that Jesus 'declared that all foods are fit to be eaten'?

4. From this section and from what you have learned already, think about Jesus' attitude to the Law of Moses and Jewish tradition. Imagine you are someone who wants to be his follower, but you have been brought up as a Pharisee. Write a letter to a friend expressing how you might feel about his teaching and his behaviour. (You must use some incidents from Mark. The most useful ones have already been mentioned in this unit.)

Jesus and the Gentiles

📖 READ MARK 7:24–37

If you look at the map, you will see that both these healings take place in Gentile areas. We have seen that many people thought when the Messiah came, Gentiles would be included in the Kingdom of God. Many of Mark's readers were non-Jews, and so this idea would be very important to them. Here, Jesus shows that his mission includes the Gentiles.

Let's look at the two stories in more detail.

The woman from Phoenicia in Syria (verses 24–30)

In the last section of Mark (7:14–23), Jesus said there was no difference between clean food and unclean food. This story seems to say there is no difference between 'clean' people (Jews) and 'unclean' people (Gentiles). Jesus goes to both of them. It seems that the news about Jesus had travelled as far as Tyre. Even in this Gentile area people had heard of him. One of them, a woman, comes to see him.

We have already said that people in Jesus' time thought women were second-class citizens. A *Gentile* woman, who did not even worship the same God, was even worse! But Jesus did not think like this. For him, people are people. It does not matter what race or sex they are.

The woman knows who Jesus is, and calls him 'sir'. In Greek, the word is *kyrie*, which can also mean 'Lord' (a title used for God: see the 'Titles of Jesus' section in this unit). She asks him to help her daughter.

Jesus' reply looks very strange at first: 'Let us first feed the children. It isn't right to take the children's food and throw it to the dogs.' In other words, 'Let's give the Jews what they need first of all. It's not fair to give what the Jews need to dogs like you Gentiles.' (The Jews knew they were the 'children of God', and many said the Gentiles were just 'dogs'. This was meant to be extremely rude.)

The woman replies: 'Even the dogs under the table eat the children's leftovers!' In other words, 'Perhaps we are dogs. But even dogs get something!'

There are some things to notice here:

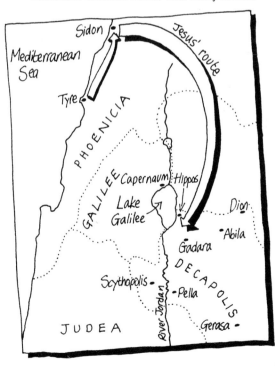

● Many people think Jesus was joking. He wouldn't really think Gentiles were 'dogs'! We can call someone an idiot without really meaning it – it depends on our tone of voice. The woman picks up on the joke, and adds a punchline. (In any case, the word Mark uses means 'pet dog', not 'wild dog'.)

Titles of Jesus

3. The Lord
This title is not often used in Mark. We find it in Mark 5:19; 7:28; 11:3; 12:36 and 12:37.

The Greek word for 'Lord' is Kyrios. You could call anyone Kyrios if they had some authority: it could just mean 'master' or 'sir', as the Good News Bible sometimes translates it. Jesus has authority, so he can be called Kyrios. But it could mean more than this.

The Old Testament was written in Hebrew. In Hebrew, God's name was Yahweh. After a time, people thought this name was too holy to say, and even today Jews will say 'the Lord' instead. When the Old Testament was translated into Greek, they used the word Kyrios for God's name. The early Christians used this translation, and would know that Kyrios was a title for God.

People in Mark sometimes call Jesus 'Lord' or Kyrios. It certainly means 'sir', but it may mean more than this. It may hint at who Jesus really is. Christians believe Jesus is God, and they will often call him 'the Lord'.

● There is a serious point, though. The woman's reply may be a joke, but it does show that, although she is a Gentile, she has faith in Jesus. Here, Jesus cures the girl without even seeing her. His power is great enough to heal from a distance.

● The early Christians believed that Gentiles were included in the Kingdom. But the Letter to the Romans shows that some of them thought the Good News should be preached 'to the Jews first, and then to the Gentiles' (Romans 1:16). That letter was written by Paul, the great missionary and writer.

The Acts of the Apostles says that when Paul arrived in a new area, he always preached first to the Jews, and then to the non-Jews. After all, Jesus was a Jew. So some early Christians thought it was only fair that Jesus' own people should hear the Good News first.

We get this idea in Mark, too. We have seen that Jesus' first followers, the twelve, were sent to preach to the Jews. But a later follower – the madman in the tombs – was sent to preach to the Gentiles. This helps us understand what Jesus means in this story.

The deaf mute
This is another Gentile healing: it takes place in the Gentile area of the Ten Towns.

Verses 33 and 34 are interesting because we have stories about other healers in the ancient world who used saliva or touch to cure people. (This may be the reason why Matthew and Luke leave this story out.) But the man was deaf. Perhaps Jesus used this sort of 'sign language' to show the man he was really healed.

This story would have reminded Mark's readers of a passage in Isaiah. Isaiah says that when the Messiah comes,
'The blind will be able to see, and the deaf will hear' (Isaiah 35:5).
And it may also have a hidden meaning. Just as Jesus makes a deaf person able to hear, he will also make people able to hear the Good News. And those people will be Gentiles, as well as Jews.

In Mark, Jesus sighs (or gives 'a deep groan') only here. It may be a form of prayer, like his looking up to heaven. Or he may be sighing because he is sad that there is so much suffering in the world.

Once again, Mark gives the Aramaic for Jesus' healing words (Ephphatha). To find out why, turn back to Unit 19.

Notes

7:27: In Greek, Jesus talks about the children's *bread*. We have seen in the feeding of the 5,000 that *bread* would have suggested the Last Supper to Mark's readers. That bread – the bread of Jesus' body – will be given to both Jews and Gentiles in the church.

There is a problem in saying that Jesus meant 'pet dog', even though Mark uses the word. In Aramaic, the language Jesus spoke, there is only one word for 'dog', and that could be used as an insult. Some scholars suggest that he spoke to the woman in Greek, which does have a word for 'pet dog'. Even if he did not, he could still be joking. It is certainly out of character for Jesus to speak like this – but he may have been using the kind of language she expected from a Jew, to test her reaction and her determination.

7:31: If you look at the map, you will see that Jesus' route is very strange. Some people think, here again, that Mark is weak on geography. Or it may be that Jesus went on a preaching tour.

7:36: Mark is again thinking of the Messianic secret. It looks very odd here. For one thing, people do not do what Jesus says: instead, they spread the news around. If Jesus normally told people to be quiet because he did not want them to get the wrong idea about what his Messiahship meant, why does he tell a Gentile crowd to be quiet? They were not expecting a Messiah. The answer may be that although the Gentiles were not waiting for the Messiah, they got very excited about people who were thought to be wonder workers, and Jesus did not want this label either.

7:37: Some people link what the crowd says to Genesis 1:31. When God made the universe, everything was perfect. His work was good (Genesis 1:31). And when God acts in Jesus, that is perfect too: everything he does is wholly good.

▲FOLLOW UP▲

1. Put these sentences into the right order:
– Jesus took him to one side.
– Jesus went to Tyre.
– Jesus told the people to keep quiet.
– Jesus groaned.
– They did exactly the opposite.
– When she went home, her daughter was cured.
– Jesus spat.
– Jesus said 'Open up!' in Aramaic.
– A woman from Phoenicia in Syria asked him to cure her daughter.
– The man was cured.
– Jesus put his fingers into the man's ears.
– Jesus looked up to heaven.
– People brought a man to him.
– She replied that even the dogs ate the children's leftovers.
– The man was deaf and could hardly speak.
– He said it was unfair to throw the children's food to the dogs.
– They were amazed by what Jesus had done.
– Jesus touched the man's tongue.
– Jesus went to the area around the Ten Towns.

2. Jesus and the woman said something about dogs.
● What did they say?
● What did they mean, and why is this important for Mark's readers?

3. What are the important ideas in the story of the deaf mute?

4. In Mark Jesus is called 'Lord', and this is what Christians call him today. Why?

5. ● Try to interview some Christians. Ask them:
what they believe Jesus thought about women
what their own views are on the women's movement.
(It might help if you prepare a questionnaire on this.)
● Do you think their ideas about women are the same as Jesus', or not? Why?

The Feeding of the 4,000

 READ MARK 8:1–10

This story is very similar to the feeding of the 5,000 in Mark 6:30–44. Like that story, the feeding of the 4,000 does two main things:
● It shows who Jesus is.
● It looks forward to the Last Supper and to the Messianic banquet.
Look back to Unit 23.

Since the feeding of the 4,000 is so like the feeding of the 5,000, a lot of scholars think Mark has included two versions of the same story. They argue that nobody could be as stupid as the disciples. If they had already seen Jesus feed a huge crowd, they would not ask:

'Where in this desert can anyone find food to feed all these people?'

(verse 4). Luke and John record only the feeding of the 5,000, perhaps because they thought there was only one occasion when a crowd was fed. Not everyone agrees with this view. Many people think Jesus did feed a large number of people on two different occasions, and that Mark has got his facts right.

Whatever we think, we should ask why Mark has decided to include both stories (after all, Luke and John did not). The answer seems to be that he is saying something about the Kingdom of God.

We have seen that the early Christians believed the Kingdom included both Jews and Gentiles.

● In the feeding of the 5,000, the Jews are given the bread.

● In the feeding of the 4,000, the *Gentiles* are given the bread.

Why the feeding of the 5,000 shows that Jews are included in the Kingdom	Why the feeding of the 4,000 shows that Gentiles are included in the Kingdom
It takes places on the shore of Lake Galilee, a Jewish area.	It takes place in the area of the Ten Towns (7:31), a Gentile area.
There are five loaves. Five may be argued to be a 'Jewish' number, as there were five books of the Torah.	There are seven loaves. To the Jews seven is a 'Gentile' number. The Jews thought the Gentile world was divided up into seventy countries (and 7×10=70!). Or it might remind Mark's readers of the seven leaders (deacons) mentioned in the Acts of the Apostles, who looked after Gentile Christians' problems.
There are twelve baskets. And there were twelve tribes of Israel.	There were seven baskets. We have just seen seven was a 'Gentile' number.
Mark uses the Greek word *kophinos* for 'basket'. This was a kind of basket used by Jewish people.	Mark uses the Greek word *spyris* for 'basket'. This sort of basket was used by Gentiles.

This may all seem a bit far-fetched at first sight. But people in Mark's time loved to find hidden meanings in numbers, which were often used as a sort of code. If we have cracked the code properly, Mark has both stories because he is saying that *both Jews and Gentiles are members of the Kingdom of God.*

We have now read a lot of miracle stories in Mark. It seems a good place to ask this question:

Did Jesus perform miracles?

The early Christians, like Mark, certainly believed Jesus performed miracles. But they did not think he was a magician, who did miracles to show off. They believed the miracles were very important to his work. They showed:

- that the Kingdom of God was near.
- that God – and Jesus – cared about people.

But people only understood this if they wanted to. Some of the Jewish leaders thought Jesus' power came from the devil.

Many people think Jesus did perform miracles. Others do not. Here are some of the most important arguments.

The Gospel writers take care to explain that Jesus' miracles were not stunts or tricks used to attract attention, but clearly linked to his care for people. This window is fake glass!

> Yes and no. Some of the miracles were done by Jesus, some were made up, some were things he did that were mistaken for miracles.

> Yes and no. Jesus did heal people, but he did not do the nature miracles. Jesus would only do miracles to heal people. The nature miracles do not do this.

> Yes. Mark was careful to check his facts, and wrote down what actually happened.

> No. The stories are all made up.

> Yes. If God can make the universe, he is not going to find it too hard to heal people or show his power over nature!

> No. If he did, God is very unfair. Why doesn't God heal everybody who is ill? Why did God let the Jews die in the Second World War, if he could have helped them?

> No. Jesus did heal people, but he used things like faith healing, hypnosis and auto-suggestion. People at the time did not understand how Jesus healed people, and thought they were miracles.

There are a few things to add. A lot of people think in certain ways without looking properly at the reasons. If we look at any problem, we should always try not to be prejudiced, and look carefully at the arguments.

Strange things do happen, which do not fit in with our normal view of the world. People can get very frightened when they hear ghost stories, even if they do not believe in ghosts. Some have *déjà vu* experiences – the feeling that you have been in a situation before, even when you have not. Some people suddenly feel very happy or very depressed for no obvious reason.

When you think about it, some people would say the whole of life is a miracle. Wouldn't it be more likely, if everything were left to chance, that we would not exist? All this could mean that there is more to life than meets the eye.

Some people argue that science can explain everything. But many scientists are believing Christians. And many say science cannot explain the great mysteries of life.

Nearly all Christians believe that Jesus performed miracles. The last and most important miracle was the resurrection.

They might ask this question:

If Jesus did not do miracles, why was he remembered? What was so special about this Jewish carpenter that made him such an important figure in world history? If he did no miracles, and the resurrection did not happen, why wasn't he just forgotten?

◤FOLLOW↓UP◥

1. Divide a page into two columns. Head one 'The feeding of the 5,000' and one 'The feeding of the 4,000'. In one colour, write down things in the stories that are the same or similar. In another colour, write down things that are different.

For example:

Things that are the same or similar:

5,000	4,000
Jesus feeds a large crowd	Jesus feeds a large crowd

Differences:

5,000	4,000
12 baskets	7 baskets

2. ● Why do some people think the two feeding stories are really two versions of the same story?
● Do you agree with them? Why?

3. ● How does Mark show that the feeding of the 5,000 is about Jewish people, and the feeding of the 4,000 is about Gentiles?
● Why is this important?

4. Look at the following ideas. What do you think of them, and why? Discuss this in your group.
'Science has disproved the Bible.'
'Scientists are biased. They have no faith, so they ridicule those who do.'
'Miracles are stupid. You might as well believe in Father Christmas, or believe that you are a fried egg.'
'It's a miracle anyone exists at all.'

Now write the following essay:
'What are the arguments *for* and *against* the idea that Jesus performed miracles? Which do you find convincing, and why?'

5. Write the following essay:
'How valuable would the miracle stories be for a Christian who wanted to convert other people to Christianity?'

Three Short Stories

READ MARK 8:11–13

The Pharisees ask for a miracle

The Good News Bible's translation of this story says that the Pharisees wanted to 'trap' Jesus. But the Greek word Mark uses can also mean they wanted to *test* him.

On the face of it this seems reasonable enough. Put yourself in their shoes. All through their history there had been people claiming to be special. How were they to tell if what Jesus said was really from God?

The Pharisees may have been thinking of passages from the Jewish Scriptures which were meant to deal with this sort of problem. For example, Deuteronomy 18:21–22:

> 'You may wonder how you can tell when a prophet's message does not come from the LORD. If a prophet speaks in the name of the LORD and what he says does not come true, then it is not the LORD's message. That prophet has spoken on his own authority, and you are not to fear him.'

The simplest way the Pharisees could test Jesus was to ask him to give them a *sign* – a miracle to see if what he said would come true. In that way they could make up their minds about him.

The Pharisees in this story could even have pointed to a precedent from the Old Testament if they had wanted to. God had told the prophet Isaiah to offer a sign to King Ahaz (Isaiah 7:10).

Why doesn't Jesus give the Pharisees the miracle they ask for in Mark's story? And why did Mark think this was important? Wouldn't Jesus have saved himself a lot of bother if he had done as he was asked?

As far as Mark is concerned all these questions miss the point. If you look back a few pages you will see that he has put this story just after the healing of the deaf mute and the feeding of the 5,000. Jesus has been performing signs all the time. The real issue is why the Pharisees feel they have to ask for one.

In the story of Jesus' rejection at Nazareth (6:1–6, Unit 20) we saw that, according to Mark, Jesus was unable to perform any miracles in his home town *because the people had no faith*. Mark thinks that the Pharisees, here, are like the people at Nazareth. They are not really interested in seeing God at work in Jesus. All they want to do is to catch him out. If they had really wanted to see miracles, they could have done so already.

Jesus is angry with the Pharisees because their attitude is wrong. Instead of accepting the Kingdom gladly, they are hanging back – so he refuses to do a special miracle, to order and just for them. This takes us back to two ideas we have already come across in Mark:

> Some people refuse to understand that the Kingdom of God is coming. They are *outside* the Kingdom (see 4:11–12, Unit 15 – there the religious authorities could not understand the parables, and here Mark seems to be saying that they cannot understand the miracles either).

Miracles do not prove anything by themselves, unless those who see them are open to God. When Jesus was performing exorcisms, the religious authorities said that he was possessed by Beelzebub (3:22, see Unit 14). If people are determined to think badly of someone, they can usually find some excuse. So, even if Jesus gave the Pharisees their miracle, he could not win against closed minds and hearts.

There is a big contrast in Mark's Gospel between the behaviour of the disciples and the attitude of the Pharisees. Although Jesus sometimes speaks harshly to his disciples (see 8;17–18, for instance), they stay with him and are willing to learn. They often fail to understand what is going on. But they are open to what God is doing in Jesus. That is why they have been given the 'secret of the Kingdom of God' (4:11). By contrast, Mark thinks that the Pharisees of Jesus' time were like the 'wicked generation' of the time of Moses. Even after God had led the people out of Egypt and fed them in the desert, they kept on asking him for more and more signs from heaven (Numbers 14:11–12.) They refused to trust him.

A warning to the disciples

READ MARK 8:14–21

This is one of the most difficult passages in the whole of Mark's Gospel. To help us understand it, we will split it into three bits:
- Jesus' warning about the Pharisees and Herod.
- The disciples' misunderstanding.
- Jesus' explanation.

● **Jesus' warning** (verse 15). The rabbis sometimes used the word 'yeast' to mean 'evil intentions' or 'bad ideas'. This is probably what Jesus' words mean here. 'Be on your guard against the yeast of the Pharisees' means 'Watch out for their ideas!'

● **The disciples' misunderstanding** (verse 16). Mark tells his readers that the disciples had forgotten to bring enough loaves with them. When Jesus started talking about yeast they thought he was warning them not to buy any bread from the Pharisees, or from Herod. They have missed the point.

● **Jesus' explanation** (verses 17–21). Jesus is irritated with the disciples because they are worrying about what they are going to eat. They really ought to know better by now: after all, they have seen the feeding miracles. There was enough food for everybody then – the disciples should learn to trust Jesus.

A deeper meaning?

Look again at verses 19 and 20. Jesus asks the disciples how many baskets of leftovers they picked up at each feeding miracle. They reply 'twelve' and 'seven'. On the surface this certainly means that the disciples should trust Jesus. He has shown that he can supply all the food they need, with plenty left over.

But we have already seen that the numbers seven and twelve have special significance for Mark. They stand for the Jews and the Gentiles (see Unit 27). What are these special numbers doing in this story?

One of the favourite ideas of the Pharisees was that the Kingdom of God was only for Jews. We have seen that Jesus disagreed with this (Unit 26). Perhaps the 'yeast' – the wrong idea – of the Pharisees is that God was interested only in Jewish people. Jesus reminds his disciples of the twelve (Jewish) baskets and the seven (Gentile) baskets, to drive home the point that the Kingdom of God is for everyone.

We do not know what Jesus meant by 'the leaven of Herod'. It seems likely that he was thinking about the ideas of the followers of Herod Antipas, but these have been lost to us, and Mark does not say any more about them.

Jesus heals a blind man at Bethsaida

READ MARK 8:22–26

This story is very similar to the healing of the deaf mute in 7:31–37 (see Unit 26).
● In both stories, the man's friends ask Jesus to help him.

● Jesus uses spittle in both miracles.
● Both stories end with Jesus trying to keep the miracle secret.

It seems likely that Mark thought of these two stories as a pair. They would have reminded his readers of some words of the prophet Isaiah about the coming of God's Kingdom:

> 'The blind will be able to see
> And the deaf hear' (Isaiah 35:5).

The story of the blind man here, however, has a symbolic meaning for Mark as well. He is about to begin a long section of the Gospel to do with how the disciples begin to realize who Jesus is, and what that means. We will be looking at this in the next two units. Up to now it is as if the disciples themselves have been blind. Now God will gradually open their eyes – just as Jesus opened the eyes of the man at Bethsaida.

Notes

8:11: The word Mark uses for 'trap' is the same as the one he uses for Satan, when he tempts Jesus in 1:13.

8:18: Jesus' words to the disciples are almost an exact quotation from Isaiah 6:9–10. He has used them once before in Mark, about people who are 'outside' the Kingdom (4:12) – although here they are put as a question. It is as though Jesus was saying, 'Surely you aren't like all the others?' The disciples ought to understand him because they have been given the secret of the Kingdom of God (4:11).

Matthew and Luke usually put Mark's miracle stories into their Gospels, but they leave out both this one and the story of the deaf mute. Perhaps they did not like the idea of Jesus using spittle to help him do miracles.

▲FOLLOW UP▲

Short answer questions
● Why do the Pharisees want Jesus to perform a miracle?
● Why is Jesus angry with the disciples in the second story?
● What is the meaning of the word 'yeast' in verse 15?
● What did Mark think was special about the numbers twelve and seven?
● The blind man had his sight gradually restored by Jesus. Mark thinks this is a symbol of something. What?

Longer questions
1. Why does Mark think that Jesus refused to perform a miracle for the Pharisees?

2. Read the notes on the Messianic secret in Unit 9. Why does Jesus tell the man not to go back to the village in verse 30?

Who Do You Say I Am?

So far in Mark, people have been asking two questions about Jesus:
● Who is he?
● Where does his authority come from?
(See 1:27; 2:7; 4:41; 6:2–3, 14–15; 8:11.)
But they have not had any answers. Only the demons know who Jesus really is, and Jesus has forbidden them to speak (1:34). Even the disciples do not yet know the truth (4:41).

Mark has been building up suspense. He has already told his readers that Jesus is the Messiah, right at the start of the Gospel. But when is Jesus himself going to say something about it? The answers begin in this story.

READ MARK 8:27–9:1

If you look carefully at the text, you will see that it has three parts:
● Jesus questions the disciples and Peter declares that he is the Messiah. This is usually called Peter's *confession* (8:27–30).
● Jesus talks about what is going to happen to him in the future (8:31–33).
● Jesus talks about what it means to follow him (8:34–9:1).

Peter's confession
(verses 27–30)
'Tell me,' Jesus says in Mark's story, 'who do people say I am?' In all the other stories he has told so far, *other people* have been asking who Jesus is. Here Jesus brings the matter up himself. He seems to have decided that the disciples are now ready to understand.

How do you think the disciples felt when Jesus asked his question? Perhaps they were confused. We know that they did not yet really understand who Jesus was (4:41). We can imagine them talking about it

among themselves, half afraid to ask Jesus straight out. Perhaps they were excited. All sorts of rumours were flying about. Was Jesus at last going to tell them?

Look at the disciples' answer in verse 28. We have already come across these ideas in the story about the death of John the Baptist. These were the three main theories about who Jesus was. Mark does not tell us which of the disciples answered Jesus. Read the notes in Unit 22 again.

Jesus listens to the disciples' answers before asking them his second question: 'What about you? Who do you say I am?'

Peter's reply is very important for Mark. It is a kind of turning-point in his Gospel:

 You are the Messiah

(verse 29).

At last, the right answer – not just to Jesus' question here, but to all the other times when people have asked 'Who is this?' Peter has got the answer right, but Jesus instantly orders the disciples, 'Do not tell anyone about me.' Who Jesus is is still a *secret*, although now the disciples have begun to share it. For the meaning of 'Messiah', look again at Unit 4.

Jesus speaks about his suffering and death
(verses 31–33)
Look again at these verses. This is the first time that Jesus talks about what is going to happen to him.

There are four things we should notice about verses 31–33:

● **Jesus calls himself the 'Son of Man,'** although Peter has just called him the

Messiah. We have already seen that Jesus prefers this title, and we shall be finding out more about it later on.

● **Jesus says that he *must* suffer and die.**
People at the time of Jesus thought that the Messiah would be a kind of victorious warrior-king (see Unit 4), but Mark says that Jesus' idea of being a Messiah is completely different. The Messiah will suffer and die. (It is very easy to forget how really shocking the idea of a suffering Messiah would have been at first, because we are used to seeing pictures of Jesus on the cross.) But why? Mark gives his readers absolutely no explanation here. However, Jesus says that it *must* happen. He is implying that it is part of God's plan, even if it seems a mystery at first.

The death of Jesus involves some extremely important ideas. We shall look at some of them later.

● **Jesus says that he will rise to life.**
Although it is part of God's plan for the Messiah to suffer, that will not be the end of the story. Jesus will rise from the dead. This too is something completely new. As far as we know, nobody at the time of Jesus expected the Messiah to die – let alone to rise again.

● **Peter cannot understand what Jesus is saying.** When Peter called Jesus the Messiah, he certainly did not mean the sort of Messiah Jesus himself had in mind. Like everybody else, he seems to have thought of a victorious king. So when Jesus talks about suffering, he cannot bear it. He had seen a great future for his friend. Now it seems that all his hopes are to be dashed. He tries to tell Jesus off, to make him change his mind, but Jesus rounds on him angrily and calls him *Satan* – the one who tempts people to do the wrong thing.

Peter and the disciples have the secret of the Kingdom of God, and now they know that Jesus is the Messiah. But they still have a lot to learn about what that means.

Following Jesus
(8:34–9:1)

These are some of the most famous verses in Mark's Gospel. Jesus says that anyone who follows him must follow him all the way, even through the suffering he has just been talking about. (The first readers of

---

The usual word used for Jesus' final suffering and death is his *Passion* (it comes from the Greek word *pathein*, to suffer). This is why passages in the Gospels like this one are called *Passion predictions*. There are three of them altogether in Mark: the other two are in 9:31 and 10:33–34. But the name is a little misleading: all of them talk about Jesus' resurrection as well as his death.

Mark's Gospel faced real dangers for being Christians. These words would have been a great comfort to them.)

Our translation of Mark is a bit misleading here. It talks about somebody 'losing his life'. We often use this expression to mean dying. 'He lost his life in the War', we say. But although what Mark wrote can mean this (and many Christians have died for their faith), that is not its only meaning. The Greek word Mark used for life is *psyche*, which means *self*. Jesus is saying that his disciples must be willing to 'give themselves up', to go with him regardless of cost. We are all self-centred. Becoming 'selfless' is a painful business – like carrying a cross. This kind of commitment means even being willing to die for Jesus.

Why should anyone bother? Look again at verses 36–38. Here, for the first time in the Gospel, is some teaching of Jesus with a sting in the tail. Although the Jews of Jesus' time did not think that the Messiah would suffer, most of them (except the Sadducees, see Unit 1) did believe that at the end of time all the dead would rise and God would judge them in his Kingdom. The good would go to be in heaven for ever, and the wicked would be punished. Some of them thought that the Messiah would be involved in this judgement.

The first Christians shared these ideas. They thought that Jesus would come again to carry out God's judgement (this is usually called the *parousia*). So it was a serious matter to refuse to follow Jesus. It was like *losing your true self*. What was really going to count in the end was whether a person accepted or refused Jesus. Because he is not just the suffering Son of Man: at the end of time, he will return in glory.

 These verses seem to contain a terrible warning for Peter. He has followed Jesus and recognized him as the Messiah, yet he is *ashamed* of what Jesus says it really means to be the Messiah.

The last verse in this section is very difficult indeed. It has caused a lot of argument among people who study the New Testament:

'And he went on to say, "I tell you, there are some here who will not die until they have seen the Kingdom of God come with power" ' (9:1).

Here is the problem. Jesus often spoke about the Kingdom of God. Sometimes he talked about it as though it had already begun with his own preaching and in his miracles. At other times he talked about it as if it were partly *in the future* (see Unit 4). It would not finally arrive until the Son of Man came in glory at the end of the world (8:38). Read 9:1 again. Here Jesus' words seem at first to mean that he expected the end of the world and the final coming of God's Kingdom *before some of his audience were dead*. Obviously, this did not happen. The world is still going on.

Some people find this very worrying. Christians believe that Jesus is God, and God knows everything. Could Jesus have been wrong about something which is at the very heart of his message – the Kingdom itself?

Here are some of the answers people have come up with:

Yes. But it does not matter. Jesus was a real man who got things wrong at times.

No. A famous British New Testament scholar, Professor C.H. Dodd, said that Mark's Greek really means that Jesus' listeners would not die until they realized *that the Kingdom of God had already come* – in Jesus' ministry.

No. Jesus was not talking about the end of the world, but about his own resurrection, or even the transfiguration (see next unit).

No. Many of the first Christians expected Jesus to return soon, and Mark was one of them. He added this bit onto 8:38 because he thought it was important. But he got it wrong. Jesus said that even he did not know the *timing* of the end of the world: the important things were to realize that it would happen, and to be ready (see 13:32–37).

Nobody has really solved this problem, but you ought to be able to discuss it. Who knows – perhaps some day you could help to sort it out!

This whole section is an extremely important part of Mark's gospel. It has introduced some really major themes which we will return to many times later on. Here are the main points again:
● Peter has realized that Jesus is the Messiah: the disciples have been let into the secret.
● The Messiah must suffer and rise from the dead.
● Following Jesus means sharing in suffering.

- Jesus is the world's final judge.
- The section ends with a difficult saying about the Kingdom of God (9:1).

Mark has ended his introduction to Jesus' ministry. From now on he will show Jesus moving towards the astonishing events at the end of the Gospel.

Notes

8:29: Jesus' question echoes the words of the disciples in the story of the calming of the storm (4:41): 'Who is this?' Mark does not make it clear why he thinks Peter suddenly realized who Jesus was, but we have already noted the strong connection between Mark's Gospel and Peter, who often appears as the spokesman of the twelve (see Unit 13). We also know from the Acts of the Apostles and from the Letters in the New Testament that Peter became the leader of the early Christian church. If you read the later account of this story in Matthew's Gospel (16:13–20) you will see that Matthew has some additional material about Peter which he adds to Mark's story. There Peter seems to appear as both the *leader* and the *symbol* of the church, and is given the 'keys of the Kingdom of heaven'. Look back to Unit 13. There we saw that most Christians believe that bishops are the successors of the apostles. Roman Catholic Christians believe that the Pope is the leader of all the bishops because he is the successor of Peter.

FOLLOW UP

1. ● Jesus said, 'Who do you say I am?' Which disciple answered him?
● What did he say?

2. Jesus said that 'the Son of Man must suffer much'. Who was he talking about?

3. 'If anyone wants to _____, he must _____, carry his _____ and _____.' Fill in the missing words.

4. ● What sort of Messiah were people expecting at the time of Jesus?
● How does this help to explain Peter's reaction to what Jesus says about his future?

5. Why does Mark think that it is dangerous not to follow Jesus? Explain your answer fully.

6. Mark 9:1 has caused a lot of problems for people who study the New Testament. Explain why, in your own words.

7. 'Does a person gain anything if he wins the whole world but loses his life?' In groups, discuss what you think Jesus might have meant by 'winning the whole world' and by 'loses his life'. Is it always good to be ambitious?

The Transfiguration

Mark tells his story brilliantly. As usual, he has packed it with meaning. Jesus again takes Peter, James and John with him, and climbs a mountain. Some scholars think this was Mount Tabor, or Mount Hermon (which is near Caesarea Philippi – see map in Unit 1). There, something extraordinary happens. It is usually called Jesus' Transfiguration, a word which means 'changing appearance'.

READ MARK 9:2–13

In this story, Mark gets across the idea that Jesus is the Son of God. But he also explains what this means: the Son of God must suffer. He thinks these two ideas are like two sides of one coin. You cannot have one without the other. How does Mark get these ideas across?

Icons are an important aspect of the Russian and Eastern Orthodox tradition. They show how God became human in Jesus, symbolizing his glorified humanity.

Jesus is the Son of God

- Jesus takes his disciples up a *mountain*. In the Old Testament, God appears to people on a mountain. He appears to Moses and to Elijah. *God, Moses and Elijah all appear at the Transfiguration, and the Transfiguration happens on a mountain.*

Exodus 24
1 Kings 19:8–9

- A '*change came over Jesus'*. The disciples realized he was the same person, but saw what he was really like. His clothes became dazzling white. Things linked with heaven were often thought to be white in colour – angels, for example, are described as wearing white clothes (why do you think this was?).

Matthew 28:2–3
Mark 16:5

Paul said that, after he was raised from the dead, Jesus had a 'glorious body': perhaps this is what Mark thinks the disciples glimpsed. *The human Jesus is also the Son of God.*

Philippians 3:21

- Peter and the disciples were scared out of their wits. People in the Old Testament, as in Mark, are often frightened when God does something. Peter wants to make three '*tents*' or ''tabernacles'. The Jewish festival of Tabernacles looks back to the

time of Moses, when they lived in tents in the desert and had a tent shrine for God. At that time, the people felt God was very close to them. The prophet Ezekiel predicted a time when God would 'live with his people', and the Hebrew word he uses means 'to live in a tent'. *Peter thinks the time has come when God, in Jesus, will live with his people.* He wants to get hold of the fantastic experience, and keep it. But Mark thinks you can't stick God's glory in a tent. *God's glory is in the man Jesus, and in his work.*

Ezekiel 37:27

- In the Old Testament, God's glory meant his beauty and power. God was so great that no one could look at him and live. So he would sometimes use a cloud to shield the people from harm. *In a similar way Mark says 'a cloud appeared and covered them with its shadow.'*

Exodus 33:20

Exodus 24:15–18. This section is worth reading, as it is very similar to the Transfiguration.

- God had said Jesus was his Son at his baptism. This is the only other time Mark says that God speaks from heaven. Here the Father *tells the disciples who Jesus is*, and that they must '*listen to him*'. The Father agrees with what the Son says. What has Jesus been saying? That the Son of God must suffer.

See Mark 1:11 and the notes in Unit 6.

The Son of God must suffer

- Elijah and Moses appear and talk with Jesus. This is very important.

The early Christians believed that both these men had something to do with the Messiah, and here they are! Moses had said God would send a new prophet, whom people should listen to. (Notice that God the Father tells the disciples to 'listen to' Jesus.) People thought Elijah would return when the Messiah came.

Deuteronomy 18:15.

Malachi 4:5
Sirach 48:10–11
(in Catholic Bibles)

- Elijah and Moses both suffered for their faith, and the Son of God has to suffer. But people believed both survived death. The Son of God will rise from the dead. The Law, represented by Moses, and the prophets, represented by Elijah, are fulfilled in Jesus. Mark says they were 'talking with Jesus'. It is as though the greatest Law-giver and the greatest prophet were saying, 'You're right! The Son of God must die for the people!'

2 Kings 2:1–17

Deuteronomy 34:5–6 was thought to mean Moses was taken up to heaven

• Jesus tells his disciples not to tell anyone what they had seen 'until the Son of Man has risen from death'. *People must not think the Messiah is all about glory. He also has to die.* Only then will people understand what his work really means.

• The disciples are confused. They can't grasp the idea that the wonderful person they saw on the mountain is one and the same as the suffering Son of Man. They were Jews. They had no problem with the idea that *everyone* has life after death. But they can't understand why one man should rise. They do not yet realize that *Jesus' resurrection shows that he was right to suffer.*

• The disciples have just seen that Jesus is the Messiah. And they have seen Elijah. But where was Elijah before Jesus came?

Jesus replies, 'Elijah has already come.' Mark's readers would know he meant John the Baptist.

But people did not realize who John

There is no known prophecy that Elijah would suffer when he returned. However, we have already seen that he suffered because of Queen Jezebel, who wanted to kill him. Perhaps the idea is that the new Queen Jezebel (Herodias) killed the new Elijah (John) – something the old Queen Jezebel failed to do.

Christians believe Jesus' suffering was predicted in the Old Testament – see Isaiah 50:4–6, 53:1–12.

was. And he was killed. People do not realize who Jesus really is. And he will also be killed. The suffering of John, and of Jesus, fits in with God's plan. This is what the Old Testament Scriptures say.

Before and after the Transfiguration, Jesus makes it clear that the Messiah has to suffer (8:27–9:1 and 9:9–13). This is what Messiahship means and Mark shows this by Jesus' being transfigured, by his meeting Moses and Elijah, and by the voice of God. The glorious Son of God is one and the same as the suffering Son of Man.

▲FOLLOW UP▲

1. Imagine you are Peter. Think about what happened at the Transfiguration, and how you felt. Write the story from Peter's point of view.

2. How do these words help us to understand why this story was important to Mark?
– mountain
– 'a change came over Jesus'
– white
– tents
– cloud
– 'Listen to him!'
– Elijah and Moses
– 'Don't tell anyone what you have seen, until the Son of Man has risen from death.'
– The Son of Man must suffer.

3. Roman Catholic, Eastern Orthodox and Anglican Christians have a festival to remember the Transfiguration. Read some of the hymns, prayers and readings used in churches on the Feast of the Transfiguration. Why do you think these hymns, prayers and readings are used? From what they say, why is the Transfiguration important for Christians today?

(Your town library or school will have the books you need. Here are some of the books you could use: *The English Hymnal, English Praise, The Alternative Services Book, The Sunday Missal.*)

The Faithless People

READ MARK 9:14–32

Jesus heals a boy with an evil spirit (verses 14–29)

In the Transfiguration, Mark shows that the Son of God and the man Jesus are one and the same. With Peter, James and John, Jesus comes down from the mountain. He returns to ordinary people and their problems.

This section is rather like Exodus 32–33:6. There, Moses has been talking to God on the mountain and, like Jesus, he comes down to find God's people behaving as though they had no faith (Moses found they had made idols to worship; Jesus finds they do not trust in God's power to heal people). Mark's readers may well have remembered this story.

The other disciples have failed to cast out a demon, and they are in the middle of an argument with the teachers of the Law. These scribes may have been criticizing them, and their master, because they cannot do anything for a boy who needs help. When Jesus arrives, Mark says, 'they were greatly surprised'. Some scholars think this was because Jesus' face was shining after the Transfiguration (in Exodus 34:30, Moses' face shone when he came down from the mountain). This may be what Mark means, but he does not make it clear.

There are two other things to look at in this story:
● What was wrong with the boy.
● The need for faith.

● **What was wrong with the boy?** People in Jesus' time thought illness was caused by demons (see Unit 7, where we discussed this idea). What was the boy suffering from?
  – He falls on the ground (verse 18).
  – He foams at the mouth (verse 18).
  – He grits his teeth (verse 18).
  – He goes rigid (verse 18) and rolls on the ground (verse 20).

These details would fit the idea that the boy was an *epileptic*. Epilepsy is a disorder of the nervous system that usually begins in childhood. In bad cases, it can be horrible. The 'fits' start with warning signals like a tingling in the face, or suddenly feeling very hot, and then very cold. Then you black out, and can hurt yourself badly when you fall – especially if there were fire or water around! Sometimes you cry out. Your muscles go rigid. After a few seconds, your arms and legs start to thrash about, and you foam at the mouth. This stage lasts a couple of minutes, and then you stay unconscious for up to half an hour afterwards.

We can imagine that in Jesus' time, people thought the violent fits were the attacks of a particularly vicious demon. But Jesus heals the boy. Curing epilepsy (let alone casting out a demon) is quite extraordinary – even today, there is treatment but no cure. Mark believes that Jesus is able to heal people because of who he is.

● **The need for faith.** Mark shows this in three ways:

The people need faith. When it comes to this boy's healing, they do not trust God. Mark shows Jesus getting angry here: in verse 19 he talks as though he were God, passing judgement on his people. (In the Old Testament, God often criticized his people through the prophets for not trusting in him – see Jeremiah 5:23.) One of the rabbis said that the Messiah's generation would be particularly faithless. And Mark believes it is because of this that they fail to recognize who Jesus is, and have him killed.

The disciples need faith. Look again at verse 29. The disciples have been given the authority to heal (3:15). But perhaps they needed to pray more – to rely more on God's power – before the healings would work. This verse may again be instructions for Christian healers: you can cast out violent demons only if you pray.

The boy's father asks for more faith. He has faith, but asks for Jesus' help because his faith is not enough. Jesus says anything is possible if you have true faith. If you think everything is hopeless, it will be. Mark's first readers may well have been very moved by what the boy's father says. They were probably being persecuted because they were Christians (see Unit 3). Like the boy's father, they need to trust God, especially when everything looks black.

The second Passion prediction (verses 30–32)

After Jesus has healed the boy, he and his disciples leave the area. They get a grim reminder of what lies ahead: Jesus speaks about his death again. This is slightly different from the first Passion prediction (8:31–33). Here, Jesus adds that he 'will be handed over' to the people who will kill him. Someone has got to do that handing over. There is a traitor in their midst.

Notes

9:26–27: Some scholars suggest that the details 'he is dead' and 'to rise' are shadows of what is to come: Jesus' resurrection. This is possible, but there is not enough evidence to be certain.

9:29: Some Greek copies of Mark say 'prayer *and fasting*'. 'Fasting' was probably added later, perhaps for the benefit of Christian healers.

FOLLOW UP

1. Copy out and correct these sentences:
– Moses and his disciples came down from the building.
– The other disciples were arguing with some teachers of geography.
– A woman came to Moses, and said her daughter had an evil eye.
– She had asked Moses' disciples to get rid of the evil eye, and they could.
– Moses said the people had lots of faith, and told them to bring the girl to him.
– When the evil eye saw Moses, it threw the girl into a river.
– The girl's mother said, 'Have pity on us and kill us!'
– Moses said that nothing was possible for the person who had faith.
– The girl's mother said: 'I don't have faith, but not enough. Help me to have less!'
– Moses got rid of the girl's evil eye.
– The disciples asked why they could do it.
– Moses said only hymns could get rid of this sort of evil eye.

2. Do you think the boy was an epileptic? Why?

3. Look again at verse 29. Why does Jesus say this?

4. The boy's father says, 'I do have faith, but not enough. Help me to have more!' Like Mark's first readers, many Christians say it is all too easy for belief in God to waver when the going gets tough. Answer these questions in full:
● Why do you think they say this?
● How might the boy's father's words be helpful for Mark's first readers?
● How far are they helpful for people in trouble today?

Some Teachings of Jesus

Mark now gives his readers some short examples of the teachings of Jesus. They seem to be very loosely connected, and it seems likely that they originally came from lots of different places in Jesus' ministry. Mark has collected them and strung them together like beads on a necklace – perhaps because he did not know when they first happened, and did not want them to be lost forever. Sometimes he has put sayings together because they have the same *theme* or key word, like 'salt' or 'fire'. That sometimes makes them hard to understand, so we will look at them one at a time.

Who is the greatest?

READ MARK 9:33–37

This is the first of two stories Mark tells about Jesus and children: the other is in 10:13–16.

Jesus and the disciples are back in Capernaum, Jesus' home base for most of his ministry. The disciples have been arguing about which one of them is the leader. It is interesting to see how well Mark tells the story. The disciples are ashamed of themselves when Jesus asks them what it was all about. They are beginning to realize that Jesus' Kingdom is not about power, even if they do not always live up to the ideal. But Jesus knows that the lesson needs to be repeated if it is to be learned properly. Patiently he sits down (a rabbi would sometimes do this when he was teaching something important) and calls his disciples to him.

Jesus' saying in verse 35 reappears in different stories and in slightly different forms in Mark 10:43, Matthew 20:16 and

Because they are powerless, children have often suffered abuse and neglect. Yet Jesus chose children as a symbol of what real greatness is in the Kingdom of God.

Luke 22:26. Perhaps it was something Jesus said several times. Real greatness in Jesus' Kingdom means being a '*servant* of all'. That's not what people usually think of! (Mark has placed this story after Jesus' second Passion prediction in 9:30–32; later in the Gospel he makes it clear that the best example of service was given by Jesus himself in giving his life for others, 10:45.)

Jesus' Kingdom turns all the usual values upside-down. If someone is ambitious, he or she should look for the lowest place and the best opportunity to serve others. In Mark's story Jesus makes this clear by showing the disciples a *child*. The point is that children need to be looked after. They are not powerful, or rich, or influential . . . But by welcoming them, Jesus says, the disciples welcome him. The child stands for all who need help and are too easily overlooked.

'Whoever is not against us is for us'

READ MARK 9:38–41

The disciples are being selfish here. They do not want people outside their group to do the things they can do. But Jesus says the outsiders are really on their side. They may become his followers, so the disciples should not tell them off. In fact, Jesus' followers should be grateful for even a cup of water, given because they belong to Jesus. The kind person who gives it will be rewarded.

The early church had a problem with non-Christians who claimed to drive out demons using Jesus' name. The idea was that Jesus' name was so powerful that demons left someone when they heard it. Things were more difficult when the exorcisms looked like black magic (see Acts 19:11–20), so the early Christians needed Jesus' advice here to solve the problem.

Temptations to sin

READ MARK 9:42–48

If we do evil things, what will happen to us after death?

Jesus gives some frightening warnings here. Some things people do mean they

The Valley of Hinnom ('Gehenna'), where the rubbish of Jerusalem burned endlessly, provided a frightening picture of hell.

will go to hell. Our English word 'hell' translates the word 'Gehenna'. Gehenna was a valley to the east of Jerusalem. In ancient Israel, children were burnt alive there as sacrifices to the god Molech (2 Kings 23:10). This had stopped by Jesus' time, and the place had become a dump where rubbish was burnt. Because of this, Gehenna was thought of as a place of fire, and the word was used to describe the place where evil people would be punished after death.

The idea in these verses is this. If you cause someone – including yourself – to stumble, you will be punished. Jesus is not talking about tripping people up, so what does he mean by 'stumble'?

● It may mean 'make someone lose their faith'. This is how the Good News Bible understands it.

● It may mean 'make someone do what's wrong'.

First, Jesus warns his followers not to make other people stumble. It is terrible to be drowned with a millstone round your

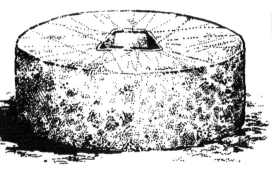

Millstones like this were used for grinding corn in Jesus' day.

neck, but it is even more terrible to cause 'one of these little ones' to stumble. If anyone does so, they will have to answer for it to God. The 'little ones' may mean children. However, Jesus called his followers 'little ones', so it probably means Christians. A millstone was a huge piece of rock

turned by a donkey to grind corn. People were sometimes killed this way in the Roman Empire, of which Israel was part.

Jesus then warns his followers not to let themselves stumble. Jesus' followers want to enter '*life*'. This means eternal life in the Kingdom of God. But they must be careful not to stumble. If Mark's first readers were being persecuted for their faith, it must have been very easy to 'stumble' and fall away from Christianity. Here, they are warned not to.

Jesus is not telling his followers to cut their hands or feet off if they do something wrong! What he means is that *the life of the Kingdom is the most important thing there is*. It is worth far more than a hand, or a foot, or an eye.

People in Jesus' time thought that different parts of the body tempted people to different sins. For example, the eye tempted people to lust (see Proverbs 6:16–19).

Salt

These verses are very hard to understand, and we can only guess at what they mean.

READ VERSE 49

Sacrifices to God were held in the Temple in Jerusalem. They were made *pure* (acceptable to God) by adding *salt* to them (Leviticus 2:13). If you heat metal in a *fire*, the *pure* metal will separate from everything else. The verse may mean, then, that *Christians should be pure*, too. Jesus may also be using 'fire' as an image of persecution. If so, Mark's first readers would have found this idea very important. *Christians may have to suffer the fire of persecution to be made pure.*

READ VERSE 50a

There was another reason why people in Jesus' time thought salt was *pure*. It came from the purest things: the sea and the sun (which evaporates the sea water and leaves the salt behind). The verse may mean that the followers of Jesus must not lose their purity, or they will fail in their job to make the world pure. If they become impure, how can they become pure again?

Someone might point out that salt cannot lose its saltness. This is not a problem. The salt from the Dead Sea is not pure. There are other things in it. So it is possible to have something that looks like salt when the real salt has dissolved!

READ VERSE 50b

The Greek says here: 'Have salt in yourselves, and live in peace with one another.'
    The 'salt' may mean:
    – salt of friendship (which is what the Good News Bible thinks)
    – salt of kindness
    – salt of being willing to be persecuted
    – salt of purity.
It is difficult to know, and we can only guess.

Notes

Verse 41: 'Because you belong to me' is really 'because you are in Christ's name'. This is one of the very few times when Jesus refers to himself as 'Christ'.

Verses 44 and 46: These are left out of the main text by the Good News Bible. They are both identical to verse 48, and some early copies of Mark leave them out too. They were probably added later. Verse 48 is quoting Isaiah 66:24.

Verse 49: Some Greek copies of Mark have this version of the verse. Others have: 'For everything will be salted with fire.' This is probably what Mark wrote. Whichever is original, though, our explanation of the verse is still possible.
    It is interesting that this is the only passage in Mark where Jesus talks directly about hell. The later Gospels include a lot more material. Perhaps Mark did not think the subject was as important as some other Christians did.

FOLLOW UP

1. What does Jesus tell his followers to do in this passage?

2. What might Jesus mean when he talks about salt?

3. Interview some Christians about what they think about hell. Find out things like
    – whether they think it exists
    – what they think it is like
    – who they think goes there.

You might want to use a questionnaire for your research. (It would be interesting to talk to Christians who go to diferent kinds of churches.) How do they understand the idea of hell, and what are the differences in their views?

4. Write the following essay: 'If everyone believed in hell, how do you think people's behaviour would change? Why do you think this?'

5. What does Mark think about greatness and service?

Marriage and Children

In the last unit we saw how Mark may have put together some of the sayings of Jesus in chapter 9 because they dealt with the same *theme* or contained the same key word. In chapter 10, Mark arranges his material in another interesting way. In a lot of the Christian literature of his time (and especially in the Letters of the New Testament) it was quite common for an author to work through a list of advice for different people in the church: husbands and wives, children, slaves, church leaders and so on. You can look up an example of this in Ephesians 5:22–6:9.

In the same way, Mark now tells a series of stories about things Jesus said and did. Each has an important meaning for a different group of people among his first Christian readers, as well as telling them more about what happened during Jesus' ministry. Together they form a kind of list of *house rules* for Mark's church. He has got four sorts of people in mind. They are:

● Married people (10:1–12).
● Children (10:13–16).
● Wealthy people (10:17–31).
● Leaders in the church (10:32–45).

In this unit, we look at the first two.

Marriage and divorce

READ MARK 10:1–12

Mark says that the Pharisees were out to get Jesus again. Perhaps they already knew what he thought about divorce and were trying to get him into trouble with Herod, who had divorced and remarried (see Unit 22). At any rate, they are trying to drag him into an argument.

The rabbis disagreed violently about divorce. One side followed a rabbi called Shammai and was very strict. They said that a man could not divorce his wife unless she had committed adultery. (Jewish law did not allow a woman to divorce her husband.) The other side followed Rabbi Hillel. They said that a man could divorce his wife for almost any reason: for spoiling a meal, for instance, or for talking to a man she did not know. Both sides said that they were keeping the Law of Moses, which allowed a man to divorce his wife if she was 'guilty of some shameful conduct' (Deuteronomy 24:1). The question was, how bad did this 'shameful conduct' have to be?

Not surprisingly, Hillel's ideas were much more popular than Shammai's. As a result, women were frequently very badly treated. Some were divorced for very minor reasons. Women were insecure within marriage and divorce brought terrible disgrace.

A burnt meal could be grounds for divorce, according to Rabbi Hillel. Women were badly treated in Jesus' day.

The Pharisees in Mark's story probably wanted Jesus to get tangled up in the argument between the rabbis, and hoped that they would be able to trip him up over some legal point. Jesus neatly side-steps their trap. (We have seen him do something very similar in the story of the Sabbath corn in 2:23–28, see Unit 12.) Instead of arguing with them about the rules in Deuteronomy, he takes them to the heart

---

Marriage

If you look up Matthew 19:11–12 you will see that there Jesus says that his teaching on marriage 'does not apply to everyone, but only those to whom God has given it'. And he seems to allow divorce if adultery has taken place.

Mark does not mention this, but he does try to make things clearer for his Gentile readers. He seems to have added verse 12 because Roman law – unlike Jewish law – *did* allow women to divorce their husbands.

Christians have always had a hard time trying to square the experience of ordinary men and women with the teachings of Jesus. Even in the New Testament, the different Christian authors often seem to disagree with one another about divorce, as though very early on the church was struggling with the problem and could not make up its mind.

Among the Christian churches today, this confusion is still going on. The Church of England is changing its rules, but until recently it took a very dim view of divorce and did not allow divorced priests to remarry and stay in the full-time ministry. The Roman Catholic Church does not recognize divorce at all, although it has its own process for the *annulment* of marriages in some circumstances.

What seems to have happened is that Jesus' teaching was originally intended to protect women and to emphasize that marriage was a good thing, which God wanted. The churches have had problems protecting this teaching while at the same time caring for people who have found themselves in difficult and distressing circumstances.

---

of the matter – right back to what God intended when he created men and women in the first place (verses 5–9). The laws Moses gave on divorce came about only because things had gone wrong: marriage itself is built into the framework of the universe. It is how God has created the world. For this reason, divorce should not

happen at all. The women of Jesus' time ought to be able to live in love, security and respect.

Children and the Kingdom

READ MARK 10:13–16

This is one of the best-loved stories in Mark. He does not tell us why the disciples tried to stop the people bringing their children to Jesus. Perhaps they wanted to protect him from being bothered by what they thought were unnecessary demands on his time. But Jesus tells them off (Mark says that he was 'angry'), welcomes the children, and blesses them.

If you look carefully at the story you will see that it contains two sayings of Jesus, one in verse 14 and the other in verse 15.

> Verse 14: 'Let the children come to me, and do not stop them, because the Kingdom of God belongs to such as these.'

Why does Jesus say that the Kingdom of God belongs to 'such as these'? One answer is that Jesus thought that his disciples should learn from some of the qualities children have. Young children (the word Mark uses means someone under twelve) are generally eager to learn, trusting, and loving towards their parents. These are the attitudes the disciples should have towards God.

But this does not seem to be enough. It is easy to be sentimental about children – but any teacher or parent will tell you how difficult the nicest child can be on a bad day. In 9:37 (Unit 32) we saw that Jesus welcomed children because they were needy and powerless. The same idea applies in this story. Children had no standing in Jewish society or in the eyes of the religious authorities. The disciples behave in the way we would expect men of their time to behave. Because of this Jesus makes children the symbol of all the people the Kingdom is really for: the weak, the oppressed, the poor and the outcasts.

Children had no standing in the Jewish society of Jesus' time. For this reason Jesus makes children the symbol of the weak and oppressed – those the Kingdom is really for. The picture shows a child being baptized – welcomed into the Christian family.

This verse has two possible meanings:
– Children like to be given things – they very rarely turn up their noses at something done especially for them. This childlike openness is the proper attitude Jesus' listeners should have to God's gift of the Kingdom.
– People should welcome the Kingdom of God as they would welcome a child who brings joy to a married couple, and as Jesus himself welcomes the children in this story.

It is difficult to tell which of these Mark meant. The idea of welcoming the Kingdom as if it were a child is close to the thought we have already had in 9:37. But most people usually understand it the other way. In Matthew's Gospel Jesus actually says, 'Unless you change and become like children, you will never enter the Kingdom of Heaven.'

Notes

10:5: Look again at the notes on the Pharisees' attitude to the Law of Moses in Unit 1. They thought that it perfectly expressed what God wanted for all time. But Jesus' attitude is different. Moses' laws were only given for a while, and sometimes even as a sort of second-best because people would not do what God really wanted. Now that the Kingdom has come, the Law is not enough. People must look behind religious rules and regulations to God himself.

10:7–8: Rabbis argued with one another from Scripture. The Pharisees ask Jesus about Deuteronomy 24:1, but he refers them back to two texts from Genesis: 1:27 and 2:24.

10:14: Most major churches today baptize babies and some count them as full members of the church from then on. This is called *infant baptism*. We do not really know whether this happened at the time when Mark was writing, but it certainly began very early on. Origen, a Christian theologian who lived between about AD185 and 254, said it was an ancient custom which had been handed down from the apostles.

However, down the centuries, some Christians have said that infant baptism is wrong: only people who can understand what is going on should be baptized. (This is the position of *Baptist* churches today – hence their name.)

Our story from Mark has often been used to defend infant baptism from criticism. When Jesus says to the disciples, 'Do not try to *stop* them', he uses the same word as we find in Acts 8:36, when somebody asks, 'What is to *stop* me from being baptized?' Some people have even suggested that both of these texts are echoes of a question which was asked about people in the early church before they were baptized, and during the baptism service.

FOLLOW UP

1. ● What did Jesus say about marriage and divorce in Mark's story (verse 9)?
● How did he back up what he said?

2. ● What did Jesus say about the laws Moses gave on divorce (verse 5)?
● How do you think Jesus' attitude to the Law was different from the Pharisees'?

3. Using the information in this unit, explain in your own words how the Pharisees might have been trying to trap Jesus.

4. Why did the disciples scold the people (verse 13)?

5. ● Who does Jesus say that the Kingdom of God belongs to (verse 14)?
● Why do you think he said this?

6. Divide your class into two groups: the followers of Rabbi Hillel, and the followers of Rabbi Shammai. Stage a debate on divorce. Remember that the argument was about Deuteronomy 24:1.

7. In Britain today, one in three marriages ends in divorce. What do you think a Christian's attitude to this might be? (You might like to discuss this with your teacher.)

The Rich Man

Should people be rich?

What do you think?

People at the time of Jesus, including the disciples and the rich man in this new story, thought Opinion 1 was right. But what did Jesus think?

Opinion 4
NO. If you are rich, you should give your money to the poor.

Opinion 1
YES. If you are rich, it is because God is pleased with you. God made the good things in life, and he wants people to enjoy them.

Opinion 2
YES. If you are rich, it is because you have earned the money.

Opinion 3
NOT REALLY. If you are rich, it is because you are lucky – it has nothing to do with talent.

We live in an unequal world. When many are poor, is it right to be rich?

📖 READ MARK 10:17–31

Jesus was pleased that the rich man kept the Jewish Law. But he did not go far enough. Jesus told him to give his money away – all of it. Do you think it was fair that he had money to spare, while other people were hungry? In the story, his money seems to stop him getting closer to God. He had made money, not God, the centre of his life.

No wonder he was gloomy and the disciples were shocked! They all thought God wanted some people to be rich. If it is hard for the rich to enter the Kingdom, it must be even harder for the poor! 'Who, then, can be saved?' the disciples asked.

But the coming of the Kingdom changes things. People have to decide whether or not they want to be in the Kingdom. God's Kingdom is the most important thing there is. If they want to be in it, nothing must get in the way. Money may be in the way. Family may be in the way. But people who give things up for the sake of the Kingdom will be rewarded. There may be persecution to go through, but there will be new 'brothers', 'sisters' and 'mothers' among their fellow Christians. And there is the promise of 'eternal life'. (This is very like what Jesus says in Mark 3:33–35.) It is impossible for anyone – even the rich – to enter the Kingdom on their own efforts. But God is ready to help, and 'everything is possible for God'.

Jesus says, 'Many who now are first will be last, and many who now are last will be first.' What does this mean?

● The 'first' are the 'important' people in the world: the rich and the powerful.

● The 'last' are the 'least important' people in the world: people like the poor, the tax collectors, the sinners and 'bad characters' whom Jesus met.

Many Christians, following Jesus' teaching and example, have given their lives to work among the poor and disadvantaged. Some, like Mother Teresa, have become well known, but many are known only to those they serve.

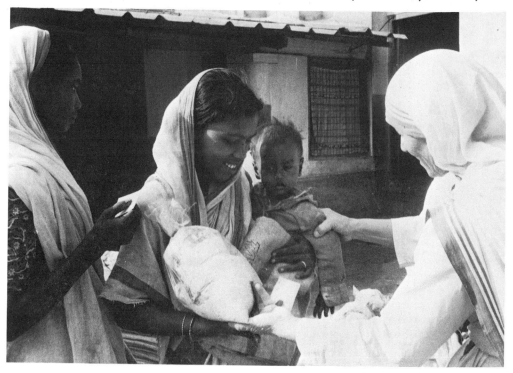

They will change places:

● The 'first' will be last. They will either be last to squeeze into the Kingdom, or they will be the least important people in the Kingdom.

● The 'last' will be first. They will either be the first to enter the Kingdom, or they will be the most important people in the Kingdom.

Why do you think this idea would have shocked people who listened to Jesus?

We know that many of the early Christians were poor. If Mark was writing for Christians in Rome, most of them were very poor, and hated by the authorities. Jesus' words here would have comforted Mark's readers.

Like all the major world religions, Christianity says the poor should be cared for. All through the Bible the poor and the needy are looked on as being under God's special care and protection. Jesus says to the rich man, 'Go and sell all you have and give the money to the poor, and you will have riches in heaven; then come and follow me.'

How do Christians today think Jesus' words apply to them? Some of their ideas are set out in the diagram.

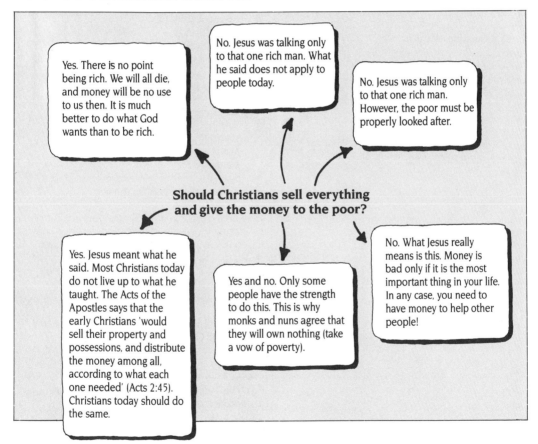

Yes. There is no point being rich. We will all die, and money will be no use to us then. It is much better to do what God wants than to be rich.

No. Jesus was talking only to that one rich man. What he said does not apply to people today.

No. Jesus was talking only to that one rich man. However, the poor must be properly looked after.

Should Christians sell everything and give the money to the poor?

Yes. Jesus meant what he said. Most Christians today do not live up to what he taught. The Acts of the Apostles says that the early Christians 'would sell their property and possessions, and distribute the money among all, according to what each one needed' (Acts 2:45). Christians today should do the same.

Yes and no. Only some people have the strength to do this. This is why monks and nuns agree that they will own nothing (take a vow of poverty).

No. What Jesus really means is this. Money is bad only if it is the most important thing in your life. In any case, you need to have money to help other people!

What do you think? Which of these ideas best explains what Jesus' words mean for Christians today?

Notes

10:18: Christians believe Jesus is God. Why, then, does he say 'Why do you call me good? No one is good except God alone'? Perhaps he did not like the man's flattery. If Jesus knew he was God, he did not tell everybody. If he had, they would have thought it was blasphemy. But Mark knows the answer his readers ought to give to Jesus' question. When he calls him 'good', the rich man has hinted at Jesus' true nature – even though he does not realize it.

10:24: Some translations have here 'how hard it is *for those who trust in riches* to enter the Kingdom of God.' The words in italics were probably not written by Mark, but were added later. We should leave them out.

10:25: Some scholars have missed the point of this vivid language. Some say we should alter the Greek a little to read 'cable' instead of 'camel'. Others say Jesus was talking about a gate in Jerusalem called 'The Needle's Eye', which was just wide enough to squeeze a camel through. (The problem is that there was no such gate!) Jesus' sense of humour is showing through here. He is saying, 'Ever tried to push a huge great camel through a sewing needle? If you think that's difficult, it's even harder to get a rich man into the Kingdom of God!'

FOLLOW UP

1. ● Fill in the gaps:
'It is much harder for a _____ person to enter the Kingdom of God than for a _____ to go through the eye of a needle.'
● Who said these words?
● Why do you think he said this?
● How was Jesus' view of riches different from that of other people at the time?

2. Jesus said, 'This is impossible for man, but not for God; everything is possible for God.' *What* is impossible for man, but not for God?

3. Peter said he and the other disciples had left everything to follow Jesus. What things did Jesus say his followers would receive?

4. How do you think
– the rich man
– the disciples
felt before, during, and after Jesus spoke with the rich man?

5. Look up these Bible passages:
– Ecclesiastes 5:10   – Matthew 6:19–21
– Luke 12:15–21   – Luke 3:11
– Luke 6:20   – 1 Timothy 6:10
– Matthew 25:31–46   – 1 John 3:17
– Matthew 6:24
How far do these verses help us to understand what Jesus means in the story of the rich man?

6. ● Make a list of all the things that you want out of life (not just material things). Put them in order – most important one first, and the least important one last.
● Why did you choose these things?
● How do you think a Christian would react to your choices?
● Would you agree with their reaction or not? Say why.

7. The great Hindu teacher Mahatma Gandhi said the problem with Christians was that he had never met one. Write an essay on whether you think it is possible to be a Christian and rich.

8. EITHER Do some research on poverty in Britain and the world today
OR Do some research on a Christian who has given his or her life to helping others (such as Mother Teresa, Desmond Tutu, or Eric Liddell). You should be able to get some information from television or newspapers, or from your R.S. department, or school or town library.

The Road to Jerusalem

Jesus now starts his journey to Jerusalem – the journey to his death and resurrection.

The third Passion prediction

READ MARK 10:32–34

This is the third time Jesus speaks about his death, and it is the most detailed. The disciples and his other followers are confused and frightened. They recognize that Jesus is the Messiah, but they still do not understand what that means. They thought the Messiah's job was to throw the Romans out of Israel. They still do not understand that instead he is to suffer and die for others.

This is what lies at the end of their journey. Jesus will be tortured and killed by the Roman (Gentile) rulers of Israel, but this will not be the end of him. Three days later, he will rise from the dead. Mark says Jesus was walking ahead of his followers: he knows what is going to happen, but still strides on. We can imagine how much courage this took.

James' and John's question

READ MARK 10:35–45

If you were invited to a meal in Jesus' time, the most important guests would usually sit on the left and right hand sides of the host. James and John want top places like these in the Kingdom. After all Jesus has taught them, they still want power – and they were among Jesus' closest followers (5:37; 9:2; 13:3; 14:33)! They may even think that Jesus is going to Jerusalem to set up a human kingdom, and they want good positions in the government.

They have completely missed the point.

● **Jesus has shown that the Messiah's job is to suffer for other people.**
● **If this is the Messiah's job, the disciples must also be ready to suffer for others.** They should not argue about who gets the best jobs.

Jesus asks the brothers, 'Can you drink the cup that I must drink? Can you be baptized in the way I must be baptized?' They seem to think he is asking them if they have the guts to be powerful, like him. Again, they are completely wrong.

> The *cup* here means suffering and death. Long before Jesus was born, if a king gave a banquet, he would hand a cup round to his guests. In the Old Testament, *God* was the true king of Israel. So a 'cup' became a symbol of what God hands out to people. This could be blessing (Psalm 23:5), or punishment (Jeremiah 49:12). Mark has been pointing out that Christians must be ready to suffer. The word 'cup' here means a 'cup of suffering'. This is the cup Jesus must drink (14:36).

> The *baptism* also means suffering and death. Here, Jesus does not mean the baptisms that John the Baptist carried out, or later the early Christians. The word 'baptism' means 'to be submerged'. So here it means 'to be submerged in suffering'.

Jesus gives James and John what they ask for. They *will* drink the same cup, and receive the same baptism. Both suffered terrible sorrow when Jesus was put to death. James was executed for his faith (Acts 12:2), loyal to the last. (The same

Titles of Jesus

4: The Son of David

David was the second, and greatest, king of Israel. He ruled the country from 1010–970BC. You can read about him in the books of 1 and 2 Samuel and 1 Kings. He was a great army leader, and during his reign Israel had its own empire. He was also very close to God, who promised him that one of his descendants would always rule (2 Samuel 7:12–13). Son of David meant 'the descendant of David', and was a title for the Messiah (see Jeremiah 30:9; Ezekiel 34:23–24).

The Psalms of Solomon and the Dead Sea Scrolls were written around Jesus' time, and they call the Messiah the Son of David. Matthew and Luke trace Jesus' family tree back to David. The title is used in only two places in Mark: by Bartimaeus here, and in 12:35–37.

thing may have happened to John, but we do not know.)

Mark's first readers would have been reminded of their own Christian baptism. The 'cup' would have reminded them of the cup used for the wine at the Eucharist (see Unit 49). We know that Mark's church may well have been persecuted. Mark is telling his readers what Christianity means.

Notes

Verse 34: Jesus says he will rise to life 'three days' after he is put to death. He died on a Friday, and was believed to have risen on a Sunday, so the 'three days' here are Friday, Saturday and Sunday. This way of counting days (taking a part of a day as a whole day) was common in Jesus' time.

Verse 38: The words 'of suffering' are not in the Greek. The Good News Bible gets across what Mark means, but we should leave these words out. Otherwise, we lose the point of James and John misunderstanding what Jesus offers them.

Verse 45: 'Many people' in Greek can also mean 'all people'.

Verses 47 and 48: It is interesting that Jesus does not tell Bartimaeus to be quiet when he calls Jesus the Messiah (Son of David). Perhaps the point Mark is making is that you can call Jesus the Messiah (Son of David) when that means that he has to suffer. Here, Jesus is on the road to his death.

Baptism and the Eucharist were very important in their faith. And their faith meant that they had to be willing to die in Jesus' service.

But serving Jesus also means serving other people. Truly great people, says Jesus, are not bigheads who want power. Instead, they give up their own interests to help others. Jesus does not have the right to give important places in the Kingdom as favours to his friends. The Father has already decided. The most important people in the Kingdom are those who do most to help others.

Even the Son of Man came to serve, not to be waited on like a king. His job is to die for the people. We will be finding out more about this in Unit 46.

Blind Bartimaeus

READ MARK 10:46–52

Jesus and his disciples are now very near to Jerusalem. Jericho was only fifteen miles away. This is the last healing miracle in Mark. He wants us to think of the disciples, not Bartimaeus, as the ones who are really blind. They still do not know what Jesus' Messiahship really means.

Bartimaeus has never met Jesus before, but he knows Jesus is there to *serve*. He asks for his sight, and Jesus gives it to him. His simple faith has saved him. (The Greek words for 'made you well' can also mean 'saved you', as they do in 5:34.) He calls

Jesus 'Son of David'. This is explained below.

Bartimaeus 'followed Jesus on the road'. Mark's words may have a hidden meaning here. It is Jesus' disciples who *follow him* (1:17; 1:18; 1:20; 2:14). And the *road* is the *road to Jesus' death* in Jerusalem. Every disciple must be like Bartimaeus, ready to follow Jesus on the road, even if it means facing death.

1. Look back at the first two predictions of Jesus' death in Mark 8:31 and 9:30–31. Now look at the third prediction. Write a list of the things the predictions have in common, and write another list of the differences.

2. ● What do James and John want from Jesus?
● What does Jesus say they will receive? Explain fully what he means.
● Why was this important for Mark's first readers?

3. ● What do James and John seem to think makes a person great?
● What does Jesus think makes a person great?
● Which view do you think is right, and why?

4. ● Tell the story of Bartimaeus in your own words.
● What is Mark saying to his readers in this story?

5. Why was the title 'Son of David' used for the Messiah?

6. Bartimaeus was blind from birth. You might like to try this exercise to help you understand a little what it is like to be blind.

Divide into groups of three. Blindfold one member of your group. The person who is blindfolded has to find his or her way around the classroom. The other two people can steer him or her, but must keep quiet. After ten minutes, take off the blindfold. Discuss with each other how you felt when you were 'blind', and how it feels to be able to see again.

You might like to vary the exercise a little. Is it easier when you have no help? How do you feel if people push you out of their way?

Jesus Enters Jerusalem in Triumph

This section marks the beginning of the end.

We have seen that an important idea in Mark's Gospel is *the secret of who Jesus is* (see Unit 9). In fact we can read the Gospel as a *slow unveiling* of that secret. So far Mark's readers have been given two stages in this unveiling:

● Before Peter's confession (8:28, Unit 29) when only Jesus and the demons know that he is the Messiah.

● After Peter's confession, when the disciples have begun to share in the secret and are being taught what Messiahship means.

In this new story Mark begins the third and final stage. Jesus enters Jerusalem in triumph and is greeted by the people as the Messiah. Mark understands this as a public confession of who he is. The Messianic secret is nearly over, and so is Jesus' life. (We have already had a hint of this in the last unit, when Jesus did not stop Bartimaeus from calling him the Son of David; 10:47.) From now on Jesus stops saying that people must not talk about him.

 READ MARK 11:1–11

This begins Mark's account of the last week of Jesus' life. We think that Jesus' ministry lasted for about three years, but Mark spends an enormous amount of time talking about a few days right at the end of it. They take five out of the sixteen chapters of his Gospel. We should notice something else as well. Until now Mark has not always been very clear about exactly when things happened in the Gospel story. But from now on he puts in *very precise timings*, to tell his readers where they are during the final

week. We get one here in 11:11, and there are others in 11:20; 14:1; 14:12; 15:1; 15:33 and 34; 15:42 and 16:1.

All this points towards two things:

● Although Mark still has some of his own stories to tell about Jesus' teaching in Jerusalem, he is beginning to follow a *set pattern*. Most people who study the New Testament think that the story of the last few days of Jesus' life was already well known in the early church before Mark wrote his Gospel. It may even have been written down.

● Like all other Christians, Mark thinks that Jesus' death is extremely important. He has already prepared his readers for it with the Passion predictions (8:31–32; 9:30–32 and 10:33–34) and with passages like 3:1–6. Because of this he is keen to spend a lot of time describing the events which led up to it.

The story of Jesus' last week begins with his entry into Jerusalem. Look at the text again. When they first read it, the people in Mark's church would have been immediately reminded of a passage from the Old Testament where the prophet Zechariah talks about the coming of the Messiah:

'Rejoice, rejoice, people of Zion!
Shout for joy, you people of Jerusalem!
Look, your king is coming to you!
He comes triumphant and victorious,
but humble and riding on a donkey –
on a colt, the foal of a donkey . . .
Your king will make peace among the nations;
he will rule from sea to sea'
(Zechariah 9:9, 10b).

Mark himself thinks that Jesus *deliberately chose* to fulfil this prophecy, and already knew what he was going to do. He doesn't just come across a colt: he sent his disciples to get one he already knew was there. (Mark does not record a previous visit to Jerusalem, and it seems very likely that he thought Jesus' knowledge about the colt was a miracle.)

There are several things to note about the story:

● The colt has never been ridden on before (verse 2). Any animal used in a Jewish religious ceremony had to be kept especially for that purpose. Jesus' entry into Jerusalem is therefore something *sacred*.

● Victorious kings used to ride war horses in great processions. But Jesus rides on a colt. He has come in *peace*.

● The people shout the normal greeting for any pilgrim arriving in Jerusalem: 'Praise God! Bless him who comes in the name of the Lord' (Psalm 118:26). But Mark says that they added something else: 'God bless the coming kingdom of King David, our father.' The people have heard Jesus teaching about the Kingdom of God, and now he has entered Jerusalem like the Messiah the prophets spoke about. This must be it! All their hopes are at last going to be fulfilled!

● Jesus' actions must have taken great courage. The crowds welcomed him as the Messiah – but Jerusalem was where his opponents had their meetings and were most influential. A public display of his Messiahship like this was very dangerous.

Jerusalem as it is today, seen from the Mount of Olives. Jesus came to the city this way, from Bethany.

Some scholars have drawn attention to two things about this story:
● It does not tell us exactly how many people welcomed Jesus.
● The religious authorities seem to be very slow to do anything about him. It is several days before he is arrested.

They have suggested that in fact the crowd at Jesus' entry may have been quite small, and mainly people who were already his followers. If there had been anything like a large demonstration the authorities would have acted much more quickly. According to this theory, Mark has made the incident seem more spectacular than it really was.

However, there are problems with this idea. A few days is not, after all, a very long time before Jesus' arrest – and in any case the religious authorities may have been scared about how the people would react if they moved too quickly (see 14:2).

The last few days of Jesus' life are as important for Christians today as they were for Mark. A week in the church's year is set aside to remember them. It is called Holy Week to underline its importance. During Holy Week the events that Mark and the other Gospel writers record (and which we will be looking at in the remaining units) are remembered at church services all over the world.

Christians around the world remember the events of the week that began with 'Palm Sunday', when Jesus rode into Jerusalem to the shouts of the crowd. Here a Palm Sunday procession gathers at Bethphage.

Holy Week begins on *Palm Sunday*, the Sunday before Easter Day. On that day the story of Christ's entry into Jerusalem is read, and most churches hold a procession before the main service or Mass of the day. The people and the clergy sing and carry palm branches to remember how the people of Jerusalem welcomed Jesus. (For more about Holy Week, see Unit 54.)

Notes

11:1 For Bethphage and Bethany, see the map in Unit 37.

The Jewish historian Josephus says that the Messiah was expected to appear on the Mount of Olives. Mark may have known this.

11:3: The Greek word for 'master' here could mean the owner of the colt, or it could mean 'Lord' (see Titles of Jesus, Unit 26).

11:10: The Good News Bible has 'Praise God' here, but Mark wrote 'Hosanna'. This Hebrew word was a traditional shout of praise by Jesus' time, but its original meaning was something like 'Save now'. The Messiah was expected to save his people from their enemies (see Unit 4).

11:11: It seems very strange that Jesus should enter Jerusalem and then leave it again so quickly. Matthew and Luke both use Mark's story but leave out this verse. However, it may very well be that Mark is right – it would be an odd thing to make up!

☛FOLLOW☛UP☛

1. How do most Christians today remember Jesus' entry into Jerusalem?

2. Give an example of how Mark's account of the last week of Jesus' life is different from the rest of his Gospel.

3. Divide a piece of paper into two columns. In the lefthand column write down what happened in the story. In the righthand column write down what each part tells Mark's readers about Jesus.

4. Mark's Gospel has been called 'a Passion narrative with an extended introduction'. Explain why you think this might be.

The Judgement of Israel

The Old Testament often said that God was angry with the people of Israel. They had become entirely self-centred and did not care about God or other people. God's messengers, the prophets, told them that what they were doing was wrong. God knew about it and he was going to punish them – this was his judgement on their crimes.

These two new stories in Mark show Jesus, like the prophets, announcing God's judgement of Israel.

READ MARK 11:12–26

In Mark, the story of the 'cleansing' of the Temple has been 'sandwiched' between the two halves of the cursing of the fig-tree. It is easiest to look at each of these stories in turn.

The cursing of the fig-tree
(verses 12–14 and 20–26)
In the Old Testament, the fig-tree was sometimes used as a symbol for Israel (see Jeremiah 8:13; Micah 7:1–6). This is the key to the hidden meaning of this story:

The fig-tree's leaves look good, but there is no fruit. Mark means, then, that the people's religion may look good, but only on the surface. God looks deeper. Good actions, and real closeness to God, must be part of religion. Otherwise it is useless.

At the end of the story, we have some of Jesus' teaching on prayer and faith:

● The idea of people moving mountains was a figure of speech used in Jesus' time. It meant overcoming problems in life that seemed difficult or impossible to face. Jesus says people can do this, if they have faith. He does not mean that people with faith will throw mountains around!

● People will receive what they ask for when they pray. God will always answer prayer (although the way he answers it will not necessarily be the way people expect).

● People have to forgive others when they pray. If they do not, they cannot receive God's forgiveness for their own sins. (This is like the Lord's Prayer – see Matthew 6:9–15.)

What happens in the story	The hidden meaning
Jesus is hungry and looks for figs.	God is 'hungry' for the 'fruit' of good actions and true religion – the 'fruit of righteousness'.
It is not the right time for figs.	It is not the right time to look for righteousness – the people will not show it.
No one will ever eat figs from the tree again.	The Old Israel is at an end. The New Israel – the Christians who form the church – now holds the key to getting right with God.
The fig-tree dies.	This may mean, again, that the Old Israel is at an end. Some early Christians thought it was a prediction of what happened in AD70, when the Roman armies destroyed Jerusalem. They thought this was God's punishment of the Jewish people.

The cleansing of the Temple
(verses 15–19)

When the Messiah came, people thought he would go to the Temple to make sure that it was used only for the worship of God (see Malachi 3:1 and Zechariah 14:21). This is what Jesus does. But the Temple and what happened there was a vital part of Judaism. So Jesus' action in the Temple showed God's judgement on Israel. He said the people had turned the house of prayer into a hideout for thieves. What had they been doing?

● Traders were selling wine, oil, birds and other animals in the Temple. These were needed for the sacrifices. Jesus went to the Temple near Passover time, when Jerusalem was crowded with people. Not all of them could bring their own animals. This was partly because of the distance they travelled, but mainly because animals for sacrifice had to be in perfect condition. The easiest way to make sure an animal was perfect was to buy it from the merchants. And the merchants made a big profit.

● Every year, male Jews had to pay a tax of half a shekel (about two days' pay on average) to keep the Temple going. The tax was paid at Passover time. Jews from many different countries came to the Passover in Jerusalem. The money-changers exchanged their foreign money for the special Temple coinage needed for the tax. It seems very likely that the money-changers, too, were making a fat profit.

● People were using the Temple as a short cut between the Mount of Olives and the eastern part of Jerusalem (see Unit 38).

Jesus was furious. The Temple was for the worship of God. It was not meant to be a short cut, or a good place to make money. There was something else, too. All these things were going on in the Court of the Gentiles. This was the only part of the Temple where non-Jews were allowed (see diagram). The Temple was not just a house of prayer for the Jews, but for 'the nations' – the Gentiles – as well. Jesus included Gentiles in the Kingdom of God. Yet they could not even get into their part of the Temple because it was full up!

Jesus' words about the Temple are not just an attack on the traders and money-changers. He is also speaking against the Jewish leaders, who let such things go on. Jesus' action here adds to the authorities' case against him. Their lives would be a lot easier if Jesus were no longer around . . .

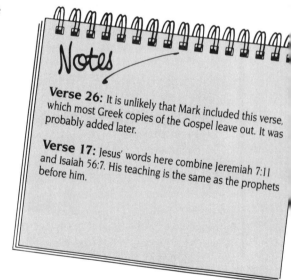

Notes

Verse 26: It is unlikely that Mark included this verse, which most Greek copies of the Gospel leave out. It was probably added later.

Verse 17: Jesus' words here combine Jeremiah 7:11 and Isaiah 56:7. His teaching is the same as the prophets before him.

⬆️FOLLOW UP⬆️

1. Draw a map of Jesus' route from Bethany to the Temple in Jerusalem and back. Write down what happened at each place. (Use the map to help you.)

2. Mark thinks the cursing of the fig-tree shows God's judgement of Israel. How?

3. Some people find the story of the cursing of the fig-tree hard to believe. Others do not. Here are some of their ideas about the story:

● It did not happen. Jesus uses his power to help people, not to destroy things when they do not give him what he wants.

● The Old Testament prophets sometimes acted out their teachings (see 1 Kings 22; Jeremiah 27). This is what Jesus is doing. His action is not evil – after all, it was only a fig-tree!

● Jesus actually told a parable about a fig-tree, which meant the same as Mark's story. (The parable may have been the one in Luke 13:6–9.) Mark, or someone before him, has changed the parable into a story about Jesus.

Which of these ideas do you think is closest to the truth? Discuss this in groups.

4. What were people doing in the Temple that annoyed Jesus? Why did these things annoy him?

5. ● What does Jesus say about prayer in this section?
● Do you think God answers prayers? Why and how?
● Some Christians say God tells them what to do when they face problems in life. What do you think they mean by this?
● There is a story about a little girl who knew Jesus had said, 'When you pray and ask for something, believe that you have received it, and you will be given whatever you ask for.' So she prayed for a bicycle. She did not get one, so she decided God did not exist.
What do you think a Christian would say to her?
● Discuss whether there is any point in praying.
You might want to discuss the second and the last questions in class.

'What right have you to do these things?'

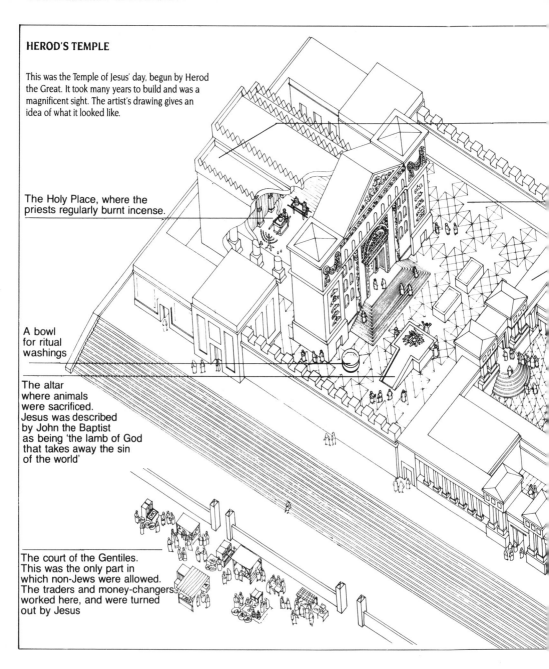

HEROD'S TEMPLE

This was the Temple of Jesus' day, begun by Herod the Great. It took many years to build and was a magnificent sight. The artist's drawing gives an idea of what it looked like.

The Holy Place, where the priests regularly burnt incense.

A bowl for ritual washings

The altar where animals were sacrificed. Jesus was described by John the Baptist as being 'the lamb of God that takes away the sin of the world'

The court of the Gentiles. This was the only part in which non-Jews were allowed. The traders and money-changers worked here, and were turned out by Jesus

Jesus has been in trouble with the Jewish leaders before. He had a lot of arguments with them in Galilee (Mark 2:1–3:6). We saw how that ended: they wanted to kill him (3:6). Now they decide to try to catch him out, so that they can arrest him.

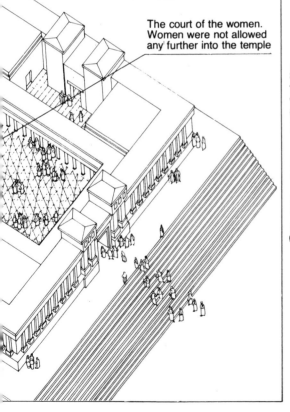

The Holy of Holies, divided from the Holy Place by a curtain. The ark of the covenant stood here in Solomon's day but no longer existed in Jesus' time

The court of the priests

The court of Israel, reserved for male Jews

The court of the women. Women were not allowed any further into the temple

READ MARK 11:27–33

This story begins a new series of Jesus' arguments with the Jewish leaders (it continues until 12:34). Jesus goes back to the Temple. Like other rabbis, he teaches his followers as he walks around the covered ways or cloisters of the Temple (see the diagram). Imagine how the chief priests, scribes and elders felt! He's only a carpenter! And not only has he just stopped people trading in the Temple, he has the nerve to come back! Who does he think he is?

So they ask him, 'What right have you to do these things?' It is not clear whether they mean things like the incident in the Temple, or everything Jesus does. But this is not the main point. The chief priests, teachers of the Law and the elders were probably sent by the Sanhedrin. This was the Jewish council, and one of its jobs was to look after religious affairs (see Unit 1). They are looking for a way to trap Jesus. They think he cannot win, whatever reply he gives:

> If he says his authority comes from God, they can arrest him for insulting God (blasphemy).

> If he says he is behaving in the way he thinks is right (acting on his own authority), they can arrest him as a dangerous maniac. No sane person would claim the right to act as he did in God's Temple!

This helps us understand why Jesus' reply is so clever. He avoids falling into their trap, and asks them a question, in return. 'Where did John's right to baptize come from: was it from God or from man?' Now it's the Jewish leaders who cannot win!

If they say John's authority came from God, Jesus will ask them why they did not believe what he said. John did not just baptize people. He also said, 'The man who will come after me is much greater than I am' (1:7). That man is Jesus.

If they say 'from man' (in other words, 'not from God'), they risk a riot. There were people listening who believed that John's authority came from God: John was a prophet.

It is the Jewish leaders, not Jesus, who are caught out. All they can say is, 'We do not know.' And because they will not answer Jesus, Jesus will not answer them. Mark thinks they refuse to see what is staring them in the face: Jesus, like John, gets his authority from God.

They lose this round of the argument, but they will soon try again.

FOLLOW UP

1. Summarize this story.

2. Jesus and the Jewish leaders both asked questions. What do these questions mean?
● How effective do you think these questions are?

The Allegory of the Vineyard

If you were criticized in front of a crowd of people, how would you react? Would you walk away? Start an argument? Start a fight? Jesus does none of these things. The Jewish leaders have attacked him, but he simply tells them a parable.

The other parables in Mark have been about the Kingdom of God, but the hidden meaning of *this* story is not. It is about the Jewish leaders, and it shows what they are really like.

READ MARK 12:1–12

Most of Jesus' stories mention things that were part of everyday life. The parables in chapter 4 use ideas about farming to talk about the Kingdom. This new story uses ideas about landlords and tenants – people

Jesus told a story about a vineyard. It was a special kind of parable, an allegory, in which each part had a deeper meaning.

who rent land. In Galilee, foreigners would often buy land and rent it to the local people. This is what the vineyard owner does here, and the tenants have to look after the vineyard for him.

Things like this often annoyed the Galilean Jews: they felt the land belonged to them! Perhaps they might get angry enough to beat up the landlord's servants. There was also a law which said that, if someone had no children and died without making a will, anything he owned would go to his tenants. This is why the tenants kill the son in the story, 'so that his property will be ours'.

This helps us understand the story a little, but there are two important questions we need to ask:
● What kind of story is it?
● What does the story mean?

What kind of story is it?

It is a parable (a story with a hidden meaning), but a special sort of parable. Most of Jesus' parables make *one* point about the Kingdom of God. This parable does not. It is like a very detailed code. Each person in this story represents a *real* person. Everything that happens represents something that *really* happened. This special sort of parable is called an *allegory*.

What does the story mean?

If the story is a code, we have to crack the code! This is how it works.

● **The vineyard owner is God, and the vineyard is Israel: the country, and its people.** In the Old Testament, the prophet Isaiah also told a story about a vineyard. His story ended like this:

'Israel is the vineyard of the LORD Almighty . . .
He expected them to do what was good,
but instead they committed murder.
He expected them to do what was right,
but their victims cried out for justice'
(Isaiah 5:7).

In Isaiah's story, the people do not do what God wants. It is the same in Jesus' story, because . . .

● **The tenants are the people of Israel, especially the Jewish leaders.** The tenants behave badly, and so do the Jewish leaders.

● **The servants (or slaves) are the Old Testament prophets, God's spokesmen and spokeswomen before Jesus' time.** God and the vineyard owner both want something. God wants the people to do good, and the vineyard owner wants his 'share of the harvest'. So they both send messengers to the people. But the people will not listen to the messengers.

● **The servants are beaten up or killed. The people treated the prophets in the same way.**
– Amos was told to keep his mouth shut.
– Jeremiah was thrown down a well and left to rot.
– Elijah had a price on his head.
In the New Testament, the Letter to the Hebrews says this happened to the prophets:

'Some were mocked and whipped, and others were put in chains and taken off to prison. They were stoned, they were sawn in two, they were killed by the sword. They went round in the skins of sheep or goats – poor, persecuted, and ill-treated' (Hebrews 11:36–37).

● **The vineyard owner (God) decides to send his son. If the people will not listen to the messengers, they might listen to him. The son is Jesus.** The story talks about the man's 'own dear son', the phrase used by the voice from heaven at Jesus' baptism and Transfiguration (Mark 1:11; 9:7).

● **The tenants kill the man's son. The Jewish leaders will kill Jesus.** They are even worse than their ancestors, who persecuted the prophets. They will not even listen to God's Son. They will hand him over to be crucified.

● **The owner of the vineyard will kill the tenants. God will not allow the Jewish leaders to get away with killing Jesus.** Perhaps they will be sent to hell, or perhaps the punishment is something else. It is not really clear how they will be punished.

● **The owner will hand the vineyard over to others. The vineyard is Israel, God's people, and the 'others' are the outcasts, the tax collectors, sinners, and Gentiles.** God's people are not just the Jews. We have seen already how Jesus showed that the 'others' were included in the Kingdom.

At the end of the allegory, Jesus quotes Psalm 118 from the Old Testament. What he says has a hidden meaning:

● People do not think a worthless piece of stone is really a building stone. But this is what it turns out to be.

● People do not think a carpenter from Nazareth is really the Messiah. But this is what he turns out to be.

The Jewish leaders understand what the allegory means, and it makes them furious. They try to arrest Jesus, but they are too frightened of the crowd, who still think a great deal of him. For the moment, all they can do is wait. But they will make a move soon . . .

▲FOLLOW UP▲

1. Draw a picture strip version of the allegory of the vineyard.

2. Imagine you are one of the Jewish leaders. How would you feel when Jesus told the story?

3. What is an allegory?

4. Divide your page into two columns. In the first column, write down what happens in the allegory. In the second column, explain the hidden meaning of the story.

5. In the allegory, Jesus says the tenants will be killed. Some Christians think this means he supported the death penalty. Others disagree, and say that the story in John 8:1–11 shows they are right.
● Read the story in John.
● From the two passages, do you think we can tell what Jesus thought about the death penalty? If so, what did he think?

Life in this World, and the Next

We now come to two more arguments the Jewish authorities had with Jesus.

The question about paying taxes

READ MARK 12:13–17

Mark says the Pharisees and the members of Herod's party 'were sent' to Jesus. He probably means that the Sanhedrin sent them. They want to put Jesus in a good mood by flattering him before they try 'to trap him with questions'. 'Tell us,' they say, 'is it against our Law to pay taxes to the Roman Emperor? Should we pay them or not?'

If you imagine that you lived in Jesus' time, you can see why the Jews hated paying the Roman taxes. The taxes were very high, and they reminded the people that they were ruled by Rome. In AD6, when they first had to pay the tax, there was a revolt led by a Zealot called Judas of Galilee. The money was paid in Roman coins, stamped with a picture of Caesar. This was against God's Law, which did not allow images (see Deuteronomy 4:16, 25 and 5:8–9). And in any case the people believed that God, not Caesar, was their king.

The Pharisees and Herodians put Jesus in a very difficult position.

If he says, 'Yes, pay the tax,' people will stop following him. No Messiah would say that!

If he says, 'No, don't pay the tax,' the Romans could arrest him as a traitor.

Jesus sees through the trick, and what he says is brilliantly clever (compare 11:29–30). 'Pay the Emperor what belongs to the Emperor, and pay God what belongs to God.'

Jesus does not agree with the Zealots' idea that the Kingdom of God means war with Rome. In his time, coins were issued by the ruler, and they belonged to him. The coin they show Jesus bears the image of Caesar and people bear the image of God (Genesis 1:27). If people pay tax, they are only giving Caesar what he owns. Yet people owe much more to God than they do to Caesar. Caesar's kingdom will pass away. God's Kingdom will not. So, God's Kingdom is far more important.

Christians and politics

This passage was very important for Mark's readers. It told them how to behave towards a non-Christian government. Jesus' words in verse 17 are also important for Christians today.

Is Jesus saying that religion and politics should be kept separate? Or does he mean that they should mix? Christians today have different ideas about this.

● Some say Jesus means that Christians should obey the government (see Romans 13:1–7). So Christians should not get involved in politics. Religion and politics are two different things, and should not mix.

● Others say Jesus means that God's laws are more important than people's laws. So Christians should get involved in politics, to try to make sure that what the government does is what God wants. There is no way that God would approve of the actions of a government like the Nazis in Germany! Most Christians would say they are called to obey God first, if there is a clash between what the government wants and what God wants.

'Is it against our Law to pay taxes to the Roman Emperor?' people asked Jesus, trying to trick him. He looked at a coin. 'Whose face and name are these?' he asked. The face and name, as on this denarius, were Caesar's. 'Pay the Emperor what belongs to him,' Jesus said, 'and God what belongs to God.'

The question about rising from death

READ MARK 12:18–27

This time it is the Sadducees who come to Jesus. The Pharisees believed in life after death, but the Sadducees did not. This was because it was not mentioned in the Torah (see Unit 1). The story they tell about the seven brothers is based on a law in Deuteronomy 25:5–6. This says that if a married man dies, and there are no children, his brother must marry the widow, so that the dead man's family line will continue.

Suppose, they say, there are seven brothers. The first one marries the woman, has no children, and dies. The second one does the same. So does the third one. Eventually, all seven have married her. If there is life after death, they say, who will be the woman's husband when they meet again? From the Sadducees' point of view, the whole thing seems daft. They think it is much easier to say there is no life after death.

This is the kind of argument about the Law that rabbis had. It is not clear whether the Sadducees' story is a serious attempt to prove there is no life after death, or is simply a silly story making fun of the whole idea. Jesus stops the argument. He says they do not understand God's power, and have misunderstood the scriptures.

Many people thought that life after death would be very much like life on earth. Jesus is saying that if you understand the new life properly, there is no problem. There will be no marriage. Instead, people will be like 'the angels in heaven'. It is very hard for us to know what it is like to be an

---

Christian belief in life after death

Christians believe that 'Christ has been raised from death, as the guarantee that those who sleep in death will also be raised' (1 Corinthians 15:20).

The New Testament seems to have two main ideas about life after death.

● After they die, people will go straight to heaven or hell.

● When people die, they will have to 'wait' for God to end the universe. (Although it is difficult to see what meaning time has beyond death.) The dead will rise, and be judged. God will make a 'new heaven and a new earth', and people will live with him there.

The New Testament is clear that people will have a body, not just a soul after death – though it will not be exactly the same as the one that died (1 Corinthians 15:35–50).

Christians today differ about what life after death will be like – although they all believe in it.

Roman Catholics believe that a very few people (the saints) go straight to heaven when they die. When others die, they have to be made pure in a place called purgatory before they go to heaven.

All Christians look forward to life in the Kingdom, when they will be with God, and sin, death and pain will no longer exist.

angel! However, this does not really matter. The important thing is that the new life will be very different from this one.

The Sadducees believed only in the laws written in the Torah. So Jesus points to a passage in the Torah, the 'Book of Moses' (Exodus), which suggests that there is life after death. In Exodus 3, God speaks to Moses from the burning bush. God says, 'I am the God of Abraham, Isaac, and Jacob.' By Moses' time, all three were dead. But God says 'I am' their God, not 'I was'. So they must somehow be alive. Therefore, there is life after death. God is too good and loving to allow his friends to be destroyed in death.

▲FOLLOW UP▲

1. The following sentences have got garbled. Unscramble them!
● The taxes pay they should if Pharisees and Herodians asked. Emperor Emperor God God to to belonged belonged the the pay pay what what and they replied Jesus should.
● Death asked about rising from the Sadducees. The woman asked heaven if they would happen what brothers in same seven married. Would she be whose wife? In marriage no heaven was there said Jesus. Will angels be like the people. Is the of the living God God.

2. ● Explain why the Pharisees' and Herodians' question to Jesus is a cunning one.
● What does Jesus say in his answer? What does he mean?

3. Look up Exodus 3:6 and Deuteronomy 25:5–6. In as much detail as you can, say what these passages have to do with the argument between Jesus and the Sadducees.

4. Try to collect some newspaper articles about Christians involved in politics. Discuss them in class.

5. Read the funeral service in a Christian prayer book. What ideas does it show about Christians' views of life after death?
● Read what Paul says about life after death in 1 Corinthians 15 and 1 Thessalonians 4:13–18.
● Christians do not usually discuss what life after death will be like. Why do you think this is?

The Greatest Commandment

If you look back carefully over Mark's story of the time Jesus has spent in Jerusalem you will see that he has told his readers about three groups of people who asked Jesus questions. They were:
● the chief priests and the Temple authorities (11: 27–33)
● some Pharisees (12:13–17)
● some Sadducees (12:18–27).

Now it is the turn of one of the scribes (the teachers of the Law) on his own.

READ MARK 12:28–34

Look carefully at verses 32 and 34. The other stories were all about people who were hostile to Jesus. The priests wanted to know what right he thought he had to teach in the Temple (11:28), the Pharisees wanted to trick him with a question about taxes (12:14) and the Sadducees did not agree with his ideas about life after death. But this story is different. The scribe is friendly – and Jesus is pleased with him. Perhaps Mark wanted to show that, although the religious officials *tended* to be opponents of Jesus, not all of them were. (In the same way, John's Gospel has a story about a friendly Pharisee called Nicodemus: John 3:1–21.)

The scribe asks Jesus which of the *commandments* is the most important. When people talk about the commandments today they usually mean the Ten Commandments which Moses brought down from Mt Sinai (Exodus 20:1–17; Deuteronomy 5:1–22). But in Jesus' time all of the rules of the Law were thought of as the commandments. The rabbis used to discuss *which of them summed up all the others.*

This is the question the scribe in Mark's

story wants Jesus to answer. He was involved with the Torah every day in his work and was asking Jesus his opinion about a professional problem. We can imagine him rather enjoying the theory of it all: he probably did not think that it had much to do with everyday life.

Although the rabbis discussed which commandment summed up the Law, they did not think that once you had discovered it you could forget all the others. The question was theoretical: a good Jew must keep the whole Law.

What Jesus says in verses 29–31 is very important. The scribe asked him about one commandment, but in reply he gives him *two.* The first (verse 30) is from Deuteronomy 6:4–5, and was already a very well-known text. It was the beginning of a prayer called the *Shema*, which Jews at the time of Jesus would recite three times a day and which still begins synagogue services. Not only that; it was written in their *phylacteries* (little leather boxes strapped to the forehead and wrist during prayer times), and *mezuzahs* (cylindrical boxes fixed to the doorposts in Jewish homes; Deuteronomy 6:8–9 explains why). Jesus' second text is from Leviticus 19:18. This one was very well-known too.

The rabbis sometimes said that one or the other of these parts of the Old Testament summed up the Torah. But in Mark's story Jesus puts them together. (It is possible that he was the first person to do this, although we cannot be sure.) For Jesus, love is the heart of the Law.

Why does Jesus tell the scribe that he is 'not far from the Kingdom of God' (verse 34)? Probably because he welcomes what Jesus has said (verse 32). The conversation started as a professional discussion, but suddenly the scribe has been struck by the truth of Jesus' words. For this reason he is not far from the Kingdom.

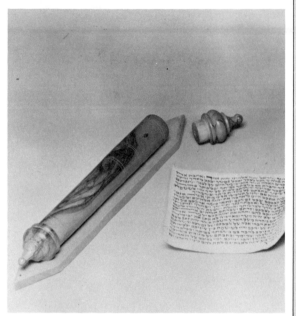

Important verses of the Law were placed inside a *mezuzah* (shown here) and fixed to the doorpost of each Jewish home.

Looking deeper

The scribe says that 'It is more important to obey these two commandments than to offer animals and other sacrifices to God' (verse 33). We have already seen that Jesus criticized the attitude of some people of his time who ignored human need and thought that pleasing God was a matter of keeping rules and regulations. (Look back to the story of the Sabbath corn in 2:23–28 in Unit 12 and the discussion about what makes a person unclean in 7:14–23 in Unit 25 to remind yourself about this.) Although Mark is always careful to say that Jesus respected the Law of Moses, it is obvious that he thought some parts of it were more important than others.

We know also that the Gentile members of Mark's church would not have kept all the laws in the Torah (see the notes on food laws in Unit 25). The early Christians in his church believed that the coming of the Kingdom meant that the Law of Moses was no longer as important as it used to be. The Law required *sacrifices* (verse 33) – but the scribe almost says that they do not matter compared with loving God and your neighbour. Some of the prophets had said things like that in the past (see Hosea 6:6), but it is still quite a surprising thing for a teacher of the Law to say at the time of Jesus. He is beginning to realize that times are changing and that the Kingdom is near. Jesus' words have helped him to draw a distinction between what really matters and what does not.

This story in Mark is an important one for Christians today. Ever since the earliest days, Christians have thought of the church as the new Israel – the people of God – who should love God and other people. This love is not just a 'feeling'. It leads to *action* and practical care for everybody, especially the poor, people who are ill, and the oppressed. One early Christian writer wrote this:

'We ought to give our lives for our brothers! If a rich person sees his brother in need, yet closes his heart against his brother, how can he claim that he loves God? My children, our love should not be just words and talk: it must be true love, which shows itself in action' (1 John 3:16–18).

Notes

12:28: The discussion the scribe has heard is the one about rising from the dead in 12:18–27.

12:31: Originally, the word *neighbour* was taken to mean just a fellow Jew. Luke's version of this story contains the parable of the Good Samaritan, where Jesus explains that a 'neighbour' means *anyone at all*, regardless of race, religion or status (see Luke 10:30–37).

12:34: Jesus has won all the arguments. He starts the next discussion himself.

Jesus summarized the Law as loving God whole-
heartedly and loving our fellow humans as we do
ourselves. Many Christians, famous – like Martin Luther
King – and unknown, have demonstrated this love for
God and love for others.

▲FOLLOW UP▲

1. ● Fill in the missing words: 'Which _____ is
the _____ _____ of all?'
● Who said this?
● Why might he have been interested in this question?

2. ● What two commandments did Jesus say were the
most important?
● Where do they come from?

3. How does this story differ from the other stories
about questions Jesus has been asked in Jerusalem?

4. Why do you think Jesus said that the teacher of the
Law was 'not far from the Kingdom of God'? Answer as
fully as you can.

5. Make a list of the ways you think Christians today try
to respond to the commandment to love your neighbour
as yourself. Do you think that there are any ways that
the churches are failing to live up to it? You may want to
discuss this in class.

6. Some Christians say that caring for the poor means
being involved in politics. Try to find out something
about Liberation Theology. Your teacher or librarian will
help you.

A Question, a Warning and an Example

This section of Mark ends Jesus' teaching in the Temple.

The question about the Messiah

READ MARK 12:35–37a

We have already seen that 'Son of David' was one of the titles of Jesus (see Unit 35). Jesus now stops answering questions, and starts asking them. Is the Messiah the Son of David, or not? (The Good News Bible translates 'Son of David' here as 'the descendant of David').

> Psalm 110:1 in the Old Testament says:
> 'The Lord said to my Lord:
> Sit here on my right
> until I put your enemies under your feet.'

Jesus' argument goes like this. David, the writer, says God was speaking to the Messiah. Yet David calls the Messiah 'My Lord'. But does Jesus mean he is David's descendant, or not? There are two main answers to this question:

● **Jesus was not a descendant of David.**
People knew this, and therefore did not believe he was the Messiah. He is defending himself by saying David did not expect the Messiah to be one of his descendants. After all, David does not call him 'My Son' but 'My Lord'. (But, if this is right, what about all the passages in the New Testament which say Jesus *is* the Son of David?)

● **Jesus was a descendant of David.**
There is a great deal of evidence for this in the New Testament. The problem with the title 'Son of David' was that it had become too mixed up with the idea that the Messiah's job was to throw the Romans out of Israel. Jesus preferred to use other titles for himself, such as 'Son of Man'. Jesus is the descendant of David, but he is much more than that. He is David's Son, but he is also David's Lord, the Son of God.

The teachers of the Law

READ MARK 12:37b–40

Matthew and Luke have much longer versions of Jesus' warnings about the teachers of the Law (see Matthew 23; Luke 11:37–52). Many were genuinely religious men, but others were two-faced (hypocrites). They pretended to be religious, but were really only interested in themselves.

Jesus says they 'like to walk about in their long robes'. The Greek can mean they 'like to walk around in porticoes', which would mean the covered walkways in the Temple, where the rabbis taught. Or it can mean that they wore large shawls (talliths), which were only usually put on for prayer. The picture we get is that the scribes had extra large versions, and wore them all the time! Or it can mean they had extra large tassels on their clothes (all male Jews had to wear these – see Numbers 15:38). It does not really matter which is right: the point is, they liked to be noticed. They wanted people to look up to them. They wanted the best seats in the synagogues and at dinner parties. They made a show of praying but extorted money from needy people.

Notes

12:36: This verse from the Psalms was a favourite with the early Christians, who applied it to Jesus. It is also rather like what Jesus says to the High Priest at his trial (Mark 14:62).

12:42: The coins the widow gave were worth a 'penny'. Mark uses the word *quadrans*, which was 1/64 of a denarius, the daily wage for a labourer.

These Jewish students are studying to become scholars of the Law. In Jesus' time, good teachers of the Law explained it to ordinary people, but some added to their burdens by making it hard to understand.

This was the absolute opposite of what Jesus wanted. It could only earn them the severest judgement.

The widow's offering

READ MARK 12:41–44

Jesus has just been talking about the scribes' attitude to widows. Now we have a story about one.

The 'temple treasury' was the money used for the daily sacrifices and running costs of the Temple. People put their gifts in thirteen trumpet-shaped boxes in the Court of Women (see diagram in Unit 38). Some scholars wonder how Jesus knew how much people gave. So they suggest this was originally a story *told by* Jesus, which was later changed into a story *about* Jesus. The point, however, remains the same. The best gift is not something you can afford, but something you cannot afford.

FOLLOW UP

1. ● What was the problem with saying the Messiah was the Son of David?
● What had the scribes (teachers of the Law) been doing?
● What was special about the widow's offering?

2. What are the arguments for and against the idea that Jesus was a descendant of David? Which do you agree with, and why?

3. When they give things away, people sometimes say, 'It's the thought that counts.' What do you think? What would you say if you were starving?

The End of the World: 1

Will the universe exist for ever, or will it end?

Will people be judged by God?

What will happen at the end of time?

The Jews and the early Christians were very interested in these questions. The Old Testament spoke of a coming 'Day of the Lord' (Amos 5:18–20; Isaiah 13:6–16). People thought this meant the day when God would wind up history and punish evil people. The Jews and the early Christians suffered terrible things. Did God care? Was he going to do anything to help? When the day of the Lord came, would God be on their side?

People wrote books which tried to give the answers. These are called *apocalyptic books* or *Apocalypses* (from a Greek word meaning roughly 'to uncover, or reveal, secrets'). Apocalyptic books are very difficult to read because of the special coded language they use. They speak of visions of strange beasts or numbers or events, which represent things that are really happening in the world. To make people take notice of what they said, the writers often claimed to be some long-dead religious hero, such as Moses, Enoch or Joseph. The Book of Daniel – the only entirely apocalyptic book in the Old Testament – was supposed to be by a Jew in the sixth century BC. Scholars think it was in fact by someone in the second century BC, and was telling its readers not to give in to the threats of Antiochus Epiphanes, the Greek ruler of Israel at the time. Scholars also say that the Book of Revelation – the only entirely apocalyptic book in the New Testament – is really about the persecution of Christians by the Roman authorities in the first century AD. Daniel and Revelation, like other apocalyptic books, say that God will triumph in the end, however bad things look now.

Christian teaching says that Jesus will return at the end of the world. But when will this happen? We know that some of the early Christians thought it would happen very quickly. Mark's church was probably being persecuted. Was Jesus going to come back soon, or would they have to wait a long time?

Mark 13 is about this question. It is the hardest chapter in the Gospel to understand, and we shall study it in three units. It will help if you read it straight through, to get the flavour of it.

In the Old Testament, heroes who were about to die often gave a final speech (such as Moses in Deuteronomy, and David in 1 Chronicles 28–29). This is Jesus' farewell speech. (In chapters 14 and 15, Mark describes Jesus' suffering and death.) Because the speech is like apocalyptic, talking of battles and earthquakes and famine, and the 'awful horror', it is sometimes called the *Little Apocalypse*. However, there are four important differences between Mark 13 and apocalyptic books:

● Mark 13 does not describe visions God gave to the writer. Jesus does not need visions. His own authority is enough.

● The language is not as strange. There are no weird beasts or special numbers.

The picture shows the ancient Temple area of Jerusalem, now crowned with a domed mosque. All that remains accessible to pilgrims is the Western or 'Wailing' Wall: the Temple itself was utterly destroyed by the Romans in AD70.

● Apocalyptic uses coded language to say exactly when God is going to act. Mark 13 does not give this kind of timetable for the end of the world.

● Apocalyptic tries to raise people's hopes. Mark 13 does this, but it also seems to want to calm them down. Perhaps some of Mark's first readers were getting over-excited, and thought the end would come very soon.

Different scholars have different views about what sources Mark used for this chapter. It is very difficult to be sure. They also disagree over how much if any of it was actually said by Jesus.

The destruction of the Temple

READ MARK 13:1–2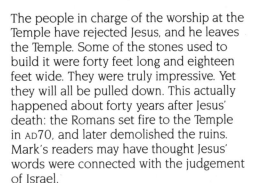

The people in charge of the worship at the Temple have rejected Jesus, and he leaves the Temple. Some of the stones used to build it were forty feet long and eighteen feet wide. They were truly impressive. Yet they will all be pulled down. This actually happened about forty years after Jesus' death: the Romans set fire to the Temple in AD70, and later demolished the ruins. Mark's readers may have thought Jesus' words were connected with the judgement of Israel.

Signs like the first pains of childbirth

READ MARK 13:3–8

Jesus speaks in private to Peter, James, John and Andrew, the 'inner group' of disciples, on the Mount of Olives. This overlooked the Temple, where the prophet Zechariah had said something very important would happen (see Zechariah 14:4). The disciples represent the church here. So, what Jesus says to the disciples, he says to all Christians.

● People will come and claim to speak for Jesus, saying 'I am he'. In Greek, these are the same words as those Jesus used when he walked on the water: 'It is I' (see Mark 6:50, Unit 24, to understand what these words mean). Acts 5:36–37 shows that many people claimed to be someone great. Others, like Bar Kochba in AD135, who led a rebellion against Rome, claimed to be the Messiah. It is even possible that some said the second coming had already happened, and that they themselves were Jesus. The Christians are warned not to be fooled by people like this.

● There will be wars, and rumours of wars. Wars were often mentioned in apocalyptic. In Mark's time there were many wars, including the Jewish rebellion against Rome which led to the destruction of the Temple.

● There will be earthquakes and famines. Both took place during the time of the Roman Emperors Claudius (AD41–54) and Nero (AD54–68).

Jesus says all these things will be 'like the first pains of childbirth'. When a woman is going to give birth, she has contractions. These are signs that the child is going to be born, but you cannot tell from the first contractions exactly when the baby is going to arrive. It may be soon; it may be some time later. So, the events Jesus speaks of show that the end is on the way. But Christians should not get too excited. It may still be a long way off.

Some rulers demand the allegiance which Christians believe is due only to God. They are like the false Messiahs described in Mark 13. Many German Christians suffered under Hitler's rule for refusing to conform.

☝ FOLLOW UP ☝

1. Do you think some people can know the future?

2. ● What is apocalyptic?
● How is Mark 13 different from other apocalyptic?

3. ● What does Jesus say is going to happen in the future?
● When did these things come true? Do you think some have not happened yet?
● 'These things are like the first pains of childbirth.' What does this mean?

4. Jesus warns about false Messiahs and false prophets. Some Christians think he means founders and holy people of other religions. Why might other Christians disagree with them?

The End of the World: 2

READ MARK 13:9–13

Jesus warns the Christians about what is going to happen to them, and what they have to do.

They will be taken to court, and will be beaten in synagogues. Each synagogue had a court of discipline (the *beth din*), that could sentence people to be whipped (Deuteronomy 25:2–3). They will stand before rulers and kings, and must preach in front of them. Paul appeared before the Roman governors Felix and Festus, and before King Herod Agrippa (Acts 24; 25:1–12, 25:13–26:32). When these things happen, they need not worry about what to say, as the Holy Spirit will give them the words. Many early Christians were uneducated people. Jesus' promise would have been very comforting to them.

Christianity will split families (compare Mark 10:28–30, Unit 34). The idea that families would break up was often found in apocalyptic; it was based on Micah 7:6. Under the Emperor Nero, Christians were executed for their faith. The Romans had to get their information from somewhere, so people may have betrayed members of their own families.

Before the end comes, 'the gospel must be preached to all peoples': the Gentiles too must hear the Good News, and become members of the Kingdom of God. Many would say that Jesus means that every single person in the world must hear the Christian message.

So, the Christians will suffer terribly. Suffering – like the persecution that Mark's church may have suffered – is part of the Christian life. But there is a great reward. 'Whoever holds out to the end will be saved.'

'The Awful Horror'

READ MARK 13:14

Mark tells the reader that he must understand this verse. If he means someone who read the passage out during worship, perhaps he expected him to explain it to the congregation. This is all very well, but what does the verse really mean? There are three possible answers:

● The words 'the Awful Horror' translate four Greek words meaning 'the Abomination of Desolation'. These words were used in Daniel 9:27; 11:31; 12:11, and 1 Maccabees 1:54. (This book is in the Apocrypha or Deuterocanonical Books included in some Bibles.) There, they meant the altar to the god Zeus set up in the Temple by King Antiochus Epiphanes in 168BC. If it means something similar in Mark, there was a time in AD40 when the Roman Emperor Caligula tried to set up his own statue in the Temple.

● The Awful Horror could be the Antichrist. This is either the Devil, or the Devil's representative, whom some people expected to arrive at the end of the world.

● Luke's version of the verse says: 'When you see Jerusalem surrounded by armies, then you will know that she will soon be destroyed' (Luke 21:20).

This is perhaps the best explanation of 'the Awful Horror', and it makes sense of the next half of the verse, 'then those who are in Judea must run away to the hills'.

Be on your guard!

READ MARK 13:15–23

It is difficult to know whether this passage is simply a prediction of a war, or is about the signs that the end is coming.

Verses 15–18 seem to be talking about a war. The description would fit the Jewish War in AD70, when the Romans surrounded Jerusalem as they got ready to storm the city. There would be no time to collect any belongings before that happened. People must leave quickly for the hills. Running way would be less easy for pregnant women or mothers with babies, and it would be very hard in winter, when the rivers were swollen. It is awful to think that many thousands of people died when the city was actually captured. Instead of running from Jerusalem, they had crowded into it.

Verses 19–20 seem to be speaking about signs of the end, although they could still be about the war. These events will be more terrible than anything that has ever happened before. God has shortened the time they will last, out of concern for his chosen people. If he had not done so, nobody would survive.

Jesus repeats his warning that people will come and claim to speak for him. False Christs and false prophets will try to dazzle and deceive God's chosen people. Even if they perform miracles, the Christians should not be taken in.

The coming of the Son of Man (the parousia)

READ MARK 13:24–27

Jesus, the Son of Man, will return *after* the signs of the end have happened, so the Christians will have to wait. He will gather God's chosen people together. The idea seems to be that the Kingdom of God will finally arrive when Jesus returns, and that people will then be judged by him (see Unit 29).

This short section is packed full of echoes of the Old Testament and apocalyptic:

● The idea of the universe breaking up – the sun and moon going dark, and the stars falling from heaven – is often found in apocalyptic. It picks up ideas from passages like Amos 8:9 and Joel 2:10.

● For Son of Man, see Daniel 7:13. (We look at this passage again in 'Titles of Jesus: 5 – the Son of Man' in Unit 45.)

● In the Old Testament, 'power' and 'glory' were used to describe God. 'Clouds' were signs of God's presence (see Unit 30).

Because of these echoes, many Christians today doubt that Jesus will return in exactly the way described here. Many say that some, or all of it, is picture language, which should not be taken literally.

FOLLOW UP

1. What was 'the Awful Horror'?

2. What are the people in Judea told to do, and why?

3. List the sufferings that Jesus says the Christians will go through.
● Now look up Acts 24–26 and 2 Corinthians 11:23–29. Which of these things did Paul go through?
● Mark's church may have been persecuted. Why would this passage have been important to them?

4. Jesus said 'the gospel must be preached to all peoples'. Is it wrong, do you think, to try to convert people to Christianity?

5. ● What will happen when the Son of Man comes?
● Try to interview some Christians about this idea. What do they think it means? (If you are doing this on your own, it will help if you can use a tape recorder or design a questionnaire so that you can share your findings with the rest of the class.)

6. If people believed that Jesus would return soon, do you think their behaviour would change? If so, how and why? If not, why not?

The End of the World: 3

Battles and earthquakes and famines are some of the signs of the end-time. Even so, Jesus says, no one can tell when it will be.

READ MARK 13:28–31

The lesson of the fig-tree

When the leaves on a fig-tree start to come out, it is a sign that summer is near. When the things Jesus describes happen, it is a sign that 'the time is near, ready to begin'. The Good News Bible uses these words to translate the Greek, which means either 'he is near, at the very gates' or 'it is near, at the very gates'. In other words, either the Son of Man is about to return, or the Kingdom is about to arrive finally. This will happen 'before the people now living have all died'.

There are problems with this passage. So far, the disciples have been warned not to get too excited about the signs or to think the end is coming too quickly. Now, they are told it is going to be soon, and they can tell when it will be from the signs. Jesus seems to be contradicting himself. How can we explain this? Some would say that Jesus is wrong or that Mark made it up. But there are other possibilities.

● Mark may be using a different source for 13:28–30, which says the end will be soon.

Titles of Jesus

5: The Son of Man

Mark's Gospel uses the title 'Messiah' or 'Christ' only 7 times. The title Jesus uses for himself is 'the Son of Man'. This appears 14 times in Mark. It is one of the most important titles of Jesus, and is also the most difficult. Scholars still argue about what it means. Christians sometimes say that 'Son of Man' means the human side of Jesus, and 'Son of God' means the God side of him. However, it is more complicated than this. We have to look at what the words 'Son of Man' meant before Jesus' time, and how Jesus used the title.

● **How was 'Son of Man' used before Jesus' time?**
We can find the answer by looking at the Old Testament and Jewish apocalyptic. You will need to look up the Bible passages. (Sometimes, English Old Testaments translate 'Son of Man' as 'mortal man', 'a human being' or simply 'man'. The Hebrew, though, always says 'Son of Man'.)

Look up

1. 'Son of Man' can just mean 'a human being'. In Hebrew and Aramaic (the language spoken by Jesus), 'son of man' can mean this. It can be used to contrast people's weakness with God's power. Numbers 23:19 In the Book of Ezekiel, God calls the prophet 'son of man', which Ezekiel 2:1 just means 'man'. So Jesus could have used the title to mean simply 'this man' or 'I'. He is a man of the people.

2. The Son of Man was someone from heaven. Daniel had a vision of 'someone like a Son of Man', who was given power Daniel 7:13–14 by God. Later apocalyptic books said the Son of Man was someone from heaven whom God would send to judge people. However, we have two big problems with these later apocalyptic books: First, we do not know whether they thought the Son of Man was the same as the Messiah. Second, many scholars say that they were written after the time of Jesus. Others disagree.

The sources he used for the rest of the chapter say the end will be later.
● 'It is near' may mean 'the destruction of Jerusalem is near', or even Jesus' resurrection is near.
● Jesus may mean his followers will realize the Kingdom has already come.

Jesus told his followers to learn the lesson of the fig-tree, whose leaves are a sign of summer. There are other signs which will herald the end of the world.

● **How did Jesus use the title of 'Son of Man'?** Jesus seems to have preferred the title 'Son of Man' to 'the Messiah'. Perhaps this was because people had fixed ideas about the Messiah's job: they thought he would get rid of the Romans. If people did not know what 'Son of Man' meant, or disagreed about it, they would not automatically think Jesus would start a war with Rome.

In Mark, Jesus uses the title in three main ways. Scholars argue over this. Some say that only one, or two of these ways were actually used by Jesus, and the rest have been made up by the early Christians. Others disagree.

Look up

1. The Son of Man has authority on earth.
The Son of Man has power on earth to forgive sins, and he is Lord of the Sabbath.

Mark 2:10

2:28

2. The Son of Man must suffer, die, and rise again.

This is the most important idea. Most of the sayings about the Son of Man are about this.

In the Old Testament and apocalyptic books, there is no real mention that this is the *Son of Man's* job. However, the book of Isaiah says that the *Servant of the Lord* must suffer and die for people's sins. People in Jesus' time were not sure who the Servant of the Lord actually was. It is unlikely that they thought the Servant was the Messiah. Even so, it is possible that Jesus used ideas about the Servant of the Lord when he talked about the Son of Man,

	Mark	8:31
		9:9
		9:12
		9:31
		10:33
		10:45
		14:21
		14:41

Isaiah 52:13–53:12

although some scholars would disagree.

3. The Son of Man will return.
The Son of Man will return at the *parousia*. This seems to echo Daniel's vision and possibly other apocalyptic books, if these were written before Jesus' time.

Mark 8:38
13:26
14:62
Daniel 7:13–14.
It will help if you compare this with the passages in Mark.

(Scholars used to say that Jesus was talking about someone else when he said the Son of Man would come. Few of them now agree with this.)

In some ways, the background to the 'Son of Man' title does not matter. If we look at the way he used it, we can see that 'the Son of Man' sums up Jesus' life and work very well.

You will understand these suggestions much better if you look back to Mark 9:1, and the notes on it in Unit 29. We had a very similar problem there. (Bear in mind, though, that 13:28–30 cannot be about the Transfiguration.)

Even if heaven and earth pass away, Jesus' words will stand for ever. What he says is not just for his own day: it is for all time.

No one knows the day or the hour

READ MARK 13:32–37

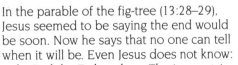

In the parable of the fig-tree (13:28–29), Jesus seemed to be saying the end would be soon. Now he says that no one can tell when it will be. Even Jesus does not know: only God the Father does. The 'servants' (Christians) do not know when the 'master of the house' (Jesus) will return. He could come at any time. While Jesus is 'away', they must not 'fall asleep' and fall away from their faith. If people in Mark's church were persecuted, we can imagine how easy it must have been to do this. The Christians are told they must 'watch', which means 'keep awake'.

Some scholars have suggested this passage was used in a service in Mark's church, when they remembered Jesus' words by keeping awake all night (through 'evening', 'midnight', 'before dawn' and 'sunrise'). This is an interesting idea, but we cannot really be sure that it happened. We can be sure, though, that Mark wanted his readers to be ready for the *parousia*. They should not get over-excited, but they must be prepared to meet the Lord when he comes.

▲FOLLOW↟UP▲

1. ● Complete the following sentence:
Heaven _____ _____ will pass away, but my _____ will never pass away.
● Who said this?

2. ● What does Jesus say about the fig-tree?
● What does he mean?

3. Jesus talks about a man going on a journey and leaving his servants in charge. What does he mean?

4. Why are the Christians told to 'watch'? Why might this have been important in Mark's church?

5. Some scholars say Mark 13:28–37 has two different ideas about when the end will come. Why do they say this?

6. Write the following essay:
'What does the title "the Son of Man" mean?'

7. Jesus says: 'No one knows, however, when that day or hour will come – neither the angels in heaven, nor the Son; only the Father knows.'

Right through history, some Christians have claimed that the end of the world was about to happen. So far, they have always been wrong. But even today some people say that the signs of the end are happening now. They might point out that we have wars, 'false prophets', and the idea of the Son of Man coming on clouds sounds like a nuclear disaster. So, they think, Jesus will return soon. Now that you have read these units, do you think this is what Mark 13 is about?

8. Design a poster or painting about the end of the world. You can use your own ideas, or things taken from Mark 13, or both.

Why Did Jesus Die?

In the next few units we are going to be looking at Mark's passion narrative (14:1–15:47). It is almost certain that the story of Jesus' suffering and death was already written down by the time Mark wrote his Gospel, and that he used this earlier version as a source. There are three important clues to this:

● Mark tells the story in detail, and spends a lot of time on it.

● From 14:1 the story runs along without a break. In the rest of the Gospel Mark has written in 'chunks' which sometimes do not seem to fit together very well (see the notes in Unit 28).

● All four Gospels – including John – follow the *same pattern* in their passion narratives.

The cross is a symbol of violent death – a crucifixion. Who would wear a tiny electric chair, or a guillotine, around their necks? Yet the cross is THE symbol of the Christian faith, because the death of Jesus is at the heart of what Christians believe about him.

We have already said some of this when we were looking at Jesus' entry into Jerusalem in 11:1–11 (see Unit 36). It seems quite likely (although some people disagree) that the entry into Jerusalem was originally part of the passion narrative, which Mark separated from the rest by introducing the stories of Jesus' ministry in Jerusalem in chapters 11 and 12, and the 'Little Apocalypse' of chapter 13.

Why was the story of the death of Jesus so important to the early Christians?

The members of the early church were convinced that Jesus had not only died, but had *risen from the dead* and appeared to his disciples. They saw this as proof that he had been right when he had said that he was the Messiah.

But before Jesus came, nobody had even expected the Messiah to die (see Unit 4). Not only that – the Law said that somebody put to death was cursed by God (Deuteronomy 21:22–23). It was well known that Jesus had been executed as a criminal.

The early Christians therefore had a problem. How could they make sense of the fact that Jesus was the Messiah and at the same time that he had died a criminal's death?

This question was not just a matter of theory. The early church wanted to bring the 'Good News' of Jesus to everybody, but it was hard to get people to accept the idea of a crucified Messiah. Jewish people found it profoundly shocking; Gentiles thought that it was simply unbelievable. Paul, a former Pharisee, spent his later life as a Christian missionary and wrote many of the letters in the New Testament. He said that the message about Christ's death on the cross was 'offensive to the Jews and nonsense to the Gentiles' (1 Corinthians 1:23).

To try to solve this problem the early Christians first looked back to their collections of the words of Jesus. There they found two sorts of sayings about his death. We can see them in Mark:

● Places where Jesus had *predicted* his own death, and said that the Messiah *must suffer* (Mark 8:31; 9:30–31 and 10:33–34).

● Places where he had said that his death as the Messiah *was going to do something important* (Mark 10:45 and 14:24).

They also saw something else. Jesus had died at the time of the Passover Festival.

This was one of the most important festivals of Judaism. It celebrated the Exodus: the time when, long before, God had saved the Israelites from the Egyptians by bringing them safely through the Red Sea (see Exodus 12–16). The Jews saw this as the most important foundation of their special relationship with God – the Covenant.

The Jews' Covenant with God was something like a *contract* between two people. On the one hand, God promised to be their special God – to help them, teach them and guide them throughout their history (this is what the Old Testament is

The Samaritans, today, still sacrifice the Passover lamb as the Jewish people did at the time of Jesus, when the Temple was still standing.

about). For their part the Jews promised not to worship any other gods, and to obey the Law of Moses. They kept the Covenant by worshipping God – and especially by the *animal sacrifices* which were made in the Temple in Jerusalem. At Passover time lambs were sacrificed and eaten at a special meal at home (see Exodus 12:1–11). But there were other kinds of sacrifice as well. Some were to give thanks to God for something, like harvest or the birth of a child. Others were to stop people from being 'unclean' (see the story of Jesus and the leper in Mark 1:40–45) or *to take away sin*.

As they thought about these things the early Christians began to realize that there was a solution to their question. *The death of Jesus was a sacrifice like the sacrifices of the animals*

The Lamb of God

These ideas crop up all over the New Testament. Paul, writing earlier than Mark, says that 'Christ, our Passover lamb, has been sacrificed' (1 Corinthians 5:7), and in John's Gospel Jesus is called 'the Lamb of God, who takes away the sin of the world' (John 1:29). The New Testament letter writers began to understand that Christians should love God – not just because it was a commandment, but because of what God had done in Jesus' death. 'This is how we know what love is, Christ gave his life for us . . . Whoever does not love does not know God, for God is love. And God showed his love for us by sending his only Son into the world, so that we might have life through him' (1 John 3:16a and 4:8–9). Eventually they began to see all the sacrifices of the Old Covenant as foreshadowings or predictions of the sacrifice of Jesus. (When the Temple was destroyed in AD70 many Christians saw it as proof that the old animal sacrifices were out of date and had been replaced by Jesus.)

in the Temple. But there was a difference. The animal sacrifices only took away some sins for the Jews. Jesus' death on the cross could take away all the sins of all the world. Long ago God had saved his people from the Egyptians and given the Jews the Covenant. Now, by raising Jesus from the dead, he had saved everybody from death itself. He was offering them a new relationship with him – a *New Covenant*.

This makes sense of the two sayings in Mark where Jesus says that his death is going to do something:

● Mark 10:45: 'For even the Son of Man did not come to be served; he came to serve *and to give his life to redeem many people.*' What does 'redeem' mean, and how does it connect up with the idea of Jesus' death as a sacrifice? Look at the table below.

The Greek word for 'to redeem' can mean:	So Jesus' death can mean:
Giving something in the place of a sacrifice you could not offer.	People owe God a sacrifice to show they are sorry for their sin. But Jesus' death is like the money that can be paid instead – and Jesus pays it.
Releasing a slave by paying money.	People are slaves to sin: Jesus' death releases them.
Paying a fine as a punishment for a crime.	By his death Jesus pays the 'fine' that is due to God as the punishment for people's sin.

● Mark 14:24: 'This is my blood which is poured out for many, *my blood which seals God's covenant.*'

We will be finding out more about this verse in Unit 49. But you can see that Jesus is talking about a new *Covenant* or relationship which God is making with the world.

These two sayings show that Mark thought about Jesus' death in the same way as other Christians of his time. It was a sacrifice which took away sin and made a new relationship with God. And they show that he thought that Jesus understood it that way, too.

One other thing needs to be said. As we read through Mark's passion narrative we will notice several *quotations from the Old Testament*. Like the Jews, the early Christians believed that God had spoken through the Scriptures. As they read them they looked for places which seemed to predict what had happened to Jesus. These were then woven into the story of his death. (It is almost certain that this happened before Mark wrote his Gospel.) In this way the early Christians wanted to show that what had happened to Jesus was part of God's plan for the world.

 Two parts of the Old Testament in particular seemed to predict Jesus' suffering, although they were written long before it: Isaiah 53 and Psalm 22. It might help to read these passages in the Bible before you start the next unit.

Why is the death of Jesus important to Christians now?

Christians today still believe that Jesus died to overcome the sin which separates men and women from God. What do they mean by this? They would say that no matter how hard we try, we cannot really be as good as we ought to be. If the world was judged tomorrow in a kind of cosmic law-court, none of us would do very well. But according to Christianity, God did not want this to happen. The love and obedience Jesus had in dying can still somehow make up for everything that men and women do wrong. The idea that Jesus' death puts everything right between God and the world is called the *atonement* ('at-one-ment').

Down the centuries, Christians have come to agree on the way in which most of the big ideas of Christianity work. For instance, they quite quickly realized that the idea that Jesus showed what God was like meant that he was God made man. But this has never really happened to the idea of the Atonement, although theologians have written and discussed it a lot.

All Christians believe that Jesus died for the sins of the world, and that his death was a sacrifice. The Bible teaches that sin separates people from God and leads to death. The New Testament goes on to say that Jesus' sacrifice overcame this separation. People's sins are 'buried in his death' (Romans 6:4), and they share in his resurrection from the dead. But nobody has yet come up with a way of explaining this which does not involve questions. We can see this even in what we have said about Mark 10:45. We could look on Jesus' death as the 'fine' that Jesus pays for the world's sins. But what does this make God the Father like? What sort of father would demand his son's death as payment for somebody else's crime? Or what sort of a judge would accept an innocent person's death in the place of a guilty one?

All of these ideas tell Christians something about the meaning of Jesus' death. They form a sort of picture language which helps them to understand the atonement. But all of them fall short of a complete picture – perhaps because what went on in the atonement is just too big to put into ordinary words. Perhaps it helps to remember that, in Christian teaching, God was actually present in Jesus. Many modern theologians talk about God *entering into the suffering of the world* on the cross and offering people a way out of it. But this is still only one idea among many.

▲FOLLOW▼UP▲

Short answer questions

1. Give one of the clues we have that the Passion story was probably written down before Mark used it in his Gospel.

2. ● Jesus died at the time of a Jewish festival. Which one?
● What did the Jews remember at it?

3. Why was Jesus' death as a criminal a problem for the first Christians?

4. Why are there so many references to the Old Testament in Mark's Passion narrative?

Longer answer questions

5. 'For even the Son of Man did not come to be served; he came to serve and to give his life to redeem (or, as a ransom for) many people' (Mark 10:45). How does this verse help us to understand what Mark believed about the death of Jesus?

6. What does 'atonement' mean? Explain your answer as fully as you can.

Things to do

7. Talk to some practising Christians about their understanding of the death of Jesus. It might help you if you tape record your conversations. Compare your findings.

The Last Act Begins

READ MARK 14:1–11

In the story of Jairus' daughter (5:21–42, Unit 19) and the sending out of the Twelve (6:6b–13 and 30–32, Units 21 and 23) we saw that Mark sometimes interrupts one story with another. He seems to do it again here. If you look carefully at verses 1–2 and 10–11 you will see that they follow on from one another. The passage still makes perfectly good sense if you leave out verses 3–9. Because of this most people think that verses 1–2 and 10–11 were originally part of the early Passion story which existed before Mark wrote his Gospel (see Unit 3). He has split them up and put the story of Jesus' anointing in the middle of them. We will look at the two stories in turn.

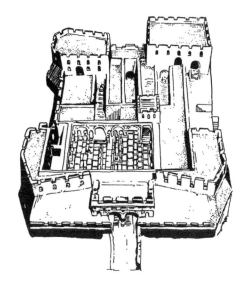

Fort Antonia was the base for the Roman garrison in Jerusalem. Being close to the Temple, soldiers were on hand in case tensions exploded into violence, in a city thronging with visitors at festival times.

The plot against Jesus and Judas' betrayal

(verses 1–2 and 10–11)

This begins with one of the precise *timings* which run through the passion narrative. Mark says that 'It was . . . two days before the Festival of Passover and Unleavened Bread.' Originally these were two separate festivals, but by the time of Jesus they had been combined. Passover was the most important part, and began the celebrations (see Unit 46). The Festival of Unleavened Bread lasted for seven days afterwards. It marked the beginning of the barley harvest. The name reminded the Jews of when God brought them out of Egypt, without time even to wait for their bread to rise (see Exodus 12:39). It was spring (normally April) and Jerusalem was crammed with pilgrims. So too were the outlying villages. Every good Jew wanted to spend at least

one Passover in Jerusalem during his life. The result was that hundreds of thousands of people were jammed into the city – which was only the size of a small town by today's standards. It was a particularly difficult time for the authorities. There were all the usual problems of crowd control. But there was the added fact that Passover celebrated the deliverance of the Jews from the Egyptians. Patriotic feelings ran high, and people with Zealot sympathies would have been thinking about God delivering his people from their new foreign rulers – the Romans.

We can imagine what it was like for the Sanhedrin in this situation. The Jewish Council was anxious to keep on good terms with the Romans, but with Jerusalem full of excitable pilgrims, anything could happen. What the chief priests and the scribes say in verse 2 of our story fits well with this. They do not want to have Jesus arrested and executed during the festival 'or the people might riot'. And they are trying to do it 'secretly' (verse 1).

Things begin to go the authorities' way when Judas offers to betray Jesus to them (verse 10). Lots of people have wondered why Judas did this. One popular idea is that he had once been a Zealot, and was disappointed when Jesus did not turn out to be the sort of Messiah he wanted. Or perhaps he did it for the money. Mark does not know – or at any rate, he does not tell us.

A woman anoints Jesus at Bethany (verses 3–9)

This is a very beautiful story. There are several things we should notice about it:

● Jesus is eating at the house of Simon *the leper* (verse 3: remember that the Good News Bible translates 'leprosy' as 'a dreaded skin disease'). We do not know who Simon was, and he does not appear anywhere else in the Gospel. It is not very likely that he was the leper Jesus cured in Galilee (1:40–45): Bethany was quite a long way away from there (see the map in Unit 37). Mark does not bother to explain, so perhaps Simon was someone quite well known to the early Christians. The story shows Jesus mixing with the *outcasts* right to the end.

● The woman breaks a jar of perfume and pours it on Jesus' head. Why does she do this? Mark thinks there are three reasons:

1. It was polite to pour a little perfume on your guests when they arrived at your house. Perfume was precious, and it showed how you welcomed them. The woman pours the *whole jar* of perfume over Jesus because she values him so much. This is the *surface meaning*.

2. When people died, their families and friends anointed their bodies with

Did Jesus die on Passover Day?

Although verse 2 fits in with what we know about Passover in Jerusalem at the time of Jesus, there are two problems. The chief priests say that Jesus' death must not be 'during the festival' (the Passover), but that is exactly what happens according to Mark's account. Jesus eats the Passover with his disciples and dies the next afternoon, still during the feast (14:12). (Jewish days did not run from midnight to midnight, like our days and Roman ones. A 'day' for the Jews went from one sunset to the next.) So what the chief priests are going to *do* contradicts what they *have* said.

But that is not all. Although all the Gospel writers agree that Jesus' death was on a Friday, John's Gospel says that this was *the day before the Passover*, and not Passover Day, as in Mark (John 18:28; 19:31). (Matthew

JERUSALEM

The picture shows a reconstruction of the city as it was in the first century, based on archaeological excavations.

The Hinnom valley, a smouldering rubbish tip which sometimes featured in Jesus' teaching

The Pool of Siloam. Jesus sent a blind man to wash here after he had been healed

and Luke follow Mark's timing.)

This is a fascinating problem. Did Jesus die on Passover Day or not? And was the last meal he ate with his disciples a Passover meal or not? There seem to be three possibilities:

● Mark is right, and John has made a mistake. Perhaps the chief priests were *originally* afraid of having Jesus arrested and executed during the feast, but when Judas offered to help them (verse 10) they changed their minds. So Jesus dies on Passover Day, and the Last Supper is a Passover meal. (There is an alternative version of this argument. The Greek words Mark uses for 'during the festival' in verse 2 could *just possibly* mean simply 'among the crowds'.)

● John is right, and Mark has made a mistake. Jesus died on the day before the Passover. It is argued that this was also what the story said before Mark wrote his Gospel. Mark 14:2 comes from this source, and reflects what actually happened.

● Both John and Mark are right. Not all Jews kept Passover at exactly the same time. We know, for instance, that the Essenes at Qumran (see Unit 1) kept the festivals at times quite different from the official worship in Jerusalem. Perhaps Jesus and his disciples did the same thing. Mark is following their religious calendar, and John the 'official' one.

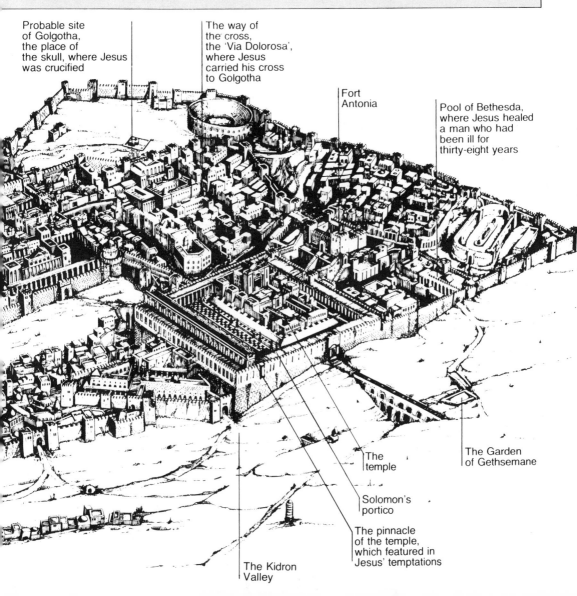

Probable site of Golgotha, the place of the skull, where Jesus was crucified

The way of the cross, the 'Via Dolorosa', where Jesus carried his cross to Golgotha

Fort Antonia

Pool of Bethesda, where Jesus healed a man who had been ill for thirty-eight years

The temple

The Garden of Gethsemane

Solomon's portico

The pinnacle of the temple, which featured in Jesus' temptations

The Kidron Valley

perfume. The jars were never used again: they were broken and the pieces were placed in the tomb with the corpse. Jesus is about to die, but there will not be time to give his body the normal care (see 16:1, Unit 54). So, perhaps without knowing it, the woman is preparing Jesus' body for burial – while he is still alive. Her action is a *prophetic sign* (see Unit 37) of what is going to happen to Jesus. This is the *second meaning*.

3. Jesus' idea of Messiahship was that the Messiah must suffer and die. We have already seen how important that was for Mark and the early Christians (Unit 46). Messiah means 'Anointed One' – and here the woman *anoints* Jesus' head. This would have been a reminder to Mark's readers that Jesus' death was his greatest act as Messiah. This is the *hidden meaning*.

Look again at verses 4–7. The people at the meal do not see any special significance in what the woman does. They simply see how extravagant she was being. It was embarrassing. They knew Jesus cared about the poor and were shocked at her behaviour. (Mark says that the perfume was 'worth three hundred silver coins' – this was nearly a year's wages for a labourer.) So they say that the perfume could have been sold to raise money for the poor. Perhaps they were trying to show off a bit as well.

Look at what Jesus says in verses 6–9. In one sense the people at the meal are right: the poor should always be helped. But that does not rule out other generous actions. And it certainly does not give the other guests the right to be spiteful to the woman. Patiently Jesus explains the meaning of her action. He appreciates the love behind it, which they are unwilling to see.

Notes

Luke and John both tell stories very similar to this one, although with slightly different characters and at different points in the Gospel story (Luke 7:36–50; John 12:1–8). Many scholars think that all three versions grew out of one original.

14:1: 'Two days before the Festival of Passover and Unleavened Bread': i.e. probably Wednesday.

14:3: Bethany was just outside Jerusalem (see map in Unit 37). Pilgrims used to stay there when Jerusalem was full up. This is probably what Jesus was doing.
Nard was a very precious perfume made from an Indian plant.

14:7: Jesus is quoting Deuteronomy 15:11. This was probably a familiar proverb. He certainly does *not* mean: 'there will always be poor people, so there is no point bothering about them' – although that is how some people have tried to understand it!

14:9: Some people have suggested that Mark added this verse to the story. Jesus does not usually talk about the 'gospel' in this way, although later Christians did. (See the note on 8:35, Unit 29.)

FOLLOW UP

1. ● What do the chief priests and the teachers of the Law say that they must not do 'during the festival' (verse 2)?
● Why do they say this?

2. ● At whose house was Jesus having a meal?
● Which village was it in (verse 2)?
● What was this village used for at Passover time?

3. ● According to Jesus, why did the woman anoint him (verse 8)?
● Give two other reasons why Mark thought she did this.

4. Which bits of Mark 14:1–11 do most scholars think Mark got from an earlier written Passion story?

5. You are Zedekiah Thaddaeus, a member of the Sanhedrin. Write a letter to your colleague Joseph Modein about the situation in Jerusalem at Passover at the time of Jesus.

6. Write a playscript of the conversation over dinner in Mark 14:3–9.

The Last Supper: 1

The story of Jesus' last meal with his disciples has always been extremely important for his followers. In this unit we look at Mark's introduction to it, and in the next we shall explore its meaning for Mark and its place in Christian life and thought today.

 READ MARK 14:12–21

Mark's story here has two parts:
● The preparations for the Passover meal (verses 12–16).
● Jesus' prediction of Judas' betrayal (verses 17–20).

We will look at each of these in turn.

The preparations for the Passover meal

These verses should remind you of something. They are very similar indeed to the story of the preparations for Jesus' entry into Jerusalem (11:1–6, Unit 36). In both of them:
● Jesus sends out two disciples to find something
● he knows what it is going to be
● he gives them something to say
● things turn out as Jesus said they would.

The stories are meant to show Mark's readers that Jesus is on top of what is happening. He is not going to his death as a victim of circumstances – he is going with his eyes open. It is not really clear whether Mark thought that Jesus had carefully arranged the room before sending the disciples out, or whether he expects his readers to think that his knowledge about it is a miracle (verses 13–15). But by the way he says that 'everything was just as Jesus had told them' it certainly seems that he

thought there was something remarkable about it. (The Old Testament has many stories about people knowing what is going to happen in advance. Look at 1 Samuel 10, for example.)

There are two other things we should notice about these verses:

> They seem to come from a different source from the one Mark uses for the verses around them. This is quite easy to spot with a bit of detective work.
>
> In the other verses Mark calls Jesus' followers by the Greek word for 'the twelve'. (The Good News Bible translates this as 'the twelve disciples', but this is a little misleading.) But here he just calls them 'the disciples'.
>
> Not only that: verse 16 does not seem to fit in very well with verse 17. Jesus has sent two of his disciples to arrange the room, presumably leaving ten. Then he turns up with twelve of them! So most scholars think that Mark has taken his story from two sources and spliced them together.

> They say that Jesus' Last Supper with his disciples was a *Passover meal*. As we shall see in the next unit, this is very important. It relates to the way Mark wants his readers to understand what Jesus did.

Look again at Unit 46 to remind yourself of the meaning of the Passover. It is still one of the most important festivals of Judaism. Jewish families and their friends gather together to remember how God brought his people out of Egypt and saved them from slavery (the Exodus). You may already have studied the modern Jewish Passover

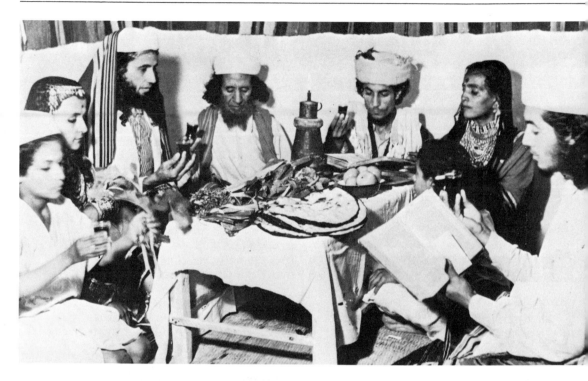

A Jewish nomad family from Arabia celebrate their first Passover in Israel. The festival continues today much as it did in Jesus' time, but without the ritual slaughter of lambs in the Temple.

celebrations. They grew out of the sort of festival which was celebrated every year in Jerusalem at the time of Jesus. But the big difference in those days was that the Temple was still standing. So, what used to happen at Passover time? And what exactly does Mark mean when he says that the disciples prepared the Passover meal?

The Passover meal was eaten in the evening, at the beginning (that's sunset) of the Jewish Passover day – 15th Nisan. At the centre of the meal was the *Passover lamb*. During the afternoon the head of the family took it up to the Temple, where it was killed as a sacrifice. Its blood was thrown against the altar by the priests, and the carcass was handed back to him to take home. This reminded the Jews of the first Passover, in Egypt. They had daubed the blood of the lamb above the door and on the doorposts of their homes, and the Angel of Death had passed over them, but the firstborn sons of the Egyptians had died (Exodus 12:21–28). (There were many thousands of pilgrims in Jerusalem at the time of Jesus. The Temple must have looked and smelled like a slaughter-house.) The lamb itself was eaten with other symbolic foods, which were specially prepared:

• **Unleavened bread** (bread with no yeast in it), because the people had had no time to wait for their bread to rise before running away from Egypt. (The house was thoroughly searched to make sure there was no yeast in it.)

• **Salt water and bitter herbs** to remind them of the tears they shed in Egypt and the bitterness of slavery.

• A mixture of apples, nuts, dates and pomegranates which looked like cement and was called **Charosheth**. This represented the clay the Jews were forced to make bricks from when they were slaves.

• **Wine** to remind them of the promises of God (the Covenant).

So you can see that Jesus' two disciples had their work cut out. The whole ceremony reminded the Jews of God's great saving act for his people in the past the Exodus.

Jesus' prediction of Judas' betrayal

Mark has already told his readers that Judas has agreed to hand Jesus over to the religious authorities (14:10–11). Now Jesus speaks about it himself. There are three things we should particularly notice:

• Jesus knows what is going to happen to him, just as he knew about the colt (11:2) and the man with the jar of water (14:13). Again Mark does not give any explanation of how this could be. But, as far as we can tell, the other disciples do not seem to have suspected Judas.

• All the disciples are upset and ask 'Surely, you don't mean me?' They are not at all sure of themselves!

Why do you think that Mark has bothered to record this particular question? The reason is probably because he thought that it carried an important message for

Christians in his own community. Even Jesus' closest disciples had things in their lives which made them feel uneasy in his presence – which made them feel as though they were capable of 'betraying' him. (As we shall see, Peter comes close to actually doing it.) Most Christians would probably feel the same. But Mark thinks that this is no reason to despair. After all, the disciples went on to become the leaders in the church!

• Jesus says: 'the Son of Man will die as the Scriptures say he will'. Jesus knows what is happening to him. His death is not some sort of wasteful tragedy. It is part of God's plan – God has spoken about it in the Scriptures. Mark wants to understand Jesus' words on two levels.

First there is the *immediate situation*. Judas is sitting with him at the meal. This calls to mind Psalm 41:9:

'Even my best friend, the one I trusted most,
The one who shared my food,
has turned against me.'

Even what Judas does is going to be used by God.

Then there is what is going to happen to Jesus *from now on*. The story of Jesus' suffering will be shot through with echoes from the Old Testament.

Before we leave this section we need to say something about Judas and who is to blame for the death of Jesus. In verse 21 of Mark's story Jesus says that it would have been better for Judas if he had never been born. That sounds fairly unpleasant. What have people made of it?

• Many later Christian writers thought that it means Judas will go to hell.

• Matthew's Gospel says that Judas became so upset by what he had done that he killed himself (Matthew 27:5). We can only imagine the terrible shame and guilt that drove him to this. Perhaps Jesus meant that it would be better never to have been born than to suffer this.

● Some say that Jesus never said these words – that they were added later. We must be very careful about saying things like this, just because we find something a bit hard to take. But there is some evidence. One of the Greek words Mark uses here is very peculiar. It appears in the Gospel only in this verse.

Mark blames Judas and the Jewish authorities for the death of Jesus. Now it is a terrible and shameful fact that

Notes

14:12: Mark says that the day the Passover lambs were killed was 'the first day of the Festival of Unleavened Bread'. In fact it was really part of the day before. It is now *Thursday*.

14:13: Water was usually carried by women. A man with a water-jug would have been very noticeable.

throughout Christian history Jews have suffered persecution, and frequently been killed, at the hands of people calling themselves Christians. Quite often, and despite the efforts of some popes to give Jewish people protection, the excuse offered was that somehow all Jews were responsible for the death of Christ. Feelings like this, at the very least, made it easier for

the Nazis to kill six million Jews less than fifty years ago, during Hitler's Third Reich – although in fairness it must be said that some Christians performed great acts of heroism to try to help them.

The idea that the Jewish nation is responsible for Jesus' death is one of the tragic lies of history. It is clearly nonsense. You might as well say that all Christians are responsible for his death, because Judas was one of Jesus' disciples. But people are rarely open to rational argument when they want to be cruel. The shame is that the idea has lasted so long and has caused so much misery.

◤ FOLLOW UP ◢

1. ● Fill in the missing words: 'I tell you that _____ _____ _____ _____ will _____ me, one who is _____ with _____.'
● Who said this?
● What part of the Old Testament is it like?

2. What was the main dish at the Passover meal?

3. Mark 14:12–16 are very like another story in the Gospel. Which one?

4. What *two* reasons are there for thinking that Mark used different sources for 14:12–16 and the rest of the story?

5. Find two places where Mark wants his readers to understand that Jesus knew in advance what was going to happen. Why do you think he emphasizes this so much?

6. Why do you think Jesus says that 'the Son of Man will die as the Scriptures say he will', and why was this important for the early church?

The Last Supper: 2

READ MARK 14:22–26

As far as we can tell, this story has always been at the centre of Christian worship. We have four versions of it: one in each of the Synoptic Gospels, and one in the letters of Paul (Matthew 26:26–30; Luke 22:14–20; 1 Corinthians 11:23–25). For once, Mark's account is not the earliest we have. Paul probably wrote his letter in about AD57. It is surprising that John's Gospel leaves it out, but he includes a long discussion about it early on: John 6:25–58.

We know that the early Christians thought that it was very important for them to meet regularly, and repeat what Mark and the other writers say Jesus did here. Down the centuries, Christians have always done the same. As we shall see, however, later Christians have not always agreed about the exact meaning of the service, where bread and wine are taken and Jesus' words repeated. They call it by different names: The Mass, Holy Communion, The Lord's Supper and The Breaking of Bread are just some of them. But most people would accept an old Greek title for it – *The Eucharist*. That has become a sort of technical name, and is what we shall call it here. (It comes from the Greek for 'to give thanks' which Mark uses when he is talking about what Jesus did with the cup.)

We shall look at modern Christian belief about the Eucharist later in this unit. First we must ask what Mark says about it.

What does Mark tell us?

From the last unit you will remember that Mark says Jesus' last meal with his disciples was a *Passover meal*. We saw there two important things about the Passover:

It celebrated the time when God had delivered his people from slavery in Egypt. This was the great saving act which showed his special relationship – the *Covenant* – with the Jews.

The centre of the Passover meal was the lamb. This had earlier been *sacrificed* in the Temple. The blood was poured over the altar and the flesh was taken home to eat.

Mark thinks that the Eucharist is a new Passover meal celebrating a new covenant. Jesus is going to make this new covenant with his death. Let's look at this in more detail.

● Jesus is going to die. He takes the bread, says a prayer of thanks to God, and breaks it. This is exactly what the head of a Jewish family did at every Passover meal. But Jesus adds something. He says that the bread is his body (verse 22). Just as the bread was broken at the Passover meal, so Jesus' body is going to be 'broken' on the cross.

● The wine at the Passover meal symbolized the promises God made with the Jews. Jesus takes a cup and again gives thanks in the usual way. But then he says another unexpected thing: 'This is my blood which is poured out for many, my blood which seals God's covenant' (verse 24).

To understand this we need to look at the Old Testament, and at three particular passages which Jesus' words echo.

The *first* is the story of how Moses long ago sealed God's original covenant with the Jews: Exodus 24:3–8. It tells how Moses read the people God's Law, and offered him animal sacrifices. Then he took the blood from these sacrifices and threw it on the people, saying 'This is the blood that seals the covenant which the LORD made with you when he gave you all these commands.'

The *second* is a passage from the prophet *Zechariah*. (We have already seen how Jesus' entry into Jerusalem was very like something in Zechariah. This new passage comes just after it.) It goes like this:

> 'The LORD says,
> "Because of my covenant with you that was sealed with the blood of sacrifices, I will set your people free"' (Zechariah 9:11).

 All this talk about blood sounds rather gruesome to us, but it would not have done in the ancient world, where animal sacrifices were very common. The Jews (and other ancient peoples) believed that the 'life' of animals and people was contained in their blood. (Quite a sensible belief when you think about it. If our blood drains away, we die.) Therefore by offering *blood* in sacrifices they were offering a gift of their *lives*: the death of the animal for the life of the person. (We still talk about people 'shedding their blood' for their country when they give their lives for it.)

The *third* comes from the prophet Jeremiah. He lived at a time when things had gone badly wrong for the Jews and they were in exile in Babylon. There they started to look forward to the new and better age which God would bring:

> 'The LORD says, "The time is coming when I will make a new covenant with the people of Israel and with the people of Judah . . . I will forgive their sins"' (Jeremiah 31:31 and 34).

So:
- The *old* covenant with the Jews was sealed by the blood of animal sacrifices, especially the blood of the Passover lamb.

- The Jews were looking forward to a *new* covenant.
- Jesus says that the wine is his *blood* which seals God's (new) covenant. And he is about to die, to be sacrificed on the cross. The promises have come true. *The new covenant has arrived.*

Mark thinks that Jesus' death is a *new sacrifice* sealing God's new relationship with his people, just as the Passover lamb 'sealed' the old covenant with the Jews. (We have already come across these ideas in Unit 46, 'Why did Jesus die?' You might like to look at it again to help you.)

When the Jews ate the Passover lamb and were sprinkled with the blood of Moses' sacrifice, they *became* and *stayed* the people of God's covenant, and shared in his first promises. Mark believes that the old sacrifices are replaced by Jesus' death, and that the Passover lamb is replaced by the Eucharist. He wants the members of his church to think that when they eat and drink at the Eucharist, they share in God's *new promises* and are members of his *new covenant.*

But this will not go on for ever. Jesus says one more thing: 'I will never again drink this wine until the day I drink the new wine in the Kingdom of God' (verse 25).

People in Jesus' time thought of heaven as a sort of enormous party given by the Messiah: the *Messianic banquet* we have already talked about. (See Units 11, 23 and 27.) This is what Jesus is talking about here. Mark wants his readers to understand that the Eucharist is a kind of *foretaste* or *promise* of the banquet they will share with Jesus in heaven, that he has made possible by his death.

The Eucharist in Christian life today

Christians still meet together for the Eucharist today, as they have done for nearly 2,000 years. Sometimes it is 'celebrated' with elaborate and beautiful ritual. Sometimes it is very simple. Everyone agrees that it celebrates and calls to mind Jesus' sacrifice on the cross and the new relationship it has made possible between God and the world.

After that, however, opinion divides into two main groups.

● **Catholic Christianity** (Roman Catholics, the Eastern Orthodox churches, and some Anglicans – 'Anglo-Catholics'). In this tradition the Eucharist is at the heart of a Christian's relationship with God, along with private prayer. It is called the Mass (or the *Liturgy* by the Orthodox) and is celebrated frequently. Christians who are serious about their faith will try to be at Mass at least on every Sunday and on the great Holy Days during the church's year, like Christmas Day (see also the notes on Holy Week in Unit 54).

Catholic teaching says that Christians remember Christ's death at the Mass. But

Christians today remember Jesus' death, and all that it means, in the bread and wine of the Eucharist. The service has many different names and forms, from the simplest 'breaking of bread' to the most elaborate Mass – yet it stands at the heart of the faith for all Christians.

more than this happens. The bread and wine themselves are miraculously changed and become a channel of God's love (a *sacrament*). Although they keep their physical properties (they would still look like bread and wine under a microscope), they really become the body and blood of the risen Christ, whose sacrifice unites the world to God. In this way Jesus is given to each Christian in a unique and special way. The Mass can be celebrated only by a priest, who stands in the place of Christ. The special ritual which has grown up around the Eucharist in this tradition of Christianity (and which can be very elaborate) emphasizes how holy the Mass is believed to be.

● **Protestant Christianity** (Evangelical Anglicans, the United Reformed Church, Baptists, Methodists, and the Free Evangelical Churches and others). This tradition places much more emphasis on the idea of the Eucharist as a *memorial* and *commemoration* of Jesus' death, and it is celebrated less frequently than in Catholic churches. Protestant Christians do not think that the bread and wine change but they symbolize the Christians' unity with Christ in his death for their sin and in his rising

again to new life, their communion with him, and their fellowship with all their Christian brothers and sisters. In this tradition the Eucharist is often celebrated with moving simplicity in church, or sometimes in 'house-groups' in people's homes. A minister or pastor usually leads the service, but not in all churches.

1. According to Mark, what sort of a meal was the Last Supper?

2. What did Jesus say his blood 'sealed' (verse 24)?

3. ● When did Jesus say he would drink wine again (verse 25)?
● What do you think this means?

4. In your own words, describe what Mark believed about the Eucharist.
OR
'It is impossible to understand what Mark thinks about the Eucharist without knowing something about Judaism.' Do you think this is true? Explain your answer.

5. Talk to some Christians about their understanding of the Eucharist, and what it means for them. Do they all agree? Discuss your findings in class.

'The Son of Man Will be Handed Over'

READ MARK 14:27–52

Jesus will die in a few hours' time. His friends will leave him, and he will face death alone.

None of the disciples believe their courage will fail them. Peter says he will follow Jesus right to the end, and the others agree. But they are wrong. God will strike the shepherd (Jesus), and the sheep (the disciples) will be scattered (Zechariah 13:7). Before the cockerel crows twice, Peter will deny three times that he even knows Jesus (see 14:66–72). The others will run away (see 14:50). The next time they will see Jesus will be 'in Galilee', after he has risen from the dead. Some scholars think this means the *parousia* will happen in Galilee, but this seems rather unlikely. John says the disciples met the risen Jesus on the shore of Lake Galilee (John 21).

Jesus takes Peter, James and John, the 'inner group' of disciples, to 'a place called Gethsemane'. This was an olive grove on the western slope of the Mount of Olives. Since Judas knew where to find it, perhaps they had been there before. There are several things to notice about verses 32–42:

● Jesus is absolutely terrified by the thought of the death that awaits him. He reacts as any other human being would. Yet he has the courage to go through with it. He has to drink the 'cup of suffering' (see Mark 10:38–39, Unit 35).

● In his prayer, Jesus calls the Father 'Abba'. The Good News Bible translates this as 'My Father!' In fact, it means 'Dad' or 'Daddy' in Aramaic. Most people in Jesus' time thought you could not call God 'Abba',

The Garden of Gethsemane, where Jesus agonized in prayer on the night of his arrest, is a grove of ancient olive-trees.

because it was not respectful enough. Mark, however, thinks Jesus is so close to God that he can use this name. The early Christians took up the idea, and they too called God 'Abba' (Romans 8:15; Galatians 4:6).

● The disciples are 'asleep'. In 13:33–37, Jesus had told them to 'watch' and 'keep awke' for the signs of the end. They cannot even keep awake here! 'The spirit is willing, but the flesh is weak': they want to stay awake, but are too exhausted.

● When trouble came, even the disciples broke. If Mark's first readers faced death, they could draw strength from Jesus' example to go through with it in spite of their fear. But if they fail, there is comfort in knowing that the disciples were welcomed back by the risen Jesus, even though they had not held out to the end.

Jesus tells the disciples to 'get up' and go to meet 'the man who is betraying me'. Either he somehow realizes that Judas is on his way, or perhaps he simply sees him in the distance.

Judas arrives with a gang of armed men, sent by the Sanhedrin. This is what Mark means by 'the chief priests, the teachers of the Law, and the elders'. Perhaps the gang was the Temple guard (the Jewish police who kept order in the Temple), or a group of ordinary people. John seems to suggest that Roman soldiers were involved (John 18:3).

They have arranged a signal: the person to arrest is the one Judas kisses. We do not know why Judas chose this as the sign, but it seems horrible. A pupil would usually show his love and respect for his master by kissing him. Here, it seems to show exactly the opposite.

They arrest Jesus. There is a brief fight, and someone cuts off the ear of the High Priest's slave or servant. John says it was Peter (John 18:10). But Jesus is not an 'outlaw' or a man of violence. He is not a warrior Messiah. They could have arrested him at any time when he taught in the Temple, but they did not. The disciples run off, frightened that they will be arrested as

Notes

Peter is mentioned in verses 29, 30, 31, 33 and 37. He does not behave very well. So, some scholars have said Mark got many of his details straight from Peter himself, since no one but Peter would show him acting like this. Other scholars disagree.

Maundy Thursday is an important day for Christians (see Unit 54). In many churches, the main service in the evening remembers the Last Supper. Straight after this comes the *Watch*. Christians will stay up for all or part of the night, pray together quietly, and remember Jesus' agony in the Garden of Gethsemane.

well. In Mark, Jesus does not see them again before his death.

Mark includes something in this story which Matthew, Luke and John leave out. He mentions the young man who followed Jesus (14:51–52). Why does Mark have this detail when the other Gospel writers do not? It is often said that this young man was actually Mark himself. This is an attractive idea, but there is no evidence. The young man may have been an eyewitness, who passed on his information. Or it may look back to Amos 2:16, which says that strong men would flee away naked when the Day of the Lord came. We do not know.

FOLLOW UP

1. ● Who said he would never leave Jesus, even if all the others did?
● What did Jesus say to him?
● Where did Jesus and his disciples go to?
● Why was Jesus terrified?
● What did Jesus pray?
● What were the disciples doing?
● Who arrived to arrest Jesus?
● What was the sign Judas gave the men?
● What happened to the High Priest's servant or slave?
● What did the disciples do after Jesus was arrested?

2. Jesus tells his disciples he will go before them to Galilee. What does he mean?

3. Jesus and the early Christians called God 'Abba'. What does this tell you about their idea of God?

4. Why might the story of Jesus in Gethsemane have been important to Mark's church?

5. Mark mentions the young man who followed Jesus (verses 51–52). Why do people think he included this detail?

6. Jesus says 'the Scriptures must come true' that speak about his death (verse 49). Look back at Unit 46. What scriptures might he mean?

Jesus' Trial
before the Sanhedrin

READ MARK 14:53–72

Mark records three trials of Jesus:
● the trial before the Sanhedrin (14:53–65)
● the 'second trial' before the Sanhedrin (15:1, see Unit 52).
● the trial before Pilate.

The *Sanhedrin* was the Jewish council (see Unit 1), and Mark says they were looking 'for some evidence against Jesus in order to put him to death'. The meeting was held in the High Priest's house, so where did Mark get his information from? This is not an easy question. Some scholars think the whole of the trial before the Sanhedrin was made up by the early Christians, who did not know exactly what happened. However, we know that some members of the Sanhedrin – Joseph of Arimathea, for example (Mark 15:43) and perhaps Nicodemus (John 3:1, 19:39) – were friendly towards Jesus. If they later became Christians they may have told others what had happened.

Mark says the witnesses told lies about Jesus. The first charge they try to fix on him is speaking against the Temple. They say that Jesus threatened to pull the Temple down and rebuild it. Any sensible court would throw out the idea. Was Jesus going to do it with his bare hands? In 13:2, Jesus had predicted the destruction of the Temple, but he had not said *he* was going to do it. The witnesses seem to have confused the saying in 13:2 with a prediction of Jesus' resurrection, which would take place 'after three days' (see John 2:19–22). But the witnesses do not agree, and the charge has to be dropped.

Things are going on too long, so the High Priest stands up. In the time of Jesus, the High Priest was *Caiaphas*, although some

people thought of his father-in-law Annas as the real High Priest. (Matthew says Caiaphas did the talking, although John suggests Annas was also involved: Matthew 26:57; John 18:13, 24.)

Is Jesus going to say nothing to the charges? There is no reply. On the surface, this seems fair enough. The 'charges' so far have been trumped-up nonsense, so why should Jesus reply to them? However, Mark's readers would have remembered what the Book of Isaiah said about the Servant of the Lord.

> 'He was treated harshly, but endured it humbly;
> he never said a word.
> Like a lamb about to be slaughtered,
> like a sheep about to be sheared,
> he never said a word.' (Isaiah 53:7).

This is just what happens to Jesus here. (It is also worth looking at Psalms 27:12 and 35:11.)

The Sanhedrin is getting nowhere, so the High Priest tries a direct question. He asks Jesus point blank whether he is the Messiah. The reply is very important: 'I am, and you will all see the Son of Man seated on the right of the Almighty and coming with the clouds of heaven!'

Notice:
● The time for the Messianic secret is now over (see Unit 9). It seems that Jesus had not wanted people to go around saying he was the Messiah because he did not want them to get the wrong idea. The Messiah was not going to start a war with Rome. His job was to suffer and die. *Jesus replies 'I am' here because this is what it means to be the Messiah.*

Jesus would have climbed this stepped road on his way to trial.

● The words 'I am' are the same words Jesus used in 13:6 and 6:50. God had called himself 'I am' when he spoke to Moses (see Exodus 3:14 and Unit 24).

● They will see the Son of Man sitting at the Father's right hand, and coming with the clouds of heaven.

We still talk about someone's 'right-hand man': a helper he or she can't do without. Jesus will sit at God's right hand: he will share in what the Father does.

Jesus' reply is very like 13:26, and so some scholars think he is telling the Sanhedrin they will see him again at the *parousia*. This brings us back to the old problem of whether Jesus, or Mark, thought the *parousia* would be soon. But we do not have to understand Jesus' words to the High Priest in this way. We sometimes use the words 'you see' to mean 'you understand'. So Jesus could mean they will understand that he will be at God's right hand, that he is the Son of Man who will eventually return on the clouds of heaven. They will come to realize who he really is.

The High Priest tears his robes. He was supposed to do this when he heard blasphemy. There is a problem here. Did blasphemy mean swearing against God, or could it just mean lying about him? The Torah said cursing God was blasphemy (Leviticus 24:16). Jesus does not do this, and although claiming to be the Messiah might be wrong, it was not blasphemy. There are four possible solutions to this problem:

● The Sanhedrin were so desperate to get rid of Jesus that they did not care what the Law said.

● Jesus was actually found guilty of being a false or lying prophet. This crime carried the death sentence (see Deuteronomy 13:1–5).

● The Sanhedrin took Jesus' words ('I am' and 'the Son of Man . . . seated on the right hand of the Almighty') to mean that he was claiming authority that belonged to God. *This* was the blasphemy.

● The early Christians did not know what really happened, and have made the story up.

So Jesus is found guilty. For Mark, his one 'crime' was being the Messiah. The Temple guards beat him and spit at him. This may echo the prediction of the Servant of the Lord's suffering in Isaiah 50:6. According to John 18:31, the Sanhedrin was not allowed to execute people. So the Council gets ready to hand him over to Pontius Pilate, who will ratify and carry out the death sentence.

Meanwhile, Peter is outside the High Priest's house (verses 54 and 66–72). Mark tells the story of Peter's denial so well that there is little to say. We should just note a few points:

● Jesus' prediction that Peter will deny him (14:27–31) comes true.

● The people know Peter is from Galilee because of his accent.

● Peter seems to deny Jesus at the same moment that Jesus admits he is the Messiah.

● When Jesus rises from the dead, he forgives Peter (see 16:7; John 21:15–22). This would have been important for Mark's church.

Notes

Verses 61 and 62: In the Greek, the High Priest calls God 'the Blessed' and Jesus calls God 'the Power'. These are both respectful ways of referring to him.

Verse 65: Some Greek copies of Mark leave out the words 'Guess who hit you!' Many have 'Prophesy!' instead, and some have both. Others add extra words. It is difficult to know what Mark actually wrote here.

● This story can only have come from Peter himself (see Unit 3). Peter seems to have been one of Mark's sources.

FOLLOW UP

1. Design a 'charge sheet' for Jesus. You might want to include details like 'name', 'age', 'occupation', 'charge', 'verdict', 'sentence'.

2. ● What did Jesus reply to the High Priest's question?
● Why is this important?

3. What was Jesus found guilty of?

4. ● Tell the story of Peter's denial in your own words.
● Why would this have been important for Mark's church?

5. The Sanhedrin acted as a court. When a person was accused of a crime that carried the death penalty, it had to follow certain rules. The *Sanhedrin Tract*, which is part of the Mishnah – a collection of Jewish teaching – describes them. The *Sanhedrin Tract* was written in the second century AD, when the council no longer existed. Scholars are not sure whether the laws it lays down actually went back to Jesus' time. However, if they did, and if Mark does describe a trial, it is very interesting to see whether the Sanhedrin broke its own laws.

The rules the *Sanhedrin Tract* describe are listed below. Check them with Mark 14:53–65. Write out the rules. Next to each one, write:

YES if the Sanhedrin seemed to break its own rules
NO if the Sanhedrin did not seem to break its own rules
UNCLEAR if it is not clear.

1. The court had to meet in a place called the Hall of Hewn Stone, which was inside the Temple buildings. _____

2. The trial should not be held the day before the Sabbath. _____

3. The trial had to be held in the daytime. _____

4. The witnesses' evidence should be heard before the trial. _____

5. The evidence of at least two witnesses had to be exactly the same. _____

6. The case for the defence had to be heard. _____

7. The accused person could not be asked a question which would show he was guilty. _____

8. Each member of the Sanhedrin had to give his verdict separately, starting with the youngest person and ending with the oldest. _____

9. A verdict had to be reached in the daytime. _____

10. The court had to meet again the next day to check they still agreed the person was guilty. _____

Jesus' Trial before Pilate

 READ MARK 15:1–20

This part of the story is very beautiful and very terrible. Look carefully at it and you will see that it has four parts:
• A morning meeting of the Sanhedrin (verse 1).
• Jesus' trial before Pilate (verses 2–5).
• The release of Barabbas and Jesus' condemnation (verses 6–15).
• The soldiers' mockery of Jesus (verses 16–20).

What does Mark want his readers to notice especially?

• **Jesus was crucified as the king of the Jews.** All four Gospels agree that this is what was written over his cross (see Mark 15:26; Matthew 27:37; Luke 23:38; John 19:19). Jesus has never been called this before. The nearest he had come to claiming to be a king was at the entry into Jerusalem (11:9, see Unit 36). But the Romans would have thought that anybody claiming to be the Messiah was calling himself a king. They had crucified a few before. So Jesus is dying as the *Messiah*.

• **The Roman authorities are not really responsible for Jesus' death.** As the church spread over the Roman Empire, Christian missionaries were faced with an embarrassing fact. Jesus had been tried and condemned by a Roman governor (procurator). This could hardly be expected to go down very well with the Roman public! (Remember, we think that Mark was written in Rome, see Unit 3.) So the Gospels tend to play down Pilate's part in the affair. They try to make it clear that the Jewish authorities pushed him into a difficult situation. This is what Mark does here.

• **Jesus is the silent victim, the Suffering Servant of God.** Mark again wants his readers to think about the words from the prophets:

'Like a lamb about to be slaughtered, like a sheep about to be sheared, he never said a word.
He was arrested and sentenced and led off to die,
and no one cared about his fate.
He was put to death for the sins of our people.'
(Isaiah 53:7–8; see also Mark 14:61, Unit 51).

This is so astonishing that even Pilate is amazed at it. God is at work.

The morning meeting of the Sanhedrin (verse 1)

The Sanhedrin has already condemned Jesus during the night (14:53–64). So why does it meet again on Friday morning? We don't know for certain, but there are three possibilities:

• A trial by night broke the Jewish Law (see Unit 51). Perhaps the Sanhedrin had to meet again at daybreak in order to go through Jesus' crimes again and make the verdict legal.

• Mark has made it sound as though this is a new meeting because he wants to emphasize that the Jewish authorities were determined to get Jesus condemned. But in fact the trial had lasted all night. The Greek words of 15:1 can just mean this.

● The meeting in the morning was not part of the trial at all.

The trial before Pilate

(verses 2–5)

The Gospels are not our only source of information about Pilate. We know quite a lot about him. The Jewish historian Josephus says that he was a cruel and stubborn man who was eventually removed from his job and sent back to Rome. He had little time for Judaism. Mark's picture of him is better than we would expect.

Mark tells the story of Jesus' trial before Pilate very quickly. Look at it again. He never tells us *why* Pilate asked Jesus if he was the 'king of the Jews'. We are left to guess that the Sanhedrin suggested it to him (see Luke 23:2). Jesus' answer is difficult to understand. It seems to mean something like, 'You're doing the talking, not me.' You can compare this with what he said to the High Priest in the last unit (14:62). Perhaps once Jesus had declared that he was the Messiah, there was nothing more to say.

The release of Barabbas and Jesus' condemnation

(verses 6–15)

There are three important things we should note about this story:

● The way Mark tells it makes it seem as though Pilate was faced with an awkward choice. He could release *either* Barabbas *or* Jesus.

● So he lets the crowd decide. This means that the Jewish authorities (verse 11) are responsible for Jesus' death, and Pilate appears almost innocent.

● Mark drives the message home by saying that Pilate 'knew very well that the chief priests had handed Jesus over to him because they were jealous'.

This stone inscribed with the name of Pontius Pilatus was found this century at Caesarea. It was the first mention of the Governor, outside of the Gospel accounts, to be discovered.

There has been a lot of argument about this story. Some people think that Mark told it this way in order to get Pilate off the hook. They would point out three things:

● We know a lot about Roman Law and the way the Romans ran Palestine. Nobody except the Gospel writers talks about a tradition of releasing prisoners at Passover time.

● The *choice* Pilate is supposed to make is silly. He could easily have released

Barabbas as a favour *and* then found Jesus not guilty – particularly if he really knew that there was no charge against him (verses 11, 14).

● Mark says that Pilate 'wanted to please the crowds' and so had Jesus crucified. But we know that Pilate had very little time for the Jews. Why should he want to please them? And would he really stand around chatting to them (verses 8–14)?

People who think like this say that Mark's story about Barabbas grew out of one simple historical fact – that a man called Barabbas had been found not guilty and released at the same time as Jesus had

In the place where Roman soldiers made mockery of Jesus after Pilate had sentenced him to death are these stones, scratched with the games the soldiers played.

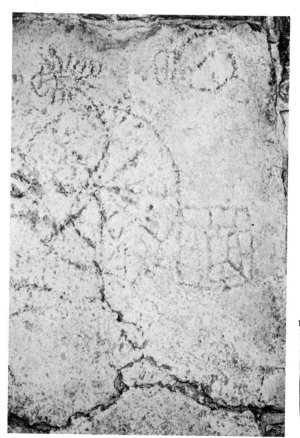

been crucified. The rest is an attempt to make the story of Jesus' death more acceptable to Roman readers.

What are we to make of this idea?

The obvious problem with it is that, if it is right, Mark took a very big risk. Pilate was a famous man, and there were crowds of people about. If the facts were changed somebody would surely have remembered what had really happened and contradicted Mark's story!

The story ends with a very brief note: Pilate had Jesus whipped. This was normal practice before somebody was crucified, but it was a very horrible thing. The weapon used was called a *flagellum*. It was a whip made of several leather strips. These strips had iron bits like hooks tied into them. The victim was bent over and bound to a post, and then beaten with this *flagellum*. It caused terrible injuries.

The soldiers' mockery of Jesus (verses 16–20)

Pilate is not involved here – perhaps that is why Mark feels able to go into detail about what went on. This part of the story would have made many of his readers remember two more passages from Isaiah about God's Suffering Servant:

'I bared my back to those who beat me,
I did not stop them when they insulted me,
when they pulled out the hairs of my beard
and spat in my face' (Isaiah 50:6).

and

'Because of our sins he was wounded,
beaten because of the evil we did.
We are healed by the punishment he
suffered,
made whole by the blows he received'
(Isaiah 53:5).

This would have reminded them that Jesus'
sufferings were part of the *atonement* (see
Unit 46).

What the soldiers do to Jesus here is the
sort of thing that very often happened to
criminals and other helpless people.

◆FOLLOW UP◆

1. ● What question does Pilate ask Jesus in Mark's
story?
● Why do you think he asks it?

2. ● Fill in the missing words: 'he knew very well that
the ___ ___ had handed ____ over to him because they
were ____ .'
● Who is this verse talking about?
● Why is it important for Mark?

3. Why have some people suggested that there may be
more to Mark's story about Barabbas than meets the
eye? What do you think of this idea?

The Death of Jesus

We have already seen why Jesus' death is important (Unit 46), and we now look at Mark's account of it.

READ MARK 15:21–39

In ancient times execution was common. Many crimes carried the death penalty, although the method of execution differed from country to country. In the Roman Empire, if you were a citizen of Rome, you were beheaded. Criminals who were not Roman citizens were *crucified*.

Crucifixion was slow: it was a way of torturing someone to death. The criminal was stripped, and then flogged to soften him up. A large beam of wood – the horizontal bar of the cross – was strapped to his arms, and he was made to walk through the town to the place of execution. A notice, stating his crime, was hung round his neck or carried in front of him. The soldiers always took the longest route, so that as many people as possible would see the offender. This was a powerful reminder not to step out of line.

When they reached the place of execution, the victim was made to lie on the ground, and his wrists were nailed or roped to the beam. The nails were not put in the hands, because they would rip out when the cross was upright. The crossbar and the criminal were hoisted up, and fixed in place on a large piece of wood planted in the ground. The notice was fixed to the cross, and the person's feet were either nailed or tied to a block which supported the weight of the body. Some criminals took a long time to die. They often hung in agony for several days.

Usually people who were crucified were left until they died from suffocation. The way the victims hung forward on their crosses made it difficult for them to breathe, except by forcing themselves up with their wrists and feet in order to gulp in air. Eventually they weakened, the pain became too great, and they gave up the struggle. (To speed things up the Roman soldiers would sometimes break the victims' legs. They could no longer push themselves up to breathe, and died very quickly. See John 19:31–33.)

Jesus was crucified.

He was beaten so badly that he could not carry his own crossbeam. Someone

else had to do it for him. We do not know who Simon was, but he came from Cyrene in North Africa. Perhaps he was a pilgrim, who had come to Jerusalem for the Passover. Mark may name him for another reason. Paul mentions a Christian named Rufus at Rome (Romans 16:13) and it may be that 'Alexander and Rufus' were known to Mark's church. If so, Mark mentions Simon to show that his information came from an eyewitness.

Jesus is crucified at nine o'clock in the morning at a place called Golgotha. 'Golgotha' is the Aramaic word for 'skull', which Mark translates for his Gentile readers. We are not sure exactly where Golgotha was. It may have been a hill that looked a bit like a skull. In Jerusalem today, you can visit the Church of the Holy Sepulchre. It is said this stands over Golgotha, but we cannot be sure. There are other, rival sites.

Two 'bandits' are crucified as well as Jesus. The word can mean 'revolutionaries'. Perhaps they were Zealots. Even at the end of his life, Jesus is found in the company of outcasts (see Unit 11).

Someone offers him wine mixed with myrrh. This was a painkiller, but Jesus would not take it. It must have taken incredible courage to refuse. The soldiers do not seem to care about the prisoner at all. They are playing dice to see who will get his clothes. Under Roman law, a crucified man's clothes belonged to his executioners. The notice stating Jesus' crime is hung on the cross: 'The King of the Jews'.

Jesus was crucified as a traitor. Perhaps Pilate's idea was to frighten any others who might claim to be the king of the Jews. Or perhaps he meant it as an insult to the Jewish authorities (see John 19:21–22). For Mark, that notice is important. Israel has rejected its king, and the Romans do not recognize him. But the crucified 'criminal' really is the king of Israel.

The passers-by jeer at Jesus. The saying about the Temple comes up again (see 14:58; 13:2 and Units 43 and 51). Nobody is interested in what Jesus really meant by

Nearly 2,000 years after Jesus' death, pilgrims carry a cross through the streets of Jerusalem in Easter procession.

it. They think he was boasting about his power. If he is so great, why does he not save himself? Even 'the chief priests and the teachers of the Law' jeer at him. If Jesus can come down from the cross, they say, *then* we'll believe in him! Mark thinks they have totally missed the point. It is because Jesus *stays* on the cross that he is the Messiah. The Messiah has to suffer and die, not dazzle people with miracles.

At noon, there is a 'darkness', which lasts until 3 p.m. What was this? An eclipse? A sandstorm? A thunderstorm? It is not really clear. The 'darkness' underlines that something terrible, yet very important, is happening. In the Old Testament Book of Amos, God had said: 'I will make the sun go down at noon and the earth grow dark in daytime' (Amos 8:9). The 'darkness', then, shows that God is at work.

Jesus has been on the cross for three hours, when he cries out, 'Eloi, Eloi, lema sabachthani?' Mark translates these Aramaic words for his readers: 'My God, my God, why did you abandon me?' This seems very strange, and it has often shocked Christians. How could Jesus be abandoned by God?

The words are a quotation from the first line of Psalm 22. Why does Jesus use them here? There are two possible answers:

● Psalm 22 is the prayer of someone in great trouble. Perhaps Jesus is thinking of the end of the psalm, where God saves the writer. He sums up the whole psalm by quoting the first line. God showed himself to be on the side of the psalm writer, and he will show himself to be on the side of Jesus.

● Jesus actually feels that God has abandoned him. Whatever else he was, Jesus was a human being, and he is dying. Christians believe that Jesus' death saves people from their sins (see Unit 46). At this moment, Jesus took on himself the sins of the world. Sin puts up a barrier between people and God. On the cross Jesus felt that barrier.

The people watching do not understand what the cry means. They mistake 'Eloi' for 'Elijah', and think that Jesus is calling for the prophet's help. People thought Elijah would return at the time of the Messiah (see Unit 5). Some also believed he would come to help good people in trouble. Someone soaks a sponge in 'cheap wine' or vinegar (this may have been the mixture of egg, water and vinegar that Roman soldiers usually drank). The sponge is held up to Jesus' lips, and they wait to see if Elijah will come to his help. This may have been an act of kindness, but Mark seems to think it was a sick, half-joking experiment.

Jesus cries out, and dies.

At that moment, the Temple curtain is torn in two. This curtain hung in front of the Holy of Holies, the most sacred part of the Temple (see diagram in Unit 38). The Holy of Holies was a symbol of God's presence among the Jewish people. Only the High Priest could enter it, just once a year, on the Jewish Day of Atonement. Now, the barrier has gone. What does this mean? Scholars have come up with three possible answers:

It is a sign that the Temple will be destroyed in the Jewish War (see Units 43 and 44).

It means that the barrier of sin which separates God from humankind has been removed by Jesus' death.

It means that the Temple, and Jerusalem, are no longer the places where people can find God. Jesus and the Kingdom have arrived. Now Gentiles as well as Jews are members of the people of God. (Some scholars suggest the detail about the curtain was invented to get across one of these ideas.)

The centurion, the Roman 'army officer' seems to realize who Jesus is. It's possible he is being sarcastic: how could a man who died on a cross be who he said he was? However, the Romans sometimes called their great heroes 'a son of God' or 'a son of the gods'. In Greek, his words can mean 'a son of God'. This may be the nearest he can get to saying who Jesus really is. If this is right, it is very important. The first person to have faith in Jesus after his death is a Gentile, and Gentiles were included in the Kingdom (see Unit 26). For Mark, for the centurion, and for Christians, the man who dies on the cross truly is the Son of God.

▲FOLLOW▼UP▲

1. Write a newspaper report of the death of Jesus. Either use the headline 'Death of a King', or the headline 'Jewish traitor executed today.'

2. Look at the representations of the crucifixion above. What point about the death of Jesus do you think each is making?

3. The story of Jesus' death in Mark is full of echoes from the Old Testament. The passages listed below are the most important. Look them up, and copy out the verses which are like the story of Jesus' death. Next to them, write the verses in Mark they remind you of. (Remember to include the references.) You will see that the passages are often almost identical. What reasons might be given to explain this?
– Psalm 22
– Psalm 69:21
– Isaiah 53, one of the songs about the Servant of the Lord.

4. Write a couple of sentences on each of the following words used in Mark's Gospel. Why are they important?
– Simon
– Golgotha
– bandits
– 'The King of the Jews'
– 'come down from the cross'
– darkness
– 'Eloi, Eloi, lema sabachthani?'
– Elijah
– the curtain hanging in the Temple
– 'This man was really the Son of God!'

The Women, the Burial and the Resurrection

We have now come to the final stage in Mark's message about Jesus, and the story of the first Easter Day. Of course, Mark's first Christian readers would have already known it. The Christian teaching that God raised Jesus from the dead was at the heart of the preaching of the Gospel which had made them Christians in the first place (see Acts 2:32). Mark himself almost certainly knew at least one person who thought that he had seen Jesus and talked with him after his death – Peter (see Unit 3). For the early Christians the resurrection of Jesus meant four things:

● It showed that God approved of Jesus.
● It proved that Jesus was who he said he was – the Messiah and the Son of God – and that what he taught was true.
● It was God's new saving act – like the Exodus in the past, only much greater, because it was for people everywhere.
● It was God's guarantee that, as he had raised Jesus to life, so too he would raise his people to life as well: death was not the end.

These ideas are still at the heart of the Christian faith.

The diagram shows a rock-cut first-century tomb, like the one in which Jesus was buried. A heavy, circular stone was rolled across the entrance to seal it.

READ MARK 15:40–16:8

When Mark wrote this story he would have had in his mind all the teaching and traditions that had been handed down to him from the early church. He tells it very simply and very quickly (the other Gospels have much longer versions).

The faithful women

The women in verses 40–41 appear in the Gospel here for the first time, despite the fact that Mark says they were with Jesus in Galilee (verse 41). This makes it very likely that he is using a source of information which he has not used before. (Luke's Gospel has a number of stories about women, and some scholars have suggested that Mark could be using a document here which was later used by Luke as well.) The women must have been well known in Christian circles – Mark expects his readers to have heard of them (verse 40).

The picture is rather a sad one: they are standing some way off, no part of the action, looking helplessly on. But perhaps Mark wants to contrast their *faithfulness* with the behaviour of the men disciples, who ran away at Gethsemane and, apart from Peter, have not been heard of since (14:50,

Unit 50). We know from Paul's letters and from Acts that women played an important part in the life of the early church.

Jesus' burial

Joseph of Arimathea asks Pilate for Jesus' body and buries it. We do not really know who Joseph was, and he has become surrounded by legend (one even says that he came to England!). Marks says that he was a member of the Sanhedrin. If he later became a Christian, he may be the source of the information about Jesus' trials. At any rate, Mark says he was thinking along the right lines: Joseph was 'waiting for the coming of the Kingdom of God'.

Usually the Romans liked to leave the corpses of criminals hanging on their crosses, as a warning to others. However, this does not seem to have worked very well in Palestine, where Jewish burial customs were very strict. Bodies had to be buried on the day of death, if at all possible. Josephus wrote that 'the Jews are so careful about funeral rites that even criminals who have been crucified are taken down and buried before sunset' (*The Jewish War*, IV:5:2).

The Jews believed that it was a *good work* to bury the dead – something pleasing to God. So this is what Joseph of Arimathea is doing. But he has to move fast, because it is nearly the Sabbath (verse 43), when even burying the dead was considered 'work' and forbidden. There was not even time to anoint Jesus' corpse with the usual spices. It is simply wrapped up and placed in a tomb. A stone is rolled across the entrance.

Joseph has no trouble in getting to see Pilate, so he must have been a very important man indeed. Not all of the authorities hated Jesus. Pilate is surprised that Jesus is already dead and sends for a report. Crucifixion usually took much longer than this (see Unit 53).

This part of the story would have reminded Mark's readers of two things:
● Jesus was really dead and buried before he rose again.
● Some more words from Isaiah about God's Suffering Servant:

'He was placed in a grave with evil men,
He was buried with the rich.'
(Isaiah 53:9)

(It is interesting that this bit of Isaiah does not quite fit what actually happened. Joseph was almost certainly rich, but Mark does not think he was evil – quite the opposite. Perhaps this is an argument for the story's historical accuracy. There is no attempt to make it fit in with Isaiah's words.)

Early on Sunday morning

The women come to the tomb once the Sabbath is over, and as soon as it is light. It was usual for a dead person's family and friends to visit the grave after the burial, but Mark adds that they went there to anoint Jesus' body – which Joseph had not had time to do. (It seems a little strange that anybody should want to anoint a body which had been lying around for two days, and some people think that Mark may have made a mistake with this detail. John's Gospel says that Joseph *did* manage to do it before the burial – John 19:39–40.)

But Jesus is not there. Instead, the stone has been rolled back and a 'young man . . . wearing a white robe' is sitting inside. Mark almost certainly means an angel, which is what Matthew's version says (Matthew 28:2; Luke and John say there were two of them). Jewish writings of Mark's time often talk about angels as 'young men' and of heavenly beings as wearing white. (Jesus' clothes became dazzling white in Mark's story of the Transfiguration: 9:3, see Unit 30.) The angel says to the women that Jesus has been raised and that they must tell the disciples that he is going ahead of them into Galilee. This seems to have two meanings:

Jesus' disciples and the women (15:41) came from Galilee. Jesus will meet them in their home, away from Jerusalem with all its unhappy memories.

Jesus has gone ahead of them as their leader. The 'sheep' were all scattered (14:27), but now Jesus, the shepherd, will call them back together.

So what Jesus said just before his arrest has come true: 'After I am raised in life, I will go to Galilee ahead of you' (14:28, see Unit 50). Look again at verse 7. The young man singles Peter out. This is probably because of his importance as the leader of the apostles (see Unit 29) and to Mark's church (Unit 3). But it is also because Peter has denied Jesus. He is not to worry about it: Jesus has forgiven him. (John's Gospel tells a very beautiful story about this in John 21:15–19.)

 Some scholars have put forward the idea that the reason the angel talks about going to Galilee is because some of the earliest Christians thought that the *parousia* would happen there, and they would have to gather to meet Jesus there when he came. On the whole this seems very unlikely. Mark leaves the angel's words unchanged, despite the fact that he is writing for Christians living in Rome.

Despite the angel's attempt to calm them, the women are terrified. They run away and say nothing.

This is hardly surprising in the circumstances! But the women's *fear* is important. It is the same sort of fear (but much more intense) as the disciples felt when Jesus calmed the storm (4:41, Unit 17) and when he walked on the water (6:50, Unit 24). And it is the same kind of fear which made the Jews tremble, long before, at the signs of God's presence when he gave Moses the Ten Commandments (Exodus 20:18). It is the fear of God – the terror his actions can produce in sinful men and women.

 Christian tradition says that Mary Magdalene was the prostitute who anointed the feet of Jesus in Luke's Gospel (Luke 7:36–50).

Matthew, Luke and John all go on to tell stories about Jesus' appearances to his disciples in Galilee and Jerusalem, but this is where the original text of Mark ends. You may think that it is a bit abrupt: so do a lot of scholars. In the next unit we will discuss that problem and look at how other people tried to finish Mark's Gospel for him.

The resurrection – then and now

The resurrection of Jesus is crucial for Mark's message about him, and for Christian faith today. But how reliable is Mark? Did it happen?

If this were a straightforward historical question like 'How did Wellington defeat Napoleon at Waterloo?' it would be very much easier to answer. But questions like 'Did the resurrection happen?' are not just historical questions: they are religious ones as well. So our answer will depend, not just on the written evidence, but on what we think the world is really like. Do we think there is a God? If we do, what sort of things does he do? These are *religious* and *philosophical* questions. That does not mean they do not have an answer, or that 'anything goes'. But it does mean that they

Resurrection theories

There are some peculiar theories about the resurrection. Two of the most common are that Jesus survived his crucifixion, or that his disciples stole the body. Modern research has shown that these do not really stand up.

Somebody surviving crucifixion and being well enough to walk around showing himself to people is a medical impossibility.

The theory that the disciples stole Jesus' body sounds more sensible, but still has immense problems. It is difficult to see what reason they would have for doing it in the first place – we have already noted that there was no belief among the Jews that the Messiah would rise from the dead. Matthew's Gospel says there was an armed guard (see Matthew 27:64–66). And the disciples would have had to be very lucky not to be seen heaving a dead body about, at a time when Jerusalem and the surrounding countryside was full of Passover pilgrims. If Jesus did not rise from the dead, the problem of what happened to his body still remains unsolved.

are much more complicated than questions usually are.

One thing we do know. Whatever happened, the earliest Christians believed that Jesus rose from the dead. They were prepared to stake their lives on it and they made it the centre of their faith.

Today Jesus' resurrection from the dead is celebrated by Christians in two ways:
● By keeping *Sunday* – the day of the resurrection – as their weekly holy day.
● By keeping the great festival of *Easter* once a year. Easter is the most important of all Christian festivals – even more important than Christmas.

Why do they do this? In Unit 46, 'Why Did Jesus Die?', we saw how Christians believe that Jesus' death puts things right between people and God. It begins a new relationship or *Covenant*. In the first Covenant with the Jews, God established them as his people and promised them the

Christians everywhere celebrate Easter as the most joyful day of the year. Here Eastern Orthodox Christians join in a great Easter procession, in Jerusalem itself.

homeland of Israel. In Christian thought, the resurrection is the promise God made in the New Covenant – the promise of life after death, or Heaven.

Christians believe that the love God showed in Jesus is so strong that it overcomes even death itself (see Romans 8:38–39). Jesus' resurrection is the promise that their relationship with him will continue, even after they have died. Death is still real. It is still frightening (even Jesus was frightened: see the story in Mark 14:32–35). But not even death can separate them from God's love. Jesus has made it possible for men and women to look beyond it to the Kingdom of God, when they will finally be set free from sin and suffering to enjoy God's presence. This is the Christian hope.

Easter in the churches

Easter Day comes right at the end of Holy Week, when Christians focus on the events of the Passion story. (The date is not fixed, because it follows the Passover new moon – but it is always sometime in March or April.)

Holy Week begins with Palm Sunday (see Unit 36), when Jesus' entry into Jerusalem is remembered. The next big service is on Thursday (*Maundy Thursday* or *Holy Thursday*). This was the night of the Last Supper – so in Catholic churches the Eucharist is celebrated with great ceremony and for the last time until Saturday night.

On Good Friday Christians everywhere remember Jesus' death on the cross. In the Roman Catholic Church it is a fast day. No Mass is celebrated, and instead the people take the sacrament from the previous evening. This has been put on one side, and all night, or at least part of it, people have been praying before it in church, remembering Jesus' agony in the Garden of Gethsemane. After hearing the story of the Passion and solemn prayers on Friday, everybody goes home. It is a sad and moving time.

In Catholic churches the Easter service itself (or *Vigil*) happens some time between Saturday night and early on Sunday morning, because that is when the women came to the tomb. It begins outside the church in darkness – the darkness of death. Then a new fire is kindled and blessed, and a single candle is lit to symbolize the risen Christ. It is carried into the church, and the people light their own candles from it.

Soon the church is ablaze with light, bells are rung, and the deacon (one of the clergy) sings the praises of God for what he has done in Jesus. The story of the Exodus is read, and the resurrection story from one of the Gospels.

After this the people renew their commitment to Christ by remembering the promises made at their baptisms. Mass is celebrated, and everybody makes his or her communion. It is a time of great joy and thanksgiving.

This is true for all Christians. Many Protestant churches hold services at dawn, remembering what happened on the first Easter Day. Special Easter hymns and carols are sung. The communion service takes on fresh and special meaning as Christians read and reflect on the Easter story, and all that Christ's death and resurrection means for them.

FOLLOW UP

1. ● Who buried Jesus' body in Mark's story?
● Why did he have to do it quickly?

2. Why does Mark say that Pilate was surprised that Jesus was dead?

3. Why is it important for Mark to record Jesus' burial?

4. ● What reason does Mark give for the women's visit to the tomb?
● What two things do they see there?

5. What is the meaning of the women's fear in verse 8?

6. Why is the resurrection important for Christian faith? Answer as fully as you can.

7. Try to find out something about the teachings of other world religions about life after death. Discuss how they are similar to, and how they differ from, Christian ideas.

The Other Endings

READ MARK 16:9–20

Mark's work finishes with 16:8: 'So they went out and ran from the tomb, distressed and terrified. They said nothing to anyone, because they were afraid.' He did not write either of the other endings to the Gospel. We know this for the following reasons:

● The best Greek copies of Mark leave out the other endings. Mark stops at 16:8.

● Other Greek copies of Mark have verses 9–20, or the shorter ending (verses 9–10). Some have both, and include the words 'this is also current', which means 'we also have this ending'. This makes it look likely that they were added later.

● Every writer has his or her own way of writing, and so does Mark. The other endings are not in Mark's style. They do not use the sort of words Mark would have chosen, and the way they put sentences together is different. For example, Mark never calls Jesus 'the Lord Jesus', and he does not end sentences with 'Amen'. The other endings use these words.

● The other endings' ideas about God (theology) seem different from Mark's.

● Matthew and Luke used Mark as a source, but they do not seem to have used the other endings. So the copies of Mark they used ended at 16:8, before the other endings were added on.

● We are not sure that Mark meant to finish at 16:8 (see below). Some early writers saw this problem too, and added one or other of the endings. They thought this would round the Gospel off better.

● Verses 9–20 look as though they are using material from Matthew, Luke and John, who wrote later than Mark. If this is so, they cannot have been written by Mark! (Not all scholars agree with this point. Some say verses 9–20 look like stories in the other Gospels, but did not get their information from them. The writer of verses 19–20 may have used a different source.)

This wooden pen-case with its reed pens, and the ink-well half-filled with black ink, comes from the time when Mark was writing his Gospel.

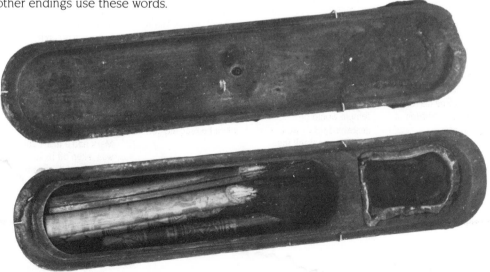

(Catholic Christians say these verses are part of the Bible, although most Catholic scholars agree they are not by Mark. Other Christians are not so sure that they are part of the Bible.)

There are two other questions we need to look at:
● Did Mark intend to finish at 16:8?

● What are we to make of the other endings?
Let's examine these in turn.

Did Mark intend to finish at 16:8?

Different scholars have different views on this question. The arguments are set out in the table below.

Mark did not intend to end at 16:8	Mark did intend to end at 16:8	Mark did not intend to end at 16:8	Mark did intend to end at 16:8
1. Mark calls his book a 'Gospel', which means 'good news'. We would expect him to end with better news than the women running away from the tomb.	**1.** The news that 'he has been raised' in verse 6 *is* good news! The whole Gospel has been leading up to this moment.	**4.** The last word in 16:8 is the Greek word *gar*, which means 'because' or 'for'. You never used this word at the end of a sentence. It looks as though Mark did not intend to finish there.	**4.** This is not true. There are other examples of *gar* ending sentences in other Greek books. In any case, Mark's Greek was not brilliant, so he might put a word in the wrong place. The end of his Gospel, 'they were afraid', sums up well the *wonder* that people should feel when they hear the news that Jesus is still on the move. Mark does not need to say anything more.
2. Mark 16:8 says the women 'said nothing to anyone'. We would not expect them to keep silent: the story would come out. All the other Gospels include stories of Jesus appearing to his disciples after he had risen from the dead. Mark would have wanted to include stories like this, too.	**2.** Mark may not mean that the women 'said nothing to anyone' *ever*. He may leave out the stories of Jesus appearing to his followers because his readers knew them so well anyway. Perhaps Mark only wanted to write about the life of Jesus *before* he was raised from the dead.		
3. Jesus predicts his resurrection (8:31; 9:9; 9:31; 10:34). In 16:7, the young man says 'he is going to Galilee ahead of you; there you will see him' and Peter is given a special mention. Mark would have wanted to say all this came true by telling his readers of Jesus' resurrection appearances.	**3.** Not necessarily! After all, Mark does not always record other things Jesus predicted coming true. Obviously, he does not record the *parousia* coming true (8:38; 13:26; 14:62), because it had not happened yet. But Jesus also predicts that the Temple would be destroyed (13:2), and Mark does not tell the story of how that actually happened. In any case, the young man's words in 16:7 show Jesus has risen from the dead, and this is enough.	**5.** Mark intended to write more, but either the ending he actually wrote was lost, or something happened. Books in Mark's time were either written on scrolls (rolls of paper), or sheets of papyrus (an early form of paper). This tore easily, so the verses Mark wrote after 16:8 could have been torn off accidentally, or damaged in some way. Or, if something happened, perhaps Mark died or was arrested by the Romans when he reached 16:8.	**5.** Quite a coincidence! Especially as Mark stops at a place where he could have *meant* to stop anyway. It does not seem likely that the ending was lost. There were probably lots of copies of Mark, and any 'lost ending' could have been copied up from these. Or someone in Mark's church would have known the book so well that they could reproduce any 'lost ending' more or less from memory. It seems *very* unlikely that Mark had a heart attack or was taken off by the Romans while the ink on 16:8 was still wet!

Did Mark intend to end his Gospel at 16:8? If not, what happened . . .?

What are we to make of the other endings?

• **The long ending** (verses 9–20). There is a clear break between verses 8 and 9, which shows that this section was added on to the end of Mark. It may originally have been a short document used to teach people who had been converted to Christianity. A document from the tenth century AD says it was written by someone called 'Ariston the presbyter', but since this 'evidence' is so late, it is not very reliable. We do not really know who wrote it. All we do know is that it was written by AD180, since Irenaeus, another Christian from that time, quotes from it.

Verses 9–20 may be made up from details taken from Matthew, Luke and John. Or it may have used a source similar to the resurrection appearances in these Gospels. It gives very brief details of the risen Jesus' appearances to:

• *Mary Magdalene* (see Luke 8:2; John 20:11–18).

• *Two travellers* (Luke 24:13–35. The note that the disciples did not believe the reports is like Luke 24:11; John 20:24–25).

• *The eleven disciples* (Luke 24:36–49; John 20:19–29).

The risen Jesus tells them they will preach the Gospel (Mark 13:10; Matthew

28:19–20), and that they will have the power to:
– drive out demons
– heal people
– speak in strange tongues
– pick up snakes
– drink poison and survive.

All of these powers (except drinking poison) are mentioned in Acts, which describes the work of the apostles. Some Christians think they need not be taken literally: they are just picture language to

The Freer Logion
One Greek copy of Mark has some extra material after verse 14. This is called the *Freer Logion* after the person who used to own the manuscript. We know that some other old copies of Mark included these words, but we only have one copy left. It is not written in very good Greek but, as far as we can tell, this is what it says:

'They said to Christ, "Nobody keeps the laws today, and nobody believes anything. Satan is in charge! People do not understand God's true power, because Satan's evil spirits are stopping them. So you must make people see what is holy and right straight away!"

'Christ answered, "The time when Satan was in charge is over. But even the sinners I died for will suffer other terrible things. These will make them turn to the truth and stop sinning, so that they will go to heaven and share in the spiritual holiness that will last for ever." '

These words are very different from anything Mark ever wrote, or (as far as we can tell) Jesus ever said. We do not know when or why they were written, but we can guess. Most scholars say they were written in the second or third century AD. They are difficult to understand, and there are two ideas about what they mean:
• The church was going through a difficult time. People wanted to know why everybody did not become Christians, and wanted the *parousia* to happen quickly.
• The idea behind them is really rather horrible. There are two sorts of Christians (or people). For one sort, Jesus' death is enough to save them. For the other sort, it is not enough. They had to suffer 'terrible things', and perhaps be punished for their sins before they could be saved. This would fit in well with the church's problems after the end of the first century. Some people were saying they were much better than other Christians, who were just idiots who would have a hard job getting to heaven.

say that Christians will have a special power or ability to cope with life. Other Christians say these powers are rather odd, and the last two are just silly. They doubt that Jesus actually said anything of the sort.

After his appearance to the disciples, Jesus is taken up to heaven (Luke 24:50–53; Acts 1:6–11). Not all Christians take this literally (although it is remembered every year on the Christian festival of Ascension Day, forty days after Easter). Some say he simply stopped appearing to the disciples. All Christians, however, agree that Jesus is risen, and that he is alive.

● **The shorter ending** (the other verses 9–10). These two verses were another try at rounding Mark off. Unlike 9–20, they were certainly originally written to do this. Mark did not write them: the style is too different.

FOLLOW UP

1. Look again at the table in this unit. Do you think Mark intended to finish his Gospel at 16:8, or not?

2. How do we know that the other endings were not written by Mark?

3. What does the 'longer ending' say happened after Jesus was raised from the dead?

4. What is the Freer Logion? What is it trying to say?

Mark wrote down the 'Good News about Jesus Christ' so that his readers – then and now – might come to terms with him for themselves. Many have found a new quality of life by believing in Jesus as the Son of God.